BECOMING A
SUCCESSFUL
STUDENT

BECOMING A SUCCESSFUL STUDENT

SECOND EDITION

Laraine E. Flemming   *South Central Community College*

Judith Leet

HarperCollinsCollegePublishers

Acquisitions Editor: Mark Paluch
Project Coordination and Text Design:
  Proof Positive/Farrowlyne Associates, Inc.
Cover Design: Molly Heron
Production Manager: Kewal Sharma
Compositor: Black Dot Graphics
Printer and Binder: R. R. Donnelley & Sons Company
Cover Printer: The Lehigh Press, Inc.

Becoming a Successful Student, Second Edition

Library of Congress Cataloging-in-Publication Data

Flemming, Laraine E.
  Becoming a successful student / Laraine E. Flemming, Judith Leet.
  —2nd ed.
    p.   cm.
  Includes bibliographical references and index.
  ISBN 0-673-46831-3.
  1. Study skills.   2. Reading (Higher education)   I. Leet, Judith.
  II. Title.
  LB2395.F54   1993   93–32728
  482.4'3—dc20   CIP

94 95 96 9 8 7 6 5 4 3 2

CONTENTS

UNIT 2   Listening and Remembering

UNIT 3   Learning from Textbooks

UNIT 4   Preparing for and Taking Exams

Unit 5   Becoming a Critical Thinker and a Thoughtful Writer

■   CHAPTER 16   Writing as a Learning Tool: The Writing Process and the Research Paper   364

■   APPENDIX   Suggestions for Reading Science Textbooks   394

PREFACE

Our goals, like yours, are to improve the performance of students in the classroom and to produce tangible results in the form of better grades. No less important, however, is our commitment to promoting intellectual growth and enthusiasm for learning. We want our student readers to find excitement in the process of learning and knowing.

This second edition of *Becoming a Successful Student* provides step-by-step guidance on how to study; for such guidance to work, we encourage students to internalize the advice and put it into practice throughout each semester of their college career. We want students to realize that there are no quick cures; they must develop stamina and remain motivated over the long haul—from the first class to the last exam.

The comprehensive advice we provide is recommended by present-day researchers and educators to help students improve their reading, writing, critical-thinking, and problem-solving skills. We have taken the results of well-accepted research, both the more recent and the time-tested, and have translated it into accessible tips that every student can understand and apply.

Since students have their own individual ways of learning, we encourage them to discover their own best learning styles. To help them, we offer a choice of strategies, all of which will produce good results when implemented thoughtfully. To help students become independent learners and thinkers, we urge them to experiment—by, for example, using a learning journal to observe themselves—and to select those strategies that are most appropriate to the task at hand.

Throughout the text, we prod students to make the most of their opportunities at college by stretching themselves in many new directions and becoming all that they can be.

Coverage: The Essential Skills

Unit 1, Making Yourself a Productive Student, orients students to college life and provides them with numerous suggestions for staying motivated throughout their college years. We acknowledge differences among students and gear our advice both to younger students directly out of high school and to mature students returning after an absence. Two other essential topics—managing time and maintaining concentration—

are broken down into manageable steps. Students learn how they can study and work productively yet still find time for friends and fun.

Unit 2, Listening and Remembering, covers three crucial topics: (1) how to learn from lectures, (2) how to take useful lecture notes, and (3) how to remember over time.

Unit 3, Learning from Textbooks, shows students how to get the most from reading textbooks. We describe three different reading strategies in depth: prereading, intensive reading, and analytical reading. Students are encouraged to decide which strategy best suits their particular purpose and assignment. Unit 3 offers three strategies for taking notes: (1) underlining and annotating pages, (2) making informal outlines, and (3) creating concise summaries. The unit concludes with a chapter on how students can learn to increase their reading rate for those times when it's appropriate.

Unit 4, Preparing for and Taking Exams, has been thoroughly revised to offer detailed advice for taking every kind of exam from multiple-choice to short-answer to essay exams. Throughout, we emphasize the role active learning plays in exam preparation and offer numerous reviewing techniques for students to choose from. For those who suffer from test anxiety, we include a variety of strategies to help them overcome their fear and believe in their own abilities.

Unit 5, Becoming a Critical Thinker and a Thoughtful Writer, emphasizes that the ability to think critically is what distinguishes a good student from an average one. A good student applies critical thinking to all areas of life—whether to studying productively, making personal decisions, reading textbooks, or writing papers. Above all, critical thinking encourages students to think for themselves after taking into account other viewpoints.

Also in Unit 5, **"Using the Library for Research"** and **"Writing as a Learning Tool"** advise students on ways to carry out research and to improve their writing. To allow for the discovery and development of their best ideas, students are urged to understand the writing process from prewriting to proofreading. We hope to convince students that writing is a vital skill, one that allows them to communicate their point of view both in college and beyond.

New to This Edition

Orientation: Chapter 1, "Adjusting to College Life," is all new. For students just finishing high school or returning after raising a family, we offer both reassurance and information. Step by step, we show them how to become accustomed to college life and how to believe in their ability to succeed. A series of innovative exercises helps them reflect on their personal strengths and long-term goals.

Motivation: Chapter 2, "Motivating Yourself to Study," has been expanded to include more extensive discussion of developing and reaching long-term goals. We also include new exercises that encourage personal analysis and reflection.

Concentration: A brand-new Chapter 3, "Improving Your Concentration," takes aim at a topic that worries incoming students of all ages—how to ignore distractions and maintain concentration. To allay their worries, we show students exactly how to set the stage for concentration and how to stay focused even in the most distracting circumstances.

Listening: This edition offers two chapters on listening instead of one: Chapter 5, "Becoming a Good Listener" and Chapter 6, "Taking Notes on Lectures." We now offer a more comprehensive discussion on how to improve listening behavior and how to take legible and complete lecture notes.

Remembering: The original chapter on memory has been completely revised to expand our discussion of why forgetting occurs and to provide additional strategies for remembering over time.

Self-Analysis: All new charts and questionnaires emphasize the role self-reflection plays in achieving academic success.

Test Taking: The two chapters in Unit 4 have been thoroughly revised and now give useful and current tips on preparing for and taking multiple-choice and other objective and essay exams. Three effective techniques for relieving test anxiety are discussed in detail.

Research Paper: In Chapter 16, step-by-step explanations on how to carry out library research and write a thoughtful research paper will help make this major assignment more manageable and more appealing.

New Readings: Most of the readings are new. Drawn from a variety of sources (textbooks, magazines, and newspapers), the readings reinforce and elaborate upon the concepts introduced in the chapter.

Acknowledgments

We are indebted to the following reviewers for their helpful suggestions and comments: Barbara Beauchamp, County College of Morris,

Randolph, N.J.; Michael Hannaford, Indiana State University; Patricia Crone, Hazard Community College; Ellen Galligan, Sullivan County Community College; Michael Hrico, Community College of Allegheny County; Nancy Mills, University of Hartford, College of Basic Studies; Dom Garino, Irvine Valley College; Annette Brittain, Tarrant County Jr. College; and Rosa Rivera Sharboneau, Gavilan Community College.

We would particularly like to thank Mark Paluch and Jane Kinney of HarperCollins, and project editor Lisa Dillman and designer Lauren Cohn for their invaluable assistance.

To the Student

Nothing would please us more than if you put our advice to work and become a highly successful student.

This book offers many tips on how to study productively and how to master the material of your various courses. If you follow the advice spelled out here and if you have a strong commitment to reaching your long-range goals, you will make the most of yourself and your future.

Laraine Flemming
Judith Leet

1

UNIT

Making Yourself a Productive Student

CHAPTER **1**

Adjusting to College Life

"I know that if I don't get my education, I won't have anything—and I want everything."

—Ladeeta Smith, student

You may be entering college straight from high school, or you may be coming back to school after some work experience. In either case, you are now enrolled in college and adapting to new classes, friends, teachers, and much more.

The topics we cover in Chapter 1 will help you adjust smoothly to your new college life.

- Finding yourself at college
- Learning your way around the campus
- Taking charge of your education
- Developing a repertoire of learning strategies
- Shifting to thinking at the college level
- Locating the help you need
- Managing stress

Finding Yourself at College

"How do I become myself?"

—Alva Myrdal, winner of the Nobel Peace Prize, 1982

Simply put, college is the place to become *your best self.* At college, you can lay the groundwork to reach your fullest potential. Think about it; college will help you make the most of the rest of your life.

College allows you time to think about who you are now—and who you want to be in the future. You can build on your skills by learning more about things you are already good at, and you can also acquire some wholly new skills.

Some of your courses will prepare you for your professional life. Others, such as courses in the arts, will enrich the rest of your life. The drama or film course you take at college, for example, will enable you to recognize and experience much more in every play and movie you see in the future.

Now is your opportunity to take advantage of all that is offered on a college campus; but no less important is meeting new people. Making an active effort to extend your circle of friends to include people of diverse backgrounds will enrich *your* life.

Try to make as many new friends as possible and learn about their lives and their experiences. Stretch yourself in many directions and see if you like your new expanded self.

Plunge into the limitless possibilities of college life. Your opportunities will never be greater.

Moving Straight from High School to College

If you have come to college straight from high school, college represents a transition from a fairly supervised life to a more independent adult one. In high school, your decisions and problems were monitored by other people. In college you are now much more responsible for how you use your time and for keeping up with your assignments.

With a sigh of relief, you can now make your own major decisions. But you want to use your new freedom well by showing *yourself* that you can behave maturely at critical times and that you have the necessary determination to put your schoolwork first. Then when the pressure is off, you can enjoy yourself fully, knowing that you have earned some relaxation.

Distractions are everywhere. Your biggest challenge will be to avoid being distracted from your overall goal of making the most you can out of your time at college.

Returning to College from the Work World

After some years away from school, many students are returning to college to get more training or to earn a degree. If that is your case, you have different obstacles from students entering college straight from high school. You may worry that you don't remember how to study, that you have waited too long and are too old, or that you have too many other responsibilities and demands on your time, such as a spouse or children.

But, in fact, you have some advantages younger students don't have. You now know exactly what you need from college, and you have the maturity and perseverance to achieve it. Chances are you will be less easily diverted from your goals. In addition, you can take advantage of skills you have acquired and the real-life work experiences you have picked up and apply those experiences and skills to every course you take.

PRACTICE 1   Use this self-evaluation to help sort out what you hope to accomplish in college. Check any of the following statements that apply to you.

_____   1.   I want to prepare for a career that pays well and offers future potential.

_____   2.   I want to improve my basic skills (reading, vocabulary, writing, math, other).

_____   3.   I want to learn how to help others (social worker, physical therapist, psychologist, dentist, other).

_____   4.   I want to work in some creative field (film, advertising, architecture, other).

_____   5.   I want to learn how to be my own boss.

_____   6.   I want to use college to explore various options for my future.

_____   7.   I want to become a productive, self-reliant person.

_____   8.   Even in some small way, I want to make the world a better place.

9.   I want to (add anything else you hope to accomplish):

_____

_____

10. In broad terms, describe what you hope to accomplish with your life after you finish college.

_____

_____

PRACTICE 2   What are your interests? Check any of the following that interest you and explain briefly.

_____ Social issues (such as AIDS, homelessness, poverty, illiteracy). Which ones?

_____

_____ Environmental issues (such as pollution, wildlife preservation). Which ones?

_____

_____ Math, science, research (such as computers, telecommunications, new technologies). Which?

_____

_____ Business (sales, marketing, finance, management). Which?

_____

_____ Politics (campus, local, state, national, international). Which?

_____

_____ Health care (care of elderly, nursing, mental health). Which?

_____

_____ History (American, Western, world). Which?

_____

_____ Education (research, teaching). Explain:

_____

_____ Arts (literature, graphic arts, interior design). Which?

_____

_____ Languages. Which?

_____

_____ Economics. Explain:

_____

_____ Accounting, taxes. Which?

_____

_____ Law (corporate, criminal). Which?

_____

_____ Other. Explain:

_____

Learning Your Way Around the Campus

Many students do not bother looking at a map to get themselves oriented, but maps will help, especially during your first semester. Get maps both of the campus and of the nearby town or city.

With map in hand, take a walk around the campus to find out where things are *before* you need them. Before each term starts, find out where each of your classes and labs will meet. Locate the computer center, your adviser's office, a photocopying machine, the library, the post office, and so forth. Once you find the computer center, you will know where to go to type your papers on a word processor and where to learn how to run new computer programs.

Find out where the swimming pool or other recreation areas are—and the hours they are open. Investigate opportunities to participate in your favorite sports and find out where they are played.

Several days before you have to take any final exam, make sure you know where it is being held and how to get there. There is no point in missing valuable minutes while you are lost. Arriving late and in a panic also can ruin your ability to think clearly.

Your goal is to *feel comfortable, confident, competent*—and knowing your way around the campus is a first step.

Taking Charge of Your Education

Since each student's courses, work hours, and home responsibilities are different, it is up to you to develop your own strategies for coping with college life. Whatever your situation, you want to **make a commitment to yourself that a certain amount of time and energy per week will be devoted to classes and studying.**

If you have limited time because of heavy job or family responsibilities, you will have to be even more efficient in how you use your time. Find new ways of squeezing the most from your waking hours. Experiment with getting up an hour earlier to study or going to bed an hour later. If you are walking somewhere, try to recall and review as much as you can of the lecture you just heard. If you are waiting to meet someone, pull out your lecture notes and review them. Always have some reading or reviewing with you in case time opens up.

To do well in college, you must attend all classes, get all the course work completed, and review in depth for tests. Unlike high school, no one supervises your attendance or monitors whether or not you complete your weekly assignments. The teacher will suggest what work should be covered but will leave it up to you to complete the assignments—or not.

With this new freedom comes responsibility to yourself. You are now in charge of what happens to you, so from the outset, take charge of your education and **make a pact, or contract, with yourself to do everything you can to succeed in college.**

✳   If you have limited time because of heavy job or family responsibilities, you will have to be even more efficient in how you use your time.

PRACTICE 3

1. To ensure your college success, check off which of the following strategies apply (or can be adapted) to your personal situation. Then make a pact with yourself to put them into practice.

_____ Except for emergencies, I plan to attend all classes, even if I feel like cutting a class.

_____ I will hand in assignments when due, whether graded or not, so I don't fall behind.

_____ I will keep up with the textbook assignments and will spend extra time studying on weekends if I fall behind.

_____ I will prepare for each class by reviewing the last lecture or by reading the pages to be discussed in class.

_____ I will review my lecture notes shortly after each lecture to fill in missing words and to review what was covered.

_____ I will study actively at least three hours each day, including Saturdays or Sundays.

_____ I will start studying for exams at least one week in advance.

_____ At the library, I will get right to work and use my time to the fullest.

2. Fill in additional strategies that apply to your personal situation, such as "ask for extra help at the writing lab."

I need to _____

Developing a Repertoire of Learning Strategies

When you take lecture notes, do you always make an outline? Do you always work alone when you study? If you rely exclusively on one method of learning, you may be shortchanging yourself. The more learning strategies you have at your disposal, the easier it is to tailor the strategy to the task at hand.

Outline form may be perfect for taking notes on your government text but you may want to make a simple list for a class discussion that has less structure. For science texts, you often may want to draw diagrams or sketches. Similarly, reading aloud may be an ideal way to understand poetry, but this method is less effective when you're studying longer forms of literature.

What Every Successful Student Knows

1. **Attend the first class.** Instructors usually use the first class to provide an overview of the course, its objectives, and its organization. Don't miss this important overview. You also need to pick up the handouts and course syllabus.

2. If you're sure you're taking the course, **buy the textbook immediately,** even if there's no assignment yet. The beginning of the semester is often chaotic and textbook shortages do occur.

3. **Get to know a friend in each class,** someone with whom you can discuss assignments or clarify questions. You can also borrow or lend notes when either of you misses a class.

4. **Go to every class.** It's tempting to cut class on a beautiful day, but don't do it. Each class provides new information, and you can't afford to have a gap in your knowledge.

5. **Talk to your instructor.** If you have questions or feel confused, don't be afraid to ask for help. Most instructors will be happy to provide it.

6. **Understand the course requirements**—the kinds of exams and papers you will be responsible for. Make sure you know these course requirements *before* you register for the course. Also before enrolling, ask your instructor if you have the right background for any course that might pose problems for you. For example, do you have enough math background for the chemistry course you want to take?

To be a successful student, develop a repertoire of study strategies. As the list in Practice 4 shows, many different ways to learn are available to you. Through a process of trial and error, decide which ones are most effective for you and for your specific classes. It's up to you to decide which methods work best.

Then, too, certain subjects lend themselves more readily to particular learning strategies. For example, it's relatively easy to create mental pictures of biological processes, but visualizing philosophical theories is another matter altogether. To be a successful student, you need to decide which learning strategies produce the best results.

Tailor the learning strategy to the task at hand.

□ PRACTICE 4   Here are some strategies for learning in college. Put a check next to the study strategies you already use. Put an x next to those you plan to try out in the coming week. (All these learning strategies are discussed later in the text.)

1. Make informal outlines _____

2. Reread difficult passages _____

3. Take notes on reading _____

4. Make charts, pictures, or diagrams _____

5. Explain material to someone else to clarify it for yourself _____

6. Create your own concrete examples of abstract theories _____

7. Participate in study groups _____

8. Visualize what you're reading _____

9. Put key definitions and concepts on tape and play them back _____

10. Make lists of key words and try to recall the full discussion they represent _____

11. Develop potential test questions and self-test _____

12. Annotate and underline your texts _____

13. Ask a friend to question you on the reading _____

14. Write summaries of the material _____

15. Make lists that compare and contrast opposing ideas _____

16. Make flash cards _____

17. Recite key points _____

18. Memorize key math formulas _____

19. Review regularly throughout the term _____

20. Make notes synthesizing lecture notes and reading _____

Keeping a Learning Journal

Keeping a learning journal is essential for discovering which study strategies work best for you. Your journal is the place to evaluate and analyze various strategies, as in these sample entries from student Jason Benedict's journal.

10/12/94   For a week now, I've been doing my computer science homework in a study group. At first I had doubts. George likes to fool around—he's pretty sharp so he can afford to waste some time. But somehow I seem to understand and remember the material better when we talk about it. George turns out to be a big help explaining what I don't get.

10/16/94   Studying poetry for my intro to literature class in a group isn't working. We get sidetracked; we don't agree on what the poem means. I'm going to study alone again. Otherwise I won't do well.

By means of his journal, Jason is figuring out what works best for him.
    But you can also use your journal to keep track of your progress. Writing regularly in your journal will help you identify both problems and solutions.

10/22/94   I'm having a hard time in English composition. I keep getting C's. I try to do everything Professor Levin asks for, but it's slow. I'm going to go over my papers first with him, and then I'm going to go to the writing center for extra help.

Keeping a learning journal will help you take control of your education. Your journal will help you discover how you learn best and how you can overcome difficulties that develop during the semester.

Shifting to Thinking at the College Level

It may surprise you to find out that college instructors want more than rote memorization of dates, names, facts, and formulas. Instead, some instructors will expect you to **synthesize** or pull together many pieces of information you have learned, and to explain how the pieces are related and why they are meaningful. Other teachers will expect you to analyze raw data and interpret what these bits of data mean. Although teachers realize there are often no simple answers to the questions they ask, they want to see how you analyze a relatively complex problem, how you support your views, and what conclusions you draw. They are interested in what you make of the facts they provide and how you develop your own point of view.

For example, one student in an American history course worked tirelessly to learn the names of Civil War generals, battles, places, and dates. Another student memorized much less factual information, but had a clearer overall sense of the large social and economic issues that led to the war. The second student was able to write more convincing answers on the exam because she could analyze and interpret specifics at the level her professor was looking for.

Similarly in science courses, you will need to apply your understanding of problems, both those worked in class and in the homework, to new and unfamiliar problems. Again, that means you need not just rote memorization of formulas but a deep understanding of how the formulas can be applied in new contexts.

Developing Your Own Point of View

While you are at college, you'll constantly be exposed to controversial ideas or theories. For example, should American literature courses include more work by women and minorities? Did John F. Kennedy have a more crucial influence on the civil rights movement in this country than Lyndon B. Johnson?

To get the most out of your college experience, don't stop learning once you can compare and contrast the two sides of an issue and pass your essay exam. Instead, try to figure out where you stand by asking yourself questions like these:

1. Which side offers the best argument?
2. Does my personal experience or knowledge lend support to one side or the other?

3. Where can I get more information?
4. Do I have to be on one side or the other, or can I develop my own compromise position?

Part of the intellectual excitement of college life is being able to develop and argue your own perspective. Don't cheat yourself out of that excitement by simply learning what other people think. Take the time to discover what *you* think as well.

As we have said, doing well in college is primarily your responsibility, but you are not alone. Make use of the many advisers and counselors ready to help you, and ask for help *before* you are in trouble.

For everyone who enrolls, college represents the unknown, and some anxiety always is associated with the unknown. But remember that *help is available.* Someone on campus can help you with any and all of your questions and problems, whether academic, financial, psychological, or social.

People employed at a college have specific responsibilities; learn what tasks they handle so that you can speak to the right person about your problem or question. The people who work at your college want students to succeed, and they work very hard to that end. Here is a list of those who can help you.

Your Adviser

As an incoming student, you will be assigned an adviser who will give you individual guidance on what courses to take in your first year and which courses you must take to fulfill requirements for graduation; your adviser is the person you should keep in close touch with during the year.

Your Instructors

Your instructors are available to you after class and at assigned times, called **office hours.** During office hours, you can ask your questions about papers, tests, assigned problems, and so forth. Your instructors are more than willing to help because your questions inform them about what topics may need further explanation in class.

Also it is a good idea to make connections with some members of the faculty so that your education becomes less impersonal. Most teachers like to get to know their students and would rather write a recommendation for someone they know personally.

Registrar

The registrar keeps official records of your courses and grades, and sends your transcripts to other schools if you decide to transfer. Your grades will be mailed from the office of the registrar after each term.

Study Skills Counselor

This counselor will give you advice on the options available if you need help with basic skills, whether in math, writing, studying, or reading.

Peer Counselor

Some colleges assign upperclass students to give advice to incoming students. A peer counselor is a good person to give you information on courses and social life at the school.

Tutor

Often a student, this person can provide hands-on help with specific courses. If you feel you are doing poorly in a course, get yourself help promptly. Ask for a tutor at the learning lab or study skills center.

Department Secretary

This assistant can help you arrange to see a professor in a specific department to discuss majors or courses.

Psychologist or Psychiatrist

Most colleges and universities provide trained specialists you can consult if you are feeling stress or dealing with emotional problems that you cannot handle alone.

Resident Assistant

Consult this student for problems with your dorm room or roommate.

Reference Librarian

The reference librarian is a very good source of information when you are writing a research paper or conducting a computer search. He or she can tell you how to locate specific types of information, from the population of Buenos Aires to the letters of Mary Todd Lincoln.

Knowing the Right Place to Go

You'll adjust to college life with relative ease if you discover early in the term the various places that provide help for students. Spend a little more time trying to locate the following offices on your campus; your time will be well spent.

Financial Aid Office

If you need a loan or scholarship to finance your education, this is the place to go. The people here can tell you what financial assistance is available and how you can apply for it. They can also help solve financial emergencies.

Placement Office

The people in the placement office can help you figure out what you might want to do when you graduate. They can tell you which majors have a lot of job opportunities and which ones don't. Placement offices also usually maintain a file on current full- and part-time job openings; if you need to work while in school, check here first.

Far too often students find the placement office in their senior year when they are looking for a job. But it is more efficient to become familiar with this office in your freshman year. Most placement officers are delighted to give students suggestions about possible careers available for them. They can also provide guidance on how to prepare for a chosen career.

Student Health Center

Most colleges and universities have some type of medical clinic or infirmary on campus. Don't wait until you get the flu to find out where your health center is. Check it out early in the semester to see what services it provides.

Department Offices

Each academic discipline usually has its own department office, where you can get information about general requirements or regulations for work in the particular discipline. If, for example, you are thinking about majoring in psychology but are worried about how much statistics you will have to take, a member of the psychology department probably can tell you how many statistics courses you'll actually need.

Many of the department offices have bulletin boards where you can find announcements about everything from special scholarships to class cancellations. If you are interested in a particular department, keep an eye on what's posted on the bulletin board.

Becoming Familiar with Key College Documents

Here's some essential reading material for launching your college career.

College Catalog

The college catalog lists the courses that are available each semester, who is teaching them, and what they cover. It also explains the various majors offered at the school and lists the courses, grade point averages, and other requirements for the degree. Read the catalog thoroughly before you consult your adviser.

Student Guide

This guide, written by students to help other students, can be useful in helping you choose courses. Students who have actually taken the courses evaluate the instructors' presentation of material.

Syllabus

Each instructor hands out a syllabus covering the course requirements. The syllabus usually identifies the textbooks to be used and the homework assignments, test dates, and papers required along with their due dates. When you get the syllabus, read it through carefully to learn what's required of you to do well in the course.

Working Out Your Grade Point Average (GPA)

At times you'll want to figure out your GPA. At most schools, an A is worth 4 points, a B is worth 3 points, a C is worth 2 points, and a D is worth 1. To find your average, take the number of points you have earned and divide by the number of courses you have taken.

If you have taken ten courses and earned four A's and six B's, you would compute

4 A's at 4 points = 16
6 B's at 3 points = <u>18</u>

34 divided by 10 courses

or a 3.4 GPA.

Recognizing Signs of Trouble Early On

If you're doing poorly in a course, you're eventually going to get a warning. But there's no point in waiting for that to happen. You will know before anyone else if your grades are in trouble. Once the first few weeks of classes are finished, ask and honestly answer these questions for each of your courses.

1. Are you giving the course your best effort?
2. Have you kept up with the reading?
3. Have you already missed more than two classes?
4. Have you turned in several assignments late?
5. Does your mind wander while you're in class?
6. Do you dread going to the class?
7. Do you lack the background to take this course?

If your answer is yes to at least two of these questions, then you probably need to talk to your instructor or academic adviser. Don't wait for things to get better by themselves. Take the initiative: talk to someone about the course, figure out why you're having difficulties, and take concrete action to improve the situation.

Managing Stress

Adjusting to college is bound to bring some stress into your life. In fact, being "stressed out" ranks as one of the top ten student complaints. However, complaining about stress is useless. A better response is to figure out how you can manage it because **stress frequently goes hand in hand with achievement.**

Recognize the Power of Attitude

Stress can actually work in your favor by stimulating you to creative action. To make that happen, however, you need a "take charge" attitude toward life. If, for example, you are feeling worn down by stress, ask yourself

1. What's causing the stress in my life?
2. What can I do to change the situation?

Say that you are feeling anxious about the number of papers and exams looming at the end of the semester. Instead of wasting time worrying about how you will get everything done, **develop a plan of action.** Make out a week-by-week schedule and figure out how you can complete a series of small subtasks that will take you to your final goal.

Try not to waste time and energy worrying about situations that are out of your control. Instead, focus your energy on situations you can change or modify in some way. In addition, avoid the "what if" scenario in which you imagine the worst happening to you. Stick to problems you really have and forget about those that are possible but not particularly probable.

Don't Be a Perfectionist

Sometimes we bring stress into our lives by demanding too much of ourselves. We set impossible goals and then get exhausted trying to reach them. Be realistic about what you can accomplish without wearing yourself out. Go ahead and aim for the dean's list, but that doesn't mean you have to get all A's. Instead of working yourself into a frenzy, allow yourself one or two B's.

Maintain a Regular Work Schedule

Particularly in college, stress is often a direct result of poor time management. A student who procrastinates or postpones getting the work done on a daily basis often ends up feeling that his or her life is out of control. You can avoid such a crisis by consistently making good use of your time. (For more on time management, see Chapter 4.)

Definitely Seek Help

Often if you talk to someone about your problems, you'll get a new perspective and discover that solutions are simpler than you thought. See pages 13–15 for suggestions of people to see on campus.

Get Some Exercise

Aerobic exercise—running, swimming, and walking—helps release tension. Whenever you are feeling overwhelmed by stress, it's time to take a break and do some exercise. It doesn't have to be a long break; exercising for just twenty minutes can brighten your perspective on the world.

Learn a Relaxation Technique

The *relaxation response* is recommended by Dr. Herbert Benson, a cardiologist at Harvard Medical School. Studying various ways of relaxing, Dr. Benson found that meditation, yoga, praying, and similar kinds of activities helped people feel calmer and more in control. Drawing on these methods, Dr. Benson developed a simple technique for soothing the body during stressful times.

Other researchers have developed similar techniques to produce relaxation. The following method requires only a few minutes twice a day. Here are the steps:

1. Find a comfortable chair in a quiet room.
2. Close your eyes and take a deep breath.
3. As you inhale, say the first syllable in the word *re-lax*; as you exhale, say the second syllable.
4. Let yourself drift into thoughts and daydreams, but periodically repeat the word *relax* to deepen your breathing.
5. Don't worry about achieving a deep level of relaxation. Maintain a passive attitude, allowing relaxation to occur at its own pace. When distracting thoughts occur, don't dwell on them. Calmly return to repeating the word *relax*.
6. When you finish, sit quietly for several minutes, at first with your eyes closed and later with your eyes open.

Working Space

READING ASSIGNMENT

When you are finished reading the following article, see if you can answer the question posed by the title. Then answer the questions that follow.

What's Your Learning Style?
   —BY JANET NELSON

The conventional method of teaching recreational sports can be summed up as detection and correction—an instructor watches students perform and then tells them what they're doing wrong and how to do it right. But this can be an unpleasant and ineffective way to learn, and many instructors have turned to a kinder school of thought: people learn in many different ways, and it's up to teachers to tailor the lesson to the student.

This approach, long reserved for training elite athletes, now holds the promise of better performance for amateurs. It is built on a foundation of psychological research, originating with Carl Jung early in the century, that identifies certain basic personality types. Expanding on Jung's research, a psychologist at McBer & Company, a management consulting firm in Boston, determined that each person has a predominant learning style—watching, thinking, feeling or doing—and in the mid-1970's developed a test for use in both schools and business to identify it. "Our research found that when people are taught in all of the learning styles, they retain the information longer than if they were simply lectured to," says Jennifer Zaccaro, a sales and marketing manager for McBer.

In recent years some of the McBer findings have been appropriated by sports instructors, who have filtered them through their own teaching experiences and begun introducing them in their schools. The instructors have discovered that most people are watchers, or visual learners, who do best when they can watch a demonstration of a technique or look at drawings or photographs. Some people are thinkers, who need precise technical explanations before they can perform—for instance, the angle at which a tennis racquet should hit the ball during a serve. Other people are feelers, who want to know what it feels like to swing the racquet correctly. Still others are doers; impatient with lessons, they need to pick up a tennis racquet and hit a ball over and over again, incorporating tips from an instructor. Although everyone uses all of these styles to some degree, and none is better than any other, most people seem naturally to favor one of them, says Ed Joyce, an instructor at the Sunday River Ski Resort in Bethel, Maine, who has developed teaching methods that draw on learning-styles research.

Joyce first used the learning-styles approach in 1985 to teach academic subjects to students who were unmotivated and in danger of failing at English High School in Boston, where he is the assistant headmaster. All of them showed greater interest in school, according to Joyce. Whether instructing a high school class or a group of six skiers, Joyce is careful to make each point in different ways, to cover the four learning styles.

Joyce also relies on the tried-and-true technique of positive reinforcement. "We don't want to be dishonest or condescending in giving praise," he says, "but if a compliment is related to a person's skill, it builds self-esteem and a feeling of mastery. That's better than criticism any day."

Integral to the learning-styles approach is a technique called modeling, which also has its roots in psychological research. Modeling is a process by which a student develops a mental image of how to do something. "Mental models are really a mainstay of cognition," says David N. Perkins, co-director of Project Zero, an ongoing investigation of intelligence at Harvard's Graduate School of Education. "They're the Swiss Army knives of the mind—they help you think flexibly about a subject."

1. What are the four basic learning styles?

2. What do you think is your best style or method of learning?

3. What makes you think this particular method works best for you?

4. According to the article, what is modeling?

5. How might you make use of this technique?

6. What ideas in this article can you apply to studying?

WRITING ASSIGNMENT

Write a few paragraphs describing how you felt during your first half hour or so at college.

JOURNAL ASSIGNMENTS

1. Do you think you gave high school your best effort? Why or why not?
2. If you're a student returning to school after a long absence, make a list of the advantages you bring with you as an older student.
3. Write down three things you plan to do to take charge of your education.

✔ Checking Out: Review Questions for Chapter 1

1. Give several reasons why college is the place to become your best self.

2. Why is it helpful to sign a pact, or contract, with yourself spelling out your plans for studying?

3. What are learning strategies? Why is it useful to develop a repertoire of learning strategies?

4. Why is it important to attend the first meeting of each class?

5. How can a learning journal help you keep on top of your studies?

6. What are some limitations of rote memorization? What other kinds of learning do teachers expect of you at the college level?

7. If you are having some problems with a course and you want advice, name some of the people on campus who are available to help you.

8. What office keeps the official records of your grades? What office can help you during a financial emergency?

9. What kinds of information are available on a syllabus?

10. Describe the technique for relaxation recommended in the chapter.

▶ In Summary

Whether you come directly from high school, from the work world, or from family responsibilities, college will be a new and challenging experience. You will need to familiarize yourself with the campus and to shift to learning at the college level. More is expected of you at college than at high school (where you and your work were supervised closely). You often will be asked to develop your own point of view and to think critically about complex issues that have no easy answers.

Most students have their own learning styles that work best for them. If you can develop a repertoire of learning strategies and tailor them appropriately to each specific task, you will handle your college assignments more efficiently. If you develop a take-charge attitude and assume responsibility for your own learning, you will help yourself adapt to the new experience of college. If and when problems arise, many people on campus are ready to offer help.

Use the tips in the rest of this book to help you learn productively.

Think of college as a challenge—but a challenge that you can meet successfully.

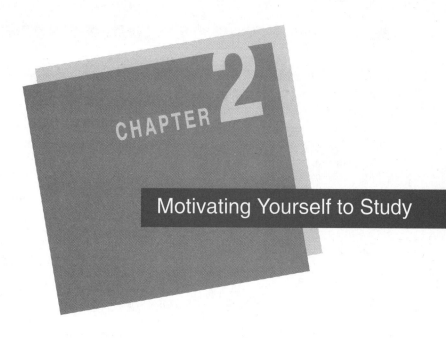

CHAPTER **2**

Motivating Yourself to Study

"The single most powerful predictor of success in the long run is commitment, a passion to pursue well-defined goals."

—*Charles Garfield*

The objective of this chapter is not simply to tell you that **motivation** or a sense of purpose is important. We also want to show you how to develop and maintain a high level of motivation—an essential ingredient for college success. The topics in Chapter 2 cover:

- Thinking about long-term goals
- Identifying *your* long-term goals
- Making a concrete plan of action for attaining your goals
- Changing unproductive habits
- Developing specific strategies for self-motivation
- Increasing your self-esteem

Thinking About Long-Term Goals

If someone asks you "Why are you in school?" would you be able to answer? Surprisingly, many students can't, or else they respond with a vague and meaningless statement such as "I need an education." If asked why, they are once again stumped. Given this response, it's no wonder that many of these students are not highly motivated to study.

Yet for most people, it is the hope of future achievements that keeps them working day after day. For example, how many Olympic athletes do you think could tolerate their grueling training without a vision of their long-term goals? To help you think about long-term goals, we have listed five ways in which college can enrich a person's life. As you read our list, think about which goals are or should be yours.

College Can Give You a Sense of Direction and Purpose

Like many freshmen, you may have arrived on campus without a clear vision of what you want to do with your life. You may not even have a solid sense of your own personal talents and gifts. It's important, therefore, that you use your college years to discover what you will do, both personally and professionally, with the rest of your life. After taking an American history course given by a particularly stimulating professor, you may discover that you are absorbed when reading history books; you might even decide that you like history enough to become a history teacher. Perhaps a biology course will introduce you to the complexity of animal behavior, and you might decide to become a veterinarian. Although you may have arrived on campus with little sense of what you can or should do with your life, you don't have to leave that way.

College Can Improve Your Chances of Getting a Good Job

Motivated students have their eyes on the future. They realize that the more college courses and credits they have on their transcript and the more specialized skills they have acquired, the more employable they will be. These students also know that people with degrees usually have the more interesting jobs—jobs in which they make decisions, earn a good salary, win promotions, and maybe even have the opportunity to travel.

College Can Give You an Understanding of Other Cultures

Americans used to describe their society as a "melting pot"; now they are more apt to speak of *diversity* or *multiculturalism* to describe the African, Hispanic, Asian, and many other cultures that contribute to American society. College is the place to study the art, history, and traditions of the many cultures of the world. It is the place to break down stereotypes and intolerance and to replace them with cooperation, compromise, and acceptance.

With all countries sharing the same finite resources, the people of the world must cooperate on how best to handle oil spills, fishing rights, air pollution, the ozone layer, disease control, and other complex global issues in order to make the world livable for all.

College Can Sharpen Your Ability to Think

The philosopher and psychologist William James once observed that the goal of education was not so much the transfer of information as the development of mental training. From James's point of view, the ultimate goal of learning was to develop intellectual habits of mind, such as the ability to evaluate conflicting opinions or to argue a point convincingly. For James, subject matter, though important, was not as critical as the ability to think hard and well.

A college or university is a unique environment, one in which you will be encouraged to spend time evaluating not just other people's ideas but your own as well. Make the most of this opportunity. Use it to learn and develop in yourself the intellectual habits scholars use in their various disciplines.

College Can Help You Discover Hidden Talents

Your college years can help you discover gifts and abilities you never knew you had. You could, for example, find yourself in a history class giving an oral report on the causes of the French Revolution. Before you give your report, you might think you can't do it because your legs feel like spaghetti and your voice has become a nervous falsetto. But afterward you feel pleased with yourself. You've discovered you have a gift for speaking in front of groups. You realize that, once started, you spoke easily and naturally; you even livened things up with a few jokes. It's important that you think of your college years as a time when you can discover gifts and abilities you never knew you had.

Once you can answer the crucial question "Why am I in college?" you will find it easier to make and maintain a commitment to studying. Hard work will no longer dismay you because your eyes will be set on the future and the promise that it holds.

☐   PRACTICE 1   In a paragraph, describe your life fifteen or twenty years from today. What do you see yourself doing both personally and professionally?

Identifying Your Long-Term Career Goals

In *USA Today* (April 29, 1993), twenty award-winning students from two-year colleges across the country listed the following long-range career goals (most of these students are moving on to four-year college programs).

physical therapy
business management
history/political science
journalism/economics
civil (environmental) engineering
high school teaching (English as a second language)
law
radiology technician
pediatrician
clinical psychology
accounting
public relations
doctorate in education
electrical engineering

Do any of these goals interest you? The advantage of having a clear-cut goal is that you don't lose time backtracking later, making up courses required to major in a given field. However, a great many students are unsure of their own interests, undecided about their major, and uncertain of their future long-term goals. In fact, many people change their majors several times during college. Many others change their careers several times after college, returning to school for additional training.

Examine Your Interests and Abilities

If you are unsure of your future career, first think of all the things that interest you most and that you most enjoy doing. Do you have a passion for photography, or do you want to work at your computer during every spare minute? Try to identify a profession in which you can do all or some of the things that you most enjoy.

Next identify your special abilities and talents, things that your teachers or friends over the years have said that you do well. If you usually get good grades in a subject, or if a subject comes to you relatively easily, this is one of your areas of strength. You should look carefully at these natural gifts and see if you can use them to advantage in one career or another.

As you search for a career goal, keep trying to match up your interests and your natural abilities. The ideal job would be one in which you enjoy the work and have a natural ability for doing it. But often people choose a profession from a more practical viewpoint, selecting a job or career that has financial or growth potential; they then plan to do something that interests them in their spare time.

Do Research on Jobs and Careers

After you consider your strengths, explore the various job possibilities that are open to you. See your career counselor to investigate the range of job possibilities, some of which you probably don't know about or have not yet considered. Find out what jobs seem suitable for you and what courses and degrees are required for each one.

As part of your research, follow the want ads in the newspaper to read the various job descriptions and salary ranges.

Whenever you can, speak to people who already have jobs in a field that interests you and ask them what the work is like, what the opportunities for growth are, how hard it is to get an entry-level job, and so forth.

Finally, think ahead and prepare for several alternate career options in case your first choice becomes outmoded by new technologies.

Try Introductory and Skill-Building Courses

Until you find your goal, take some basic skill-building courses that will get you started and will help you later in the work force. Select courses in math, English composition, basic computer programming, or statistics at the right level for you. Also try introductory courses in fields such as psychology, business, government, economics, history, and literature. Many of these courses will fill general requirements for most majors.

Take Your Time

Take time with this major decision of finding the job or career that suits you best. Your goal is to find a life's work that is stimulating and appealing—one that allows you to do your best work. People who like their jobs look forward to going to work each day, and their lives remain rewarding over the years.

PRACTICE 2   This questionnaire is to help you identify those specific abilities and interests that may lead to a major in college—and, in time, to a career or profession.

1. What are your strongest interests—things you most look forward to doing?

    1. _____

    2. _____

    3. _____

2. What are your special abilities, the things teachers or others have said you do well?

    1. _____

    2. _____

    3. _____

3. Of all the courses you have taken thus far, which three have you liked most?

    1. _____

    2. _____

    3. _____

4. Of the jobs you have had, what parts of the work have you preferred? What parts do you want to avoid in future jobs?

_____

_____

5. Are there any adults you have met or seen working who hold jobs that you may want to do? Describe their jobs.

_____

_____

6. Name three dream jobs you'd like to have—the kind everyone wants but only a few people get. (These jobs may be highly competitive, require a good deal of training, or require certain specialized abilities.)

1. _____

2. _____

3. _____

7. Name three realistic jobs you'd like to have. (These are jobs where openings will probably be available, where the salary will cover your needs, and where long-range prospects for growth and promotion are good.)

1. _____

2. _____

3. _____

8. Given your dreams and the reality of the job market, what jobs or careers do you think you should prepare for?

_____

_____

PRACTICE 3   List the future job or career possibilities you intend to explore, and some courses you might take leading to those careers. Then add the appropriate majors.

Job 1: _____

Possible courses to take:

_____

_____

_____

Possible major leading to Job 1: _____

Job 2: _____

Possible courses to take:

_____

_____

_____

Possible major leading to Job 2: _____

Job 3: _____

Possible courses to take:

_____

_____

_____

Possible major leading to Job 3: _____

Making a Concrete Plan of Action

Identifying your long-term goals is the first step toward achieving them. The next step is to **identify the intermediate steps you need to take to achieve your goals.** For example, if one of your long-term goals is to improve your chances of doing interesting and varied work in artificial intelligence, you might decide to take several computer science courses.

In mapping out a step-by-step approach to your long-term goals, you should also ask yourself if each step is both *realistic* and *attainable.* If you have decided that a knowledge of computers will improve your career choices, plan to become an expert in one or two computer languages. This is an achievable goal. Do not, however, plan to master every computer language ever devised. This is an impossible task that in the end will intimidate rather than encourage you.

Be Prepared for Setbacks

In planning for your future goals, you should also prepare yourself for an occasional setback or defeat. By definition, long-term goals take time to achieve, and there is no guarantee that every step you take toward your final objectives will be successful.

Over the course of your college career, you will have to inspire and re-inspire yourself. Expect to meet some resistance from within, some failures, some black moods. But if the general trend is one of small gradual successes, then you are on the right track.

Develop Stamina

College students have to keep up their motivation over long periods of time. To do so, they need to develop *stamina.* As opposed to a sprint that takes an intense burst of effort for a short time, think of college as a long-distance run where you need steady effort over a longer time period.

Instead of staying up too late, sleeping through classes, and being generally out of control and ineffective, rethink your life to maximize your energy for work, study, and recreation over the long haul. Create a good balance for yourself.

PRACTICE 4   Write down one of your long-term goals. Next to the goal, list some specific *intermediate* steps you can take to achieve that goal.

Example

Long-Term Goal	Intermediate Steps
Become a systems analyst	1. Take an introductory computer course
	2. Form a study group
	3. Look for a part-time job with a computer software firm
	4. Look for someone who already works in computers to be my mentor

Specific Strategies for Improving Your Self-Motivation

Here are specific strategies you can use to spark your enthusiasm for studying. Feel free to adapt them so they work for you. Act as if you are a scientist conducting research on yourself, and your objective is to figure out how to make yourself study more efficiently.

Post Your Long-Term Goals

Post your list of goals in your workplace or put it in your notebook. Every time you feel your motivation slipping, glance at that slip of paper and think about what you are working toward.

"Bachelor's degree in biomedicine and a job in a hospital research lab. My own apartment."

"First goal: degree in film. Then an internship at a TV station for practical experience. Next, job to earn money for graduate school in film. Later, direct documentary film on Native Americans."

Speak to Yourself Positively About Studying

Develop a list of mottoes or messages related to studying. If you feel your motivation flagging, use them to urge yourself on.

- "I can pass this course, and I'm going to."
- "I can make myself study; a little hard work won't hurt me."
- "I'm close to a breakthrough in precalculus."
- "I will study and prepare and perhaps my chance will come."
  —Abraham Lincoln
- "You're learning a lot; keep it up."

Psychologists confirm that positive self-talk is beneficial in all areas of your life. By the same token, do not allow yourself to make negative evaluations ("I can never do well on multiple-choice exams").

Take Someone You Admire as a Role Model

Think of someone whose achievements you admire, and find out as much as you can about that person's life. How did this person prepare for his or her career? Were there any setbacks?

Look in the library for biographies of people who interest you. Read with a focus on how they overcame obstacles and defeats. After recovering from a crippling bout of polio, which left him able to stand only with the help of braces, Franklin Delano Roosevelt went on to be elected president of the United States four times. Where did he get the inner strength to make up for his physical limitations?

Be an Effective Strategist

Spend five minutes each night reviewing that day's accomplishments and evaluating whether your study strategies worked. Ask yourself leading questions.

- Did I study for as long as I had intended? If not, why not?
- Did I use my studying time efficiently? Did I spend too long on math and not get to bio?

- Overall, am I keeping up with my assignments?
- Have I fallen behind in one course? If so, what's the best thing to do now?

Then begin to plan ahead, making use of what you've learned about yourself. See Chapter 4 for more on managing your time.

Get Yourself Mentally Ready for the Next Day

Psych yourself for tomorrow's tasks by asking yourself a series of questions before you go to sleep:

- What tasks must I accomplish tomorrow and in what order should I do them?
- What is a reasonable amount of time for each task?
- What time will I get started tomorrow? What time will I do each task?

By settling firmly in your mind what you plan to do tomorrow, you will prepare yourself to act on those plans.

Use Rewards on Yourself

Make a list of those things that you genuinely love to do—listen to music, take a long swim, take a run around the track, have a slice of pizza, whatever—and do one of these things after you have studied productively. Then you'll have the pleasant sensation of being in control, of having earned your rewards.

Review Your Accomplishments to Date

If you feel your motivation flagging, tell yourself how you've been improving.

- "Now I'm getting into this course, it's easier."
- "I'm catching on about how to take notes."
- "I did well on the first quiz—so why not again?"
- "I understand more of what I read."
- "My math skills are really coming along."

Attack Something You Are Resisting—but Only for Ten Minutes

Getting started is often the hardest part, but once you've begun, you'll find it easier to continue. Try to coordinate your tasks with your energy. Do the hardest ones when you are freshest; do the easier ones when you are fading.

Visualize the Results of Your Hard Work

Create mental pictures of what your life will be like once you have achieved some of your goals. Imagine yourself speaking at a conference, traveling on business in a foreign country, getting a promotion, or having your own home. Use these images to spur you on whenever you feel your motivation flagging.

Imagine Your Life If You Don't Achieve Your Goal

When Sarah Pallister, a nursing student, was working her way through school, she would often feel discouraged. Because she had a part-time job and two children to raise, she had more to do than she could handle without feeling pressure. But every time she got discouraged, she would think of what her life was like before—without a steady job or a secure income. Not surprisingly, Sarah graduated at the top of her class.

Look for a Mentor

A *mentor* is someone who takes a personal interest in your progress and is willing to give you advice and encouragement on reaching your goals. If, for example, you plan to be a lawyer or a paralegal, search for a legal professional who is willing to take an active role in guiding you.

Your mentor, in many cases, has taken the same career path you are planning to take, and so can give you specific practical advice on how to enter the profession. A film student, for instance, learned from her mentor that it was highly useful to network with fellow film students who had already found jobs.

Challenge Yourself

Compete only with yourself. Your goal is to do better than *you* did before, to keep learning more skills, and to master each course. Don't worry about how anyone else does.

Above all, use your determination and inner strength to keep going. Inner-city student Judith Aquilar explains how she succeeded when many of her friends did not: "I *made sure* I got to see the adviser; I *made sure* I completed my credits and got through. I *made sure* I was going to pass." With her determined attitude, she was unbeatable.

Increasing Your Self-Esteem

"There are several kinds of football players. There are those who have it and know it, those who have it and don't know it, those who haven't got it and know it, and those who haven't got it and don't know it. Those who haven't got it and don't know it have won us more games than anybody."

—Woody Hayes, football coach

As the quotation from winning coach Woody Hayes suggests, believing in yourself plays a powerful role in achieving success. The stronger and more competent you feel, the less likely you are to give up on your goals. So think about and put into practice these pointers for increasing self-esteem.

Identify your positive traits.   Take the time to figure out what's good about you. Are you a loyal friend? A good listener? A reliable employee? Do you know how to take a joke, share responsibility, say the right thing in difficult situations? Once you take stock of your strengths, you'll be amazed at how many you have.

Analyze the habits you call "faults."   After you have identified your strengths, list what you believe are your faults. Then consider what you can do to change them. Most failings are not fixed character traits. They are usually habits that can be altered through concentration and discipline. Do you consider yourself to be a disorganized or careless worker? Being disorganized or careless is not genetically determined. If you really want to be more organized, you can develop that personality trait. It just takes a little time and effort. Tell yourself, "In the past, I've been disorganized, but in the future, I'm going to schedule my time so I finish everything I start."

Meet fear of failure head-on.   To increase your self-esteem, confront the fear that plagues 99 percent of the population—fear of failure. Tell yourself you won't always meet every short-term goal or pass every test. No one does. But you don't need to think of these experiences as *failures*. If you figure out what went wrong and plan on how you'll improve the next time, you are taking positive steps and *learning,* not failing. Keep in mind that using the word *failure* represents an act of interpretation. In other words, it all depends on how you choose to evaluate the situation.

Give yourself credit.   Every time you do something you're proud of, congratulate yourself. Did you stick to your study schedule, run a mile in seven minutes, or polish the car to a high sheen? No matter how small or insignificant the accomplishment, congratulate yourself for doing it well.

Remember your past accomplishments.   Too often, people evaluate themselves solely by their current accomplishments. If things aren't going well in the present, they feel inept and inadequate. Yet remembering past accomplishments is particularly important at times like these. Whenever you're feeling overwhelmed, remind yourself of obstacles you've overcome in the past. Having a hard time mastering chemistry? Remember how you thought you'd fail eighth-grade algebra? Well, you didn't fail then, and you won't fail now.

Don't overestimate the confidence of others.   In new and challenging situations, such as the first term of freshman year, most people feel scared or anxious. But some hide it better than others. So don't criticize yourself for not feeling as confident as those around you. At one time or another, they've probably felt intimidated too.

PRACTICE 5   Use this questionnaire to evaluate your self-esteem. More than five "yes" answers suggests you need to give yourself a pep talk and follow the pointers outlined above.

1. When you make a mistake, do you think about it for days or weeks at a time?   ☐ Yes   ☐ No

2. When you have to learn something new, do you get extremely anxious?   ☐ Yes   ☐ No

3. Do you find it hard to believe that other people could admire you?   ☐ Yes   ☐ No

4. If someone compliments you, do you tend to assume he or she is just being kind?   ☐ Yes   ☐ No

5. If someone disagrees with you, do you usually think you're the one who must be wrong?   ☐ Yes   ☐ No

6. Are you easily discouraged if people don't praise you for achieving a goal or finishing a task?   ☐ Yes   ☐ No

7. Are you afraid to answer questions in class for fear you might be wrong?   ☐ Yes   ☐ No

8. Are you normally afraid of doing something you've never done before?   ☐ Yes   ☐ No

9. If confronted with a challenge, do you immediately think, "I won't be able to do this"?   ☐ Yes   ☐ No

10. If you are in a group, do you find it hard to take a position the others don't agree with?   ☐ Yes   ☐ No

11. Do you assume that most people know more than you do?   ☐ Yes   ☐ No

12. Do you get nervous when you meet new people because you wonder how they will respond to you?   ☐ Yes   ☐ No

13. In an unfamiliar setting, do you wait for someone to approach you instead of introducing yourself and starting a conversation?   ☐ Yes   ☐ No

14. Do you feel upset if you don't meet the standards you've set for yourself?   ☐ Yes   ☐ No

15. Do you think most successful people are simply a lot more talented than you are?   ☐ Yes   ☐ No

---

PRACTICE 6   Each of the following personal characteristics is marked with a plus or a minus. Circle each plus or minus that you think you possess. Then look the list over and consider how you can turn those minuses into additional pluses.

1. I'm punctual. +
2. I'm always late. –
3. I finish anything that I start. +
4. I start things, but I don't finish them. –
5. I have a sense of humor. +
6. I always look on the bright side. +
7. I tend to be pessimistic. –
8. I'm a very determined person. +
9. I give up too easily. –
10. I can't speak in front of groups. –
11. I like to figure out new solutions to problems. +
12. I tend to prejudge people and ideas. –
13. I have a lot of common sense. +

14. I tend to be disorganized. –
15. I know how to organize my time. +
16. I like to learn new things. +
17. I know how to talk to people. +
18. I'm not serious enough about my work. –
19. I have trouble concentrating. –
20. I don't have enough self-confidence. –
21. I have trouble accepting criticism. –
22. I have a very limited vocabulary. –
23. I like learning new words. +
24. I'm enthusiastic about life. +
25. I believe in myself. +

Working Space

READING ASSIGNMENT

Read the following selection (from *The Autobiography of Malcolm X*) about Malcolm X's struggle to educate himself in prison. Then answer the questions that follow.

Saved

BY MALCOLM X

I became increasingly frustrated at not being able to express what I wanted to convey in letters that I wrote, especially those to Mr. Elijah Muhammad. In the street, I had been the most articulate hustler out there—I had commanded attention when I said something. But now, trying to write simple English, I not only wasn't articulate, I wasn't even functional. How would I sound writing in slang, the way I would *say* it, something such as, "Look, daddy, let me pull your coat about a cat, Elijah Muhammad—"

Many who today hear me somewhere in person, or on television, or those who read something I've said, will think I went to school far beyond the eighth grade. This impression is due entirely to my prison studies.

It had really begun back in the Charlestown Prison, when Bimbi first made me feel envy of his stock of knowledge. Bimbi had always taken charge of any conversation he was in, and I had tried to emulate him. But every book I picked up had few sentences which didn't contain anywhere from one to nearly all of the words that might as well have been in Chinese. When I just skipped those words, of course, I really ended up with little idea of what the book said. So I had come to the Norfolk Prison Colony still going through only book-reading motions. Pretty soon, I would have quit even these motions, unless I had received the motivation that I did.

I saw that the best thing I could do was get hold of a dictionary—to study, to learn some words. I was lucky enough to reason also that I should try to improve my penmanship. It was sad. I couldn't even write in a straight line. It was both ideas together that moved me to request a dictionary along with some tablets and pencils from the Norfolk Prison Colony school.

I spent two days just riffling uncertainly through the dictionary's pages. I'd never realized so many words existed! I didn't know which words I needed to learn. Finally, just to start some kind of action, I began copying.

In my slow, painstaking, ragged handwriting, I copied into my tablet everything printed on that first page, down to the punctuation marks.

I believe it took me a day. Then, aloud, I read, back to myself, everything I'd written on the tablet. Over and over, aloud, to myself, I read my own handwriting.

I woke up the next morning, thinking about those words—immensely proud to realize that not only had I written so much at one time, but I'd written words that I never knew were in the world. Moreover, with a little effort, I also could remember what many of these words meant. I reviewed the words whose meanings I didn't remember. Funny thing, from the dictionary first page right now, that "aardvark" springs to my mind. The dictionary had a picture of it, a long-tailed, long-eared, burrowing African mammal, which lives off termites caught by sticking out its tongue as an anteater does for ants.

I was so fascinated that I went on—I copied the dictionary's next page. And the same experience came when I studied that. With every succeeding page, I also learned of people and places and events from history. Actually the dictionary is like a miniature encyclopedia. Finally the dictionary's A section had filled a whole tablet—and I went on into the B's. That was the way I started copying what eventually became the entire dictionary. It went a lot faster after so much practice helped me to pick up handwriting speed. Between what I wrote in my tablet, and writing letters, during the rest of my time in prison I would guess I wrote a million words.

I suppose it was inevitable that as my word base broadened, I could for the first time pick up a book and read and now begin to understand what the book was saying. Anyone who has read a great deal can imagine the new world that opened. Let me tell you something: From then until I left that prison, in every free moment I had, if I was not reading in the library, I was reading on my bunk. You couldn't have gotten me out of books with a wedge. Between Mr. Muhammad's teachings, my correspondence, my visitors—usually Ella and Reginald—and my reading of books, months passed without my even thinking about being imprisoned. In fact, up to then, I never had been so truly free in my life. . . .

I have often reflected upon the new vistas that reading opened to me. I knew right there in prison that reading had changed forever the course of my life. As I see it today, the ability to read awoke inside me some long dormant craving to be mentally alive. I certainly wasn't seeking any degree, the way a college confers a status symbol upon its students. My homemade education gave me, with every additional book that I read, a little bit more sensitivity to the deafness, dumbness, and blindness that was afflicting the black race in America. Not long ago, an English writer telephoned me from London, asking questions. One was, "What's your alma mater?" I told him, "Books."

1. What motivated Malcolm X to improve his ability to read and write?

2. What effect did Malcolm X's improved reading ability have on his life in prison?

3. What effect did it have on his attitude toward life in general?

4. In your own quest for an education, do you think you are as motivated as Malcolm X was? Why or why not?

WRITING ASSIGNMENT

In his autobiography, Malcolm X describes the excitement he felt at the moment he found he could really read. Write a paper in which you describe a similar learning experience, one in which you felt excited by your sense of power and accomplishment. The experience doesn't have to revolve around books or words, but it does have to represent the excitement of learning something new.

JOURNAL ASSIGNMENTS

1. Which of the strategies for motivation listed on pages 34–38 do you think are going to be useful to you? Why do you think they will work?
2. Try to come up with at least two more strategies for maintaining motivation.
3. Start a list of mottoes you can use when you feel your motivation flagging. To open your list, here's one from Hillary Clinton: "In the future what you can earn on a job will depend on what you can learn."

✔ Checking Out: Review Questions for Chapter 2

1. Why are long-term goals important?

2. When you analyze your long-term goals, what kinds of questions should you ask yourself?

3. What do we mean when we say that the word *failure* represents an act of interpretation?

4.   Name three specific things you can do to develop motivation.

5.   Explain why it is important to develop stamina.

▶ In Summary

The key to inspiring yourself to study is motivation, the idea that you are working toward some long-term goal that you hope to achieve over time. Once you know *why* you are in school, everything else will more easily fall into place. That's because your work will have a meaning and a purpose. Studying is often hard work. No one is going to deny that. But once you know why you are studying, you will find that hard work does not dismay you because you have a goal and a sense of direction. Studying is a stepping-stone toward your future.

CHAPTER 3

Improving Your Concentration

"When a distraction arises, ask yourself: would you rather have the distraction, or would you rather have your goal?"

—*John-Roger and Peter McWilliams*

Although motivation is essential to college success, so too is the ability to *concentrate*—that is, to stay focused on your work without allowing your mind to wander. From this chapter, you'll learn steps you can take to improve your powers of concentration, such as:

- Creating an environment that encourages concentration.
- Developing the right attitude toward distractions.
- Staying focused despite external or internal distractions.
- Eliminating any habits that may interfere with concentration.

Setting the Stage for Concentration

Successful students know that setting the stage for concentration is an essential first step. They know that where they study and whom they study with are just two of the factors that can contribute to (or detract from) their ability to concentrate.

Work in the Same Place

Dedicating a particular place or space just for study is crucial to maintaining concentration. To a degree, we are all creatures of habit. If you associate a specific room or area with studying, you will automatically get to work once you enter your designated work space. Studying in that particular spot will become a habit, one you won't want to break.

Choose a Quiet Spot

Although you'll eventually learn to concentrate and shut out any distractions, it will be a while before you reach that level of concentration. While you are learning how to concentrate for long periods, search out a place that is relatively free of distractions. If you can't find a quiet room at home or in the dorm, look for a spot in the library and think of it as your work space. If you are a mother of small children, or if you are a single man working two jobs to stay in school, this advice may be hard to put into practice. Just do the best you can to eliminate as many distractions as possible.

Set Time Limits for Studying

If you sit down to study assuming that you have the whole night ahead of you, you're giving your mind an open invitation to wander. To concentrate fully, challenge yourself by setting specific time limits for each task. Tell yourself you have only one hour to finish at least ten pages of your mass communications text. Knowing how much you want to accomplish in an hour will make you more conscious of how you use (or waste) your time. With only one hour to complete your reading assignment, you'll recognize that a fifteen-minute chat with your roommate is a large chunk of that time.

Gather Your Materials

Gather everything you need before you start to study—pen, paper, highlighter, dictionary, calculator, and so on. It's far too easy to interrupt your concentration and look for your favorite pen at exactly the moment you are struggling with a difficult section of your earth science text. Don't give yourself excuses for unnecessary interruptions.

Use the Proper Lighting

Work in a space where you can create what ergonomists (people who study the relationships between performance and work environments) call *task lighting*. Task lighting illuminates a specific area—the page or the paper you're working on—without lighting up the rest of the room. Long-necked reading lamps that turn in different directions will give you the kind of task lighting you need. A number of good, inexpensive ones are available on the market.

When you can't control the available light, say at work or in the library, find a light bright enough so that you don't strain to read.

Select Your Study Companions Carefully

If you study with a friend who yawns constantly, complains about studying, and asks you for the time every five minutes, we guarantee your concentration will falter. Maybe it won't happen in the first hour when you feel fresh and determined. But as soon as you get a bit tired or frustrated, your friend's complaints will contribute to your weariness, and soon you will be talking instead of studying. Therefore choose someone to study with who, like you, is determined to do well. If you feel like quitting, your friend can argue against it. Or you can be the one to say, "No, let's not give up yet; let's work another half hour." The support of friends is an invaluable resource; make the most of it.

Turn Off the Music

If you work at it, you can become so expert at shutting out distractions that your roommate could play rap music while you're studying and you could ignore it. However, it takes a lot of work and enormous self-discipline to arrive at that level of consciousness and concentration. When you are first learning how to lengthen your attention span, don't put obstacles in your path. Turn off the music.

Evaluate the Difficulty of Your Assignments

Not all texts and papers will demand the same level of concentration. Some will be more demanding than others. If an assignment sounds relatively easy, plan on reading two chapters instead of one, or on writing a complete draft instead of a partial one. But if you're assigned a chapter or a paper in your most demanding course, limit yourself to completing only half of the chapter, or only one section of the draft. Above all, don't overtax your powers of concentration and end up feeling defeated. If the assignment turns out to be easier than you expected, you can always do more.

Take Periodic Breaks

If you try to work without a pause, your eyes and your brain get overtired, and fatigue interferes with your ability to concentrate. If you allot two hours for your study session, make sure you take a fifteen-minute break after the first hour.

Make your break as different as possible from your work. If you're writing a term paper, don't write a letter on your break. Instead, walk around the room and stretch your legs. Or make a phone call or leaf through a magazine, preferably one with a lot of pictures.

Keep your breaks short. Anywhere from ten to twenty minutes is fine. More than twenty minutes and you'll feel like you're finished for the day; getting back to work will be hard.

Take Responsibility for Concentrating

A good deal of research suggests that how you respond to distractions can influence their effect on your concentration.[1] In one study, two groups of students were asked to work in a room with a lot of background noise. One group was told that the noise would facilitate their work, making it go faster. The other group was told that the noise in the room would hinder

---

[1]See Virginia Voeks, *On Becoming an Educated Person* (Philadelphia: W. B. Saunders, 1979), 167.

their performance. In the end, the students who believed that noise would not distract them performed better on comprehension tests than the students who believed that noise would bother them. What determined the students' success (or failure) was their *attitude* toward distraction, *not* the background noise itself.

If you are forced to work in noisy surroundings, don't give up on studying. Tell yourself, "I'm going to concentrate despite these distractions." You'll be surprised by the powers of concentration you can muster when you put your mind to it.

Avoid Food That Makes You Drowsy

The food you eat affects your concentration.[2] Foods high in fat (hamburgers, potato chips, hot dogs, and ice cream) diminish alertness and cause drowsiness. So if you are planning to study in the evening, eat foods like pasta, pretzels, bagels, low-fat yogurt, and fruit instead of a hamburger. The former will energize you for studying; the latter will dull your thinking and make it harder to concentrate.

Get Enough Sleep

While it's true that some people can get by with relatively little sleep, most of us need between six and eight hours to feel alert the next day. Without that amount of sleep, fatigue sets in and our concentration suffers.

To discover how much sleep you need, chart your sleeping and waking patterns for at least two weeks. For example, if you have had four hours of sleep the night before, do you nod off when your art history professor turns off the lights to show slides? On the other hand, if you have had seven or eight hours' sleep, do you stay alert and enjoy looking at the slides? Once you discover how much sleep you need to avoid fatigue, take steps to see that you get the right amount.

PRACTICE 1   Find a short novel or a long article that is easy and enjoyable to read. Start reading in a quiet room, but as soon as you reach a particularly suspenseful or important part, stop reading. Move to a noisier room or area, say the cafe-

---

[2]See Judith Wurtman, *Managing Your Mind and Mood through Food* (New York: Rawson, 1986).

teria or student lounge. Begin reading where you left off. See if you can make the external noise disappear.

Four Tips to Help You Get Enough Sleep

1. *If possible, go to sleep and wake up at approximately the same time every day.* To a large extent, getting enough sleep is a matter of habit, and your body will, over time, adjust to a certain rhythm of sleeping and waking. But to feel your best, establish a sleep routine and stick to it.

2. *Get at least thirty minutes of physical exercise every day.* While studying may fatigue your brain, it does not necessarily tire out your body. You need at least thirty minutes of aerobic exercise—walking, swimming, running—to make your body feel tired enough to rest.

3. *Tell yourself the consequences of losing sleep.* When you're tempted to stay up late, especially during the week, tell yourself that losing sleep has consequences. You will not concentrate well in class if you are tired. Can you afford to feel tired? If your friends all like to stay out late at night partying, make some new friends and see the old ones only on weekends.

4. *Avoid coffee after 5:00 P.M.* Drinking coffee, tea, or carbonated drinks—or any other beverage high in caffeine—after five may produce insomnia.

Becoming an Active Learner

Setting the stage for concentration is a good beginning. But even more to the point is your willingness to **be an active learner,** someone who digs deeply into the material, pulls it apart, and puts it back together again.

Vary Your Assignments

Even the most disciplined students find their minds wandering if they concentrate too long on a single assignment—particularly if they are working on a complicated computer program or reading a difficult text. After a while, the intensity of their concentration produces fatigue.

Varying the assignments you work on is a good way to combat this problem. When you vary your assignments, you call upon different kinds of thinking. If you are tired of working on math problems, renew your mental energy by reading a short story for your American fiction class. Both of these tasks require concentration, but each involves a different kind of thinking. Thus, while one part of your mind is taking a rest, another part can take over and maintain your concentration.

With Pen in Hand, Underline and Annotate

If you annotate the margins of a text, outlining key points or jotting down possible test questions, you have to be paying attention. The very act of annotating forces you to do so.

The same is true of underlining, but only if you underline selectively. While you are deciding what's important to underline and what's not, your attention is automatically focused.

Vary Your Learning Strategies

Just as varying your assignments will help you stay focused, varying your learning strategies will have the same effect. Feeling worn out after underlining and annotating fifteen pages? Try making a diagram or a drawing of the next section to get you back on track. There's no rule saying you must always use the same study method. On the contrary, people seem to learn best when they combine a variety of learning styles.[3]

Think Critically

When you study, don't be satisfied with simply understanding what a text says. Instead, begin to think critically by evaluating what you read. In your psychology text, does the author's explanation make sense to you? In your lecture notes, does the argument outlined by your teacher fit your experience of how humans behave? Do you find yourself agreeing or disagreeing? Asking yourself these kinds of questions will help you maintain your concentration and develop an interest in the course since you will be

---

[3]See Janet Nelson, "What's Your Learning Style?" *New York Times Magazine,* April 28, 1993, 79.

excited by the material itself. The mental activity of challenging the author's or instructor's ideas will help keep you active and alert.

Make Connections

Try to **connect what you are learning with what you already know.** For example, if you are reading about the Eightfold Path of Buddhism for your world civilization class, compare those eight steps with the Ten Commandments. Do you find a lot of similarities or differences between the two? Combining or connecting new information with previous knowledge can make your studying more meaningful and can help you remember points of similarity and difference.

Quit with a Sense of Accomplishment

Try not to stop working when you're feeling stumped. If you're in the middle of a difficult passage, reread one paragraph several times until you have at least a partial understanding of the author's message. If a draft of your paper isn't going well, put the draft aside and *freewrite* jotting down any thoughts that come to mind on your topic; more than likely, you'll discover an idea you can pursue the next day. In both cases, ending on a positive note will make it easier to return to work later.

Learn a Secret of Concentration

Rather than convincing yourself a course is just a tiresome requirement and is nothing you care about, tell yourself that *every* course can teach you something of value. It's up to you to discover what that useful information is and how to make the most of each course and each teacher.

If you can discover something of value to you, you will find the course more absorbing. If you are deeply interested, you will concentrate for extended periods without effort.

> **✳** To improve concentration, be an active learner, someone who digs deeply into the material, pulls it apart, and puts it back together again.

☐ PRACTICE 2   Here's a concentration checklist. Make two copies. Fill out one now and the other a month from now. Your goal is to turn every no into a yes.

1. Do you set specific goals before you begin an assignment?   ☐ Yes   ☐ No

2. Do you set a time limit before you begin an assignment?   ☐ Yes   ☐ No

3. As you study, do you constantly make decisions about what is important and what is not?   ☐ Yes   ☐ No

4. As you read, do you underline selectively and annotate in the margins?   ☐ Yes   ☐ No

5. Do you vary the kinds of tasks you do?   ☐ Yes   ☐ No

6. Do you use a variety of learning strategies?   ☐ Yes   ☐ No

7. Do you periodically look up and mentally review key points from your reading?   ☐ Yes   ☐ No

8. As you work, do you pace yourself to stay within the time limits you have set?   ☐ Yes   ☐ No

9. If you come across a problem in your studying, do you write down your questions and plan to ask for help later?   ☐ Yes   ☐ No

10. Do you congratulate or reward yourself when you finish your work?   ☐ Yes   ☐ No

11. Do you try hard to develop an interest in each of your courses?   ☐ Yes   ☐ No

12. If you have a lapse of concentration, do you immediately try to get back on track?   ☐ Yes   ☐ No

13. Do you try to connect what you are learning with what you already know?   ☐ Yes   ☐ No

14. As you read, do you evaluate the author's ideas and agree or disagree with the author's arguments?   ☐ Yes   ☐ No

Breaking Ineffective Habits

When you are studying, do you look up every time someone passes by? If you are reading a difficult text, do you lean back and look out the window every five minutes, wishing you were outside? Such poor habits can interfere with concentration; they need to be changed.

Although it takes some time, you can change or modify your study habits by applying the three R's of behavior modification: *recognition, refusal,* and *replacement.*

Recognition

Recognizing what you are doing is the first step in changing your behavior. In other words, you have to *monitor your concentration*. Keep a tally sheet while you are studying. Each time you find yourself looking out the window and daydreaming, catch yourself by marking the tally sheet; for a sample tally sheet, see page 59.

Refusal

As soon as you mark your tally sheet, tell yourself, "It's time to get back to work." Don't criticize yourself for looking out the window and losing your concentration. Self-criticism is negative reinforcement and does little more than make you feel bad.

If you can't stop thinking about errands or phone calls you need to attend to, take a break and write down everything you need to do *once you finish studying*. Then put the list aside and return to your studies.

Replacement

Now take the next and most crucial step— replace your ineffective habit with one that will encourage concentration. As soon as you catch yourself looking out the window, see if you can **recite** out loud or silently some part of the text you just read. Recitation, a valuable study strategy that helps maintain concentration and ensures remembering, is a good replacement for the habit of daydreaming.

PRACTICE 3   For each of the following situations, check the strategy you would use. If possible, use the blanks to suggest a strategy of your own.

Situation A
You are working on your least favorite subject and using every excuse for an interruption.

Strategies for Maintaining Concentration
1. Work on this subject first, never last. Assemble everything you need—pens, pencils, note cards—before you start studying.
2. Set a definite time limit for the amount of studying you intend to do. Work in twenty-minute stretches.

3. Jot down potential test questions while you are reading. After your break, see if you can answer them.

_____

_____

_____

Situation B
You like the material well enough, but it's dense and difficult.

Strategies for Maintaining Concentration
1. Annotate while you read, jotting down key points in the margins.
2. Make diagrams to help you picture relationships between ideas.
3. Read the material once at a normal rate of speed. Don't reread until you've reviewed the lecture covering the same material.
4. Think of a reward you will give yourself if you work for an hour.

_____

_____

_____

Situation C
You are hungry and sluggish from lack of sleep.

Strategies for Maintaining Concentration
1. Get a high-protein snack.
2. Take an exercise break—a brisk walk or a quick run—before you settle down to study.

3. Quit early to get a good night's sleep and tack an extra half-hour on to your next few study sessions.

_____

_____

_____

Situation D
Your mind wanders because you keep thinking about other things you have to do.

Strategies for Maintaining Concentration
1. Stop working for a few moments. Write down the errands or tasks that are nagging you.
2. Tell yourself that doing well in this course brings you one step closer to your long-term goal, so you can't afford to be distracted.
3. Run essential errands or make important phone calls before you settle down to work.

_____

_____

_____

Situation E
Your friends are all going to a party on a weekday night and want you to come.

Strategies for Maintaining Concentration
1. Remember the motto "When a distraction arises, ask yourself: would you rather have the distraction or your goal?"
2. Always plan some recreation for the weekend so you can look forward to it.
3. Go to the party, but tack an extra thirty minutes on to your next few study sessions.

4. Make some new friends—
   friends who share your goals.

_____

_____

_____

Situation F
You're working at home and your
family keeps interrupting you.

**Strategies for Maintaining
Concentration**
1. Get a baby-sitter and head for
   the library.
2. Have a family meeting and explain how important it is for you
   to study.
3. Close your eyes and do the relaxation technique described
   on page 19. Then tell yourself,
   "If I want to, I can ignore all external distractions."

_____

_____

_____

PRACTICE 4   Make several copies of the tally sheet shown on page 59. Use them to monitor your concentration. (1) Each time your attention drifts away from your
work, put a check in the distraction column. (2) Try to identify the cause and
(3) respond with a strategy.
At the end of the week, look over your tally sheets and analyze the results. If
your distraction checks are diminishing, give yourself a reward. If they are increasing, consider different strategies.

Example

Distraction	**Cause**	**Strategy**
✔	Material dense and difficult—chemistry reactions tough	—Make diagrams —Take break every 20 minutes

Tally Sheet

Date: _____

Beginning Time: _____

Distraction   Cause   Strategy

Ending Time: _____

Working Space

READING ASSIGNMENT

Read the following article on concentration by Daniel Goleman. As you read, underline any information you think may help you improve your concentration. Then answer the questions that follow.

Concentration Is Likened to Euphoric States of Mind
—By Daniel Goleman

The seemingly simple act of being fully absorbed in a challenging task is now being seen as akin to some of the extravagantly euphoric states such as those sought in drugs or sex or through the "runner's high."

New research is leading to the conclusion that these instances of absorption are, in effect, altered states in which the mind functions at its peak, time is often distorted and a sense of happiness seems to pervade the moment.

Such states, the new research suggests, are accompanied by mental efficiency experienced as a feeling of effortlessness.

One team of researchers describes these moments of absorption as "flow states."

According to Mike Csikszentmihalyi, a psychologist at the University of Chicago, "flow" refers to "those times when things seem to go just right, when you feel alive and fully attentive to what you are doing."

The understanding that deep absorption can be transporting will not come as news to those who readily sink into rapture at a symphony or while reading poetry, but the new research adds precision in defining the circumstances that evoke such heightened awareness.

The Chicago research on flow, which has been under way for more than a decade, began with a study of people performing at their peak. Basketball players, composers, dancers, chess masters, rock climbers, surgeons and others were asked to describe in detail times when they had outdone themselves. One of the elements that was invariably present in these descriptions was full absorption in the activity at hand, an attention that was finely attuned to the shifting demands of the moment.

Along with a full absorption, people in flow described a set of experiences that, taken together, suggest an altered state of consciousness. These include a distortion in the sense of time, so that events seem either to go very quickly or very slowly; an altered sense of one's bodily sensations or sensory perceptions; and a fine precision in gauging one's responses to a changing challenge.

With a group of colleagues at Chicago, and another group at the University of Milan Medical School, Dr. Csikszentmihalyi most recently has been studying the circumstances that draw people into the flow state. In one recent study, 82 volunteers carried beepers that would remind them, at random times throughout the day, to record what they were doing, how concentrated on it they were, and how they felt. The volunteers ranged from assembly-line workers and clerks to engineers and managers.

"People seem to concentrate best when the demands on them are a bit greater than usual, and they are able to give more than usual," Dr. Csikszentmihalyi said. "If there is too little demand on them, people are bored. If there is too much for them to handle, they get anxious. Flow occurs in that delicate zone between boredom and anxiety."

No Easy Formula

There is no easy formula for getting into the flow state, but some circumstances make its occurrence more likely, according to the research. If a situation is boring, for example, somehow making it more challenging may lead to flow. One assembly-line worker in the Chicago research, for example, had a job in which he simply tightened a set of screws all day long. But after several years he was still experimenting with ways to shave a few seconds from his time, a challenge that kept him engrossed.

On the other hand, if things are overwhelming, sometimes simplifying a complex job into manageable pieces can bring that alignment of skill and challenge that evokes a flowing concentration. And simply making the effort to pay attention, even if a struggle at first, can on occasion give way to flow.

"Most jobs have a ceiling built in—you can learn them in a few days," said Dr. Csikszentmihalyi. "Your skills for it increase rapidly, but the challenge doesn't change, so you get bored. Many people are bored much of the time, and their attention is totally scattered. When their concentration drops, so does their motivation and confidence."

"The fine focus during flow cuts out all irrelevant thoughts and sensations," Dr. Csikszentmihalyi said. "There is a mental recruitment where everything aligns in an effortless concentration, sort of a mental overdrive."

In that way, this level of concentration resembles meditation in which the desired result is often a feeling of invigoration and relaxed alertness. The essence of meditation is simply to focus attention.

Two Kinds of Attention

The "flow" state studied by the Chicago researchers needs to be distinguished from the strained concentration that is brought to bear when, for example, a person has little interest in the task at hand and must force attention. These two kinds of attention—effortless and strained—have been found to have distinctly different underlying patterns of brain function, according to findings by researchers at the National Institute of Mental Health.

The research on attention and brain activity has, in the past, revealed seemingly contradictory findings, some studies finding that full concentration increased cortical arousal, and others finding a decrease. Dr. Hamilton's research showed that the effortless concentration typical of flow brought about a lowered cortical arousal. When more effort was put into concentration, on the other hand, it seemed to increase cortical arousal.

"There seems to be a difference between effortful and effortless attention," said Jean Hamilton, a psychiatrist in Washington, who did the research with Monte Buchsbaum, a psychiatrist now at the University of California Medical School at Irvine.

The studies show that the strained concentration involves greater activity by the brain, almost as if it is in the wrong gear for the work demanded.

The scientists are finding a number of individual differences among people in their abilities to become absorbed and to make the most of it when they do.

"The ability to become completely immersed is necessary for productivity, but not sufficient," said Auke Tellegen, a psychologist at the University of Minnesota. "You also need the capacity for mental constraint, so you don't just get swept away by impulse. Many people who are prone to absorption don't have the mental discipline that allows them to be productive."

Similarity to Hypnosis

One of the most suggestive pieces of evidence linking deep concentration to other kinds of altered states is its similarity to hypnosis.

Dr. Tellegen and others have done research showing that people who easily become absorbed in, say, fantasy or a painting, are more readily hypnotized than are those more impervious to such pleasures. And research reported in a recent volume of *The Journal of Personality and Social Psychology* shows that people who are given to rapt absorption are also susceptible to altered states of consciousness.

"There is a group of people who readily get so absorbed in things that they become lost in them, or in their thoughts or fantasies, for that matter," said Ronald Pekala, a psychologist at Center and Jefferson Medical College in Pennsylvania, who did the research on altered awareness with another psychologist, Krishna Kumar. "It is these same mental processes that seem to get intensified during hypnosis."

The people who are easily hypnotized, although they may become readily absorbed in some things, have to struggle as much as anyone else when it comes to endeavors that are not so enjoyable, Dr. Pekala has found. But when he simply asked them to sit quietly for a few minutes with their eyes closed, they frequently reported feelings approaching an altered state, including a rapturous joy, a sense of some profound meaningfulness, vivid imagery, and an altered sense of time, all accompanying a deeply absorbed attention. Such people, Dr.

Pekala believes, may go through much of the day lost in a pleasant, reverie-like state.

Although it may not be possible to force oneself into a feeling of absorption, it seems possible to learn to enter that state of mind more easily. Ellen Langer, a psychologist at Harvard University, has been studying the effects of what she calls *mindfulness,* a state of active attention that seems to have much in common with flow.

One of the ways Dr. Langer has increased people's mindfulness is straightforward and simple. She has them think about what is going on from as many vantage points as possible. "We taught people to watch television mindfully by asking them to watch shows as though they were someone else—a politician, or an athlete or a criminal," Dr. Langer said. "The point is to break through people's assumptions with an active attention that stimulates their thinking."

Dr. Langer has found that mindfulness has both psychological and health benefits. In a series of studies conducted among elderly patients in nursing homes, Dr. Langer and her colleagues have discovered that compared to patients who did not receive the mindfulness training, these patients had lower blood pressure and, in a three-year follow-up had fewer physical ailments, better overall health and a better mortality rate.

Meditation training, Dr. Langer has found, produces similar effects. "We're trying to achieve the same goal as meditation, but in a Western way," Dr. Langer said. "We try to get people to see the moment more creatively by paying more active attention."

1. What is a flow state?

2. According to a number of people interviewed—basketball players, composers, rock climbers, and dancers—what was one of the elements that helped them outdo themselves?

3. According to author Daniel Goleman, when do people seem to concentrate best?

4. According to the article, what should you do if you are pursuing an activity you find altogether boring?

5. In what ways are meditation and concentration similar?

6. The experience of being in deep concentration resembles what other altered state?

7. Does the article claim that everyone has the same capacity for absorption? Explain your answer.

8. According to the article, you probably cannot force yourself into a state of deep absorption. However, what can you do?

9. Dr. Ellen Langer refers to the state of active attention as "mindfulness." What is one suggestion she makes for increasing mindfulness? Can you think of another way mindfulness might be increased?

10. According to Dr. Langer, what are some of the benefits of mindfulness?

WRITING ASSIGNMENT

Take an object that you recognize but don't see every day, a natural object like a pine cone, a mushroom, a dried flower, a colored feather, or a maple leaf, and *focus your attention on it for several minutes.* During this time, look at the object from different angles; consciously shift your perspective by turning the feather or your head. When you are finished looking at the object, use a pencil and paper to describe it in the minutest possible detail. To get you started, here is a description by student Paul Akin:

> The feather is about six inches long. When I hold it in my hand, it reaches from the beginning of my palm to the end of my fingertips. Most of the feather is black and very silky. The very tip of the feather is pure white and it comes to a point. The spine of the feather is light gray. It is strong but flexible and bends without breaking.

Once you complete your description, put it and the object aside. Find a quiet and comfortable place to sit. Close your eyes and mentally re-create the object you have described in such detail. Don't be discouraged if visualizing the object takes some time. That's natural. Your mind may wander, but as soon as you catch yourself losing sight of the mental image, tell yourself to get back to your work. Focus on the picture you are mentally re-creating. When you think your mental drawing is complete, keep it in focus for at least a minute or two. Then open your eyes and congratulate yourself on taking a giant step toward controlling both your powers of visualization and concentration.

JOURNAL ASSIGNMENTS

1. Use your journal to interpret or explain this German proverb: "Who begins too much accomplishes little."
2. List the specific steps you are going to take in order to improve your concentration.
3. Start today to analyze your patterns for sleeping and waking.
4. Describe the motivational strategies you've been using. Which ones seem to be working best for you? For Melissa Cacace, imagining her future once her goals are achieved spurs her on:

> "If I get tired or don't want to work anymore, I imagine myself teaching my classes and doing a really good job. That image usually motivates me to get back to work because I certainly can't be a professor without graduating from college first."

✔ Checking Out: Review Questions for Chapter 3

1. Why should you designate a particular place or space solely for studying?

2. What is task lighting?

3. What does research suggest about attitude and background noise?

4. Why is it important to set time limits when you study?

5. Why should you vary your assignments?

6. When you take breaks during a study session, be sure to:

7. What kinds of foods can interfere with your concentration?

8. Describe what it means to be an *active learner*.

9. Identify at least three strategies for active learning.

10. Explain the three R's of behavior modification.

▶ In Summary

The ability to concentrate can be acquired or it can be improved by following the suggestions introduced in this chapter. Before you begin to work, make sure you've set the stage for concentration. Choose a quiet, well-lit place; gather all your materials; and set specific time limits for your assignments. While you study, maintain your concentration by active learning. Dig deep into the material, analyzing, evaluating, and connecting what you're learning. Remember, too, how essential it is to monitor your concentration—to know why you've been distracted. Then you'll be in a better position to replace negative habits with positive action.

CHAPTER **4**

Taking Charge of Your Time

"Time expands for those who court it."

—*Kenneth Atchity*

Time management does not mean sacrificing all leisure activities in favor of studying. On the contrary, if you use the principles of time management we recommend, you'll find the time to study *and* enjoy yourself.

- Applying the principle of divide and conquer to all difficult tasks
- Making a weekly schedule
- Establishing your priorities
- Identifying your high-energy prime time
- Analyzing and revising your schedule so it works for you
- Using a daily To-Do list
- Finding time in unexpected places
- Breaking the procrastination habit

Divide and Conquer

It's easy to look at your course syllabi in September and feel disheartened. Faced with readings, papers, and quizzes, you may get intimidated by the amount of work you have to do. But to help yourself right from the start, apply one key principle of time management: whenever possible, **divide your assignments into smaller subtasks.**

Say it's Monday, and you have to read two chapters in your American government text by Friday. Don't plan to read both chapters Thursday night. Instead, plan on reading one chapter on Tuesday and another on Wednesday. Use Thursday to reread any sections of the text that you found difficult the first time around or that you know are vital to the course. By dividing your work into smaller, more manageable subtasks, you won't feel overwhelmed when you sit down to study.

Current research suggests that if you return to an assignment over several days instead of trying to digest it all in one day, the information will stick better in your memory. With this strategy, called *spaced* or *distributed learning,* you spread an assignment over several study sessions to review and reinforce it. Therefore, whenever possible, complete an assignment over the course of a few days rather than in one intense effort.

Breaking your assignments into more manageable bites offers an additional bonus. Each time you finish one of your subtasks, you will feel a sense of accomplishment and control—simply because you did what you set out to do. That very good feeling of accomplishment will make you more willing to tackle and complete the next assignment.

> **✳**   Each time you finish one of your subtasks, you will feel a sense of accomplishment and control—simply because you did what you set out to do.

Divide and Conquer Long-Term Assignments

The principle of divide and conquer is particularly important for end-of-term assignments.

Say that you have a ten- or fifteen-page paper due on December 21. Don't just mark the due date on your calendar and *hope* you get the assignment done on time. Instead, create a series of subtasks, each with its own specific due date; for example:

1. By September 7, jot down ideas about the topic.
2. By September 15, look at library resources and make a tentative bibliography.
3. By September 30, read at least two books, and three articles.
4. By October 15, write a tentative main idea.
5. By October 30, prepare an informal outline.
6. By November 7, write the first rough draft.
7. By November 21, revise the first draft.
8. By December 7, finish a second draft.
9. By December 16, complete the bibliography.
10. By December 17, finish editing the paper.
11. By December 19, finish typing and proofreading the paper.
12. By December 20, hand in the paper.

Working on your papers in manageable bites like this will make them much easier to complete—and with far less last-minute pressure. You'll also do more careful work because you will have the time to mull over your first draft and revise it as new and better thoughts come to you.

☐ PRACTICE 1   Select one of your end-of-term assignments and create a list of subtasks for its completion. Then schedule a deadline for each subtask. If you do not have a specific paper or report due, list the dates when you plan to review for your midterm or final exams.

Making a Weekly Schedule to Suit Your Needs

While you are learning how to manage time, make a detailed weekly schedule that organizes your time from morning until night. A detailed schedule will help you discover where you use your time productively and where you waste it.

Most of all, your schedule will help you stay up to date with your work. If you know what you want to accomplish each day, you are more likely to stick to your plans rather than be diverted from them.

To get you started with your schedule, we will follow how Tina Judson, a student known for her organizational abilities, works out her schedule.

Preparing a Master Schedule

Early in each semester, as soon as she has decided on her classes, Tina first works out a master schedule of what her typical week will be like.

She indicates the hours for her classes as well as for her other fixed commitments—her part-time job, meals, and exercise. Initially she works on a blank schedule like the one shown in Figure 4–1.

Most important of all, she wants to **block out specific hours each day for study,** as shown in Figure 4–2. The key to Tina's plan is she knows exactly when she plans to study each day; she lets nothing trivial interfere with the hours she sets aside for studying. An outstanding student, Tina explains that a good part of her success is due to being "organized." Her papers are written long before they are due; she finishes reviewing for exams with time to spare.

Preparing a Detailed Weekly Schedule

After completing her master schedule, Tina makes fifteen photocopies of it (one for each week of the semester). Each Sunday evening, she adds specific goals to accomplish in her study sessions for the next week. See Figure 4–3 for how she develops her detailed weekly schedule.

Notice what she plans for Monday:

6:00   go over biology reading notes
7:00   read sociology Chapter 7
8:00   read government assignment
9:00   freewrite on topic for English composition

Early in the term Tina likes to use Mondays to get an overview of all her courses. But as the term continues, she shifts more of her study hours to the most pressing course or assignment. Every Sunday she plots what assignments need attention in the coming week, and she plans for them on her detailed schedule, often putting down specific pages to read.

Tina also makes a quick To-Do list each morning, copying all the items for that day from her detailed weekly schedule. She puts an *A* beside her top-priority assignments. Jotting the items down, Tina says, helps her recall exactly what she wants to do that day. Then she simply works her way down the list. If she doesn't finish, she knows she has completed what most needed to be done.

Keeping a Monthly Calendar

As part of her system, Tina also has posted above her desk a monthly calendar in which she keeps track of all future assignments and appointments as well as long-term research papers, final exams, and vacation

Figure 4–1: Blank Schedule. Use a blank schedule such as this to develop your master schedule, as shown in Figure 4–2.

	Monday	Tuesday	Wednesday	Thursday	Friday	Saturday	Sunday
7–8							
8–9							
9–10							
10–11							
11–12							
12–1							
1–2							
2–3							
3–4							
4–5							
5–6							
6–7							
7–8							
8–9							
9–10							
10–11							
11–12							

Figure 4–2: Master Schedule for a Semester. Notice how blocks of time are set aside for studying.

	Monday	Tuesday	Wednesday	Thursday	Friday	Saturday	Sunday
7–8							
8–9	CLASS American Government	EXERCISE Jogging	CLASS American Government	EXERCISE Jogging	CLASS American Government		
9–10	STUDY	JOB	STUDY	JOB	STUDY	STUDY	Clean Room
10–11	↓		↓		↓	↓	Laundry
11–12	Lunch		Lunch		Errands Free	EXERCISE	
12–1	CLASS Biology	↓	CLASS Biology	↓	CLASS Biology	↓	
1–2	STUDY Review Bio. Lecture	Lunch	STUDY Review Bio. Lecture	Lunch	Lunch	Lunch	Lunch
2–3	CLASS Eng. Comp.	Study Group Biology	CLASS Eng. Comp.	Sports Basketball	CLASS Eng. Comp.	Free	
3–4	CLASS Sociology	↓	CLASS Sociology	↓	CLASS Sociology		
4–5	Free	Free	Free	Free	Free	↓	Free
5–6	Dinner	Dinner	Dinner	Dinner	Dinner	Dinner	Dinner
6–7	STUDY	STUDY	STUDY	STUDY	Sports or Movie	Free	STUDY
7–8							
8–9			↓				↓
9–10	↓	↓		↓	↓	↓	Plan next week's schedule
10–11							
11–12							

Figure 4–3: Detailed Weekly Schedule. Note how specific assignments are listed in blocks of time set aside for studying.

	Monday	Tuesday	Wednesday	Thursday	Friday
7–8					
8–9	CLASS American Government	EXERCISE Jogging	CLASS American Government		
9–10	Read Biology Assignment	JOB	Read Biology Assignment		
10–11	↓		↓		
11–12	Lunch		Lunch		
12–1	CLASS Biology	↓	CLASS Biology		
1–2	Review Biology Lecture	Lunch	Review Biology Lecture		
2–3	CLASS Eng. Comp.	Study Group Biology	CLASS Eng. Comp.		
3–4	CLASS Sociology	↓	CLASS Sociology		
4–5	Free	Free	Free		
5–6	Dinner	Dinner	Dinner		
6–7	Go over Biology notes	Draft paper for Eng. Comp.	Go over Biology notes		
7–8	Read Sociology Chap. 7	↓	Read, revise draft for Eng. Comp.		
8–9	Read Amer. Gov. assign.	Read Sociology Chap. 7	↓		
9–10	Free write on topic for Eng. Comp.	Read Amer. Gov. assign.	Brainstorm on topic for Soc. paper		
10–11		Free			
11–12					

plans. She likes the kind of calendar where she can see the whole month on a single page.

Check in the bookstore for a suitable monthly calendar to help keep yourself on track.

Establishing Priorities

You may have noticed that Tina's schedule (Figure 4–3) allots different amounts of time to different subjects. Biology, for example, receives a lot of her time; sociology receives considerably less. Tina has consciously scheduled her time in this way because biology is crucial to her goal of becoming a medical technician. In addition, she finds her biology text harder to read than her sociology text, and she needs to give it more attention.

When you work on your schedule, don't unthinkingly give each course and each assignment equal time. Instead ask questions that will help you **establish your priorities and allot your time accordingly.**

- How important is the assigned material for mastering the course? (If it is important, give it extra time.)
- How relevant is this course to my long-term goals?
- How will my grade on this assignment affect my final grade in the course?
- How much time can I allot to the task without taking time away from my other important assignments?

PRACTICE 2   Make a list of your assignments for this week. Then give each assignment a letter grade that indicates its importance. The following example shows Ellen Bernardi's list. Ellen plans to become a parole officer, and she has used that goal to establish her priorities.

Example

Priority	Assignments
C	Biology lab report
A	Criminology paper
B	World literature read pp. 206–236
A	Psychology read pp. 100–120

Priority	Assignments
_____	_____
_____	_____
_____	_____
_____	_____
_____	_____

Creating Your Own Schedule

Now that you've seen how Tina develops her schedule, start yours by drawing or photocopying (and enlarging) the blank form shown in Figure 4–1. To help you create your master schedule, here are a few pointers.

1. Fill in all the fixed times when you are in class, at your job, at meals, or at any other regular commitment, as in Figure 4–2.
2. **Mark where you have blocks of free time to study each day.** Then commit yourself to studying in those blocks of time. Rather than having to decide each day when to study, you already know which hours you are committed to studying. An established routine will help you get into the rhythm of studying; try hard to stay in your routine.
3. **Schedule your hardest subjects first** when you are freshest and when your mind can concentrate best. Leave less demanding or more routine tasks for later. Reading for your easiest course, returning library books, or photocopying articles usually can be done after the hard subjects.
4. Whenever possible, schedule your study sessions close to the actual courses for which you are doing the assignment. In Figure 4–3, see how Tina frequently does her biology assignment just before biology class meets. If you keep study and class times close together, you make it easier to connect your reading assignments to the lectures.
5. If possible, schedule an hour-long review session right after any important or difficult class. You can sort out any unclear information in your notes most quickly at this point; if you wait, deciphering your notes may take twice as long. If you have fully understood a lecture, reviewing your lecture notes right after class helps ensure remembering.

6. Fit in study breaks, sports, and free time for yourself. Don't be under the misconception that it is a good idea to study all the time. You *need* relaxation, sports, friendship; exercise will help you control stress. Even if only for brief periods, allow time for your favorite sport, for relaxing and running errands, and for catching up with friends and family. When you return to your study routine, you will feel renewed energy.

7. Most of us have a daily **prime time** or times when we study or work most efficiently.[1] By paying careful attention to how well you work at different hours of the day, you will learn to recognize the times when you feel fresher, sharper, and more energetic. Then schedule your most challenging tasks in your prime time.

---

*   Indicate on your schedule where you have blocks of time for study. Then *commit yourself* to studying in those blocks of time each day.

☐   PRACTICE 3   Draw or photocopy (and enlarge) the blank grid in Figure 4–1; then start designing your own schedule for the week, as in Figure 4–3.

Analyzing and Revising Your Schedule

At times you will have to deal with the unexpected—a cousin may arrive without warning or you may catch the flu. Such temporary interruptions are no reason to revise your basic schedule permanently.

However, you may find that you consistently fail to meet the schedule you have set for yourself. When that happens, investigate what is going wrong. Ask yourself questions like these.

1. Are you regularly underestimating (or overestimating) the amount of time you need to complete your assignments? If calculus usually takes two hours rather than one, build in an extra hour. Small adjustments are to be expected.

2. Are you sitting down to work at the times you planned, or do you waste the first fifteen minutes buying coffee?

---

[1] Alan Lakein, *How to Get Control of Your Time and Your Life* (New York: Signet, 1974), 48–49.

3. Are you letting distractions (your family, friends, telephone) throw you way off schedule? How can you eliminate or avoid these interruptions?

4. Are you doing each task with the same degree of perfection? Are you spending too much time on things not essential to your success? Yes, getting an *A* in American literature is desirable, but if your goal is to be an accountant, consider settling for a *B*. With only so many hours in the day, you may have to be less of a perfectionist.

5. Are you trying hard to follow your schedule? Initially time management is hard work, requiring determination and self-discipline. But before you give up and decide to rework your whole schedule, do some self-analysis. The problem may not be the schedule. It may be that you need to redouble your commitment to managing your time.

Using a Time Log

If you can't figure out where your time vanishes, use a **time log** for a few days to compare *what you planned to do* with *what you actually did*.

The sample time log suggests that this student's schedule is on target. She just has to *stick* to it and avoid distractions—mainly conversations with friends—that are totally within her control.

Sample Time Log

	What I Planned	What I Actually Did
9–10	Reading sociology assignment: 20 pages	Got to the library late; didn't start till 9:15. Then talked to roommate about next weekend. Read only 8 pages. 12 pages left to do.
10–11	Sociology class	Went to sociology class.
11–12	Review lecture notes, eat lunch	Started talking again after class; didn't get time to review; ate lunch.

☐   PRACTICE 4   For one day, use a time log to analyze how efficiently you use your time.

Setting Priorities with a To-Do List

"The key to successful time management is doing the most important task first, and giving it your full concentration, to the exclusion of everything else."
— Alec MacKenzie, time management consultant

As a minimum, we suggest a weekly schedule (see Figures 4–2 and 4–3) as a way of keeping track of your ongoing responsibilities while at college.

To remember far-off due dates and events, some students supplement the weekly schedule with a monthly wall calendar. Many also make a quick To-Do list, to keep track of immediate school and personal responsibilities.

When making your own To-Do list, put your most urgent tasks at the top of the list (or mark them with an *A* for highest priority), as in this example.

TO-DO LIST

PRIORITY   TASKS

A   Read 10 pages of Chap. 11, econ.

A   * Study for quiz in bio.

                Start drafting sociology paper.
                Complete half of math assign.
                Make appointment to see Prof. Atassi.

                Do laundry.
                Call about Lakers tickets.

A   Pick up toothpaste, milk.
                Pick up Sam at day care/ 5:30.
* Do first—a must

Before doing anything else, begin and complete your most important task—as soon as you have a block of free time. Don't let any small errands divert you from attacking this most urgent task of the day first. In the sample To-Do list on page 79, studying for a biology quiz comes first.

Just start. Starting is often the hardest part. Don't begin any other tasks until you finish all your A-priority items. The other tasks are things that can wait a day or so. Transfer any undone tasks to your next To-Do list.

Every time you complete one of your tasks, cross it off the list. The very enjoyable feeling that comes with completing a task, especially one you were reluctant to start, will motivate you to begin on the next item.

Avoid Retracing Your Steps

Unfortunately, without a list, most of us forget some of the supplies we need. To save time, whenever you think of things you want at the drugstore, supermarket, or bookstore, write them down on your To-Do list. And if you have several errands, organize your list so you won't retrace your steps.

PRACTICE 5   Make a To-Do list of the tasks that you expect to complete tomorrow. Remember to put the tasks with the highest priority first, or mark them with an *A*. Then put a star next to *the one task* you want to complete before you do anything else.

Looking for and Finding the Time

"Finding time begins with an act of will. You also have to look for time in the right places."

—Kenneth Atchity

Poet and author Kenneth Atchity is absolutely correct; finding time is very much an act of will. If you consciously look for ways to save yourself time, you will discover that you actually have more time than you had thought. Here are some suggestions for saving time. See if they work for you.

1. Combine two activities.
If you travel thirty minutes by bus to your part-time job, use this time to read the short stories you have been assigned in your American literature course. If you are in the shower or walking to class, mentally review the key civil rights cases mentioned the day before in your American govern-

ment class, or mentally outline your paper comparing Martin Luther King and Malcolm X.

2. Be prepared to study while you wait.

Any time you have an appointment where you might have to wait, bring work with you. If you are going to the dentist, bring along a list of Spanish verbs or notes to review for next week's quiz. Even if you're tempted, don't waste those twenty minutes flipping through old magazines.

3. Use the telephone to get information.

Before you spend time walking to the library to see if your interlibrary loan has arrived, phone the reference desk. Late at night, call to see if the computer center is still open.

4. Organize your desk.

Jeffrey Mayer, best-selling writer of a book on time management, urges his readers to make organizing their desks a top priority. Mayer knows how many minutes—or even hours—most of us waste looking for that paper, book, or article hidden beneath a pile of clutter. Follow Mayer's advice; spend one or two uninterrupted hours getting your desk in order.

5. Have a system for locating important things.

If you consistently place your sociology notebook in the right-hand corner of your desk and put your textbook on top of it, you won't misplace either one. *Be consistent about where you put what you need*—papers, pens, notebooks, textbooks, and keys—and don't waste time searching for lost items.

6. Don't let a one-hour task take three hours.

When you're working on a relatively simple task—say recopying your math homework—assume that interruptions matter. In other words, don't dawdle; spend the right amount of time on each assignment.

7. Do it right the first time.

Sometimes we put off doing a thing correctly because it seems too time-consuming. Say you decide not to make a backup copy of the paper you are typing into the computer. Making a copy would take a little extra effort, and you don't want to go to the trouble. Unfortunately, if there's a power failure and you lose that paper, rewriting the paper from scratch is going to take a lot more time than making a copy would have. To quote Jeffrey Mayer: "If you haven't got the time to do it right, when will you find the time to do it over?"

8. Ruthlessly cut down on television.

While enrolled in school, set aside specific times for watching television, say, the news and an hour-long program *after your studying is done.* Once the program is over, leave the room so you won't get caught up in watching reruns of sitcoms. Don't leave the television on while you are working; it's too tempting to start watching the screen.

PRACTICE 6   Use this checklist to decide if you need to make cleaning your desk or work space a top priority. Two or more yes answers mean you should get to work fast.

		Yes	No
1.	Are there more than ten items on your desk?	☐	☐
2.	Do you hesitate to put papers down on your desk because you might lose them?	☐	☐
3.	In the past week, have you been unable to find something you *knew* was on your desk somewhere?	☐	☐
4.	Do you frequently find missing papers or books underneath other papers or books?	☐	☐
5.	Do you tell yourself your desk looks cluttered, but *you* know where everything is?	☐	☐

Breaking the Procrastination Habit

"If you want to make an easy job seem mighty hard, just keep putting off doing it."
—Michael LeBoeuf

People who procrastinate usually have long-term goals they want to achieve. Yet they put off the daily work necessary to reach those goals. Yes, they do plan to learn Spanish, and of course they are going to learn to use a word processor. The problem is they are always going to do these things tomorrow, not today. But somehow tomorrow never comes because procrastinators keep postponing—and feeling guilty about—what they intend to do.

If procrastinating produces nothing but guilt, why are there so many procrastinators? Some people procrastinate because the tasks facing them seem so difficult and demanding that they don't know where to begin. Other people procrastinate because the goal to be achieved is someone else's goal, not their own. These people find it difficult to mobilize their energy and initiative.

There is, however, a more serious reason for procrastination—to protect a weak self-image. Unsure of their abilities and fearing failure, many people use procrastination as a way of avoiding being judged or tested. By not putting themselves to the test, they can always tell themselves that they *would* accomplish great things if they could only find the time. In this way they save face and avoid the risk of failure. What's sad about this is that procrastinators save their pride but at a terrible cost to themselves. They never work up to their potential, and they let their lives go by without experiencing the satisfaction that real accomplishment brings.

Battling procrastination is tough, but it can be done, particularly if you follow these guidelines.

Focus on a Task You Want to Complete

Target one project that you want to accomplish within a specific period of time. The project does not have to apply to a course assignment. It may be a paper for one of your classes, or it may be a short story that you want to contribute to the college magazine.

Let Other People Know About Your Project

Tell several people what you intend to accomplish and when you plan to finish it. In particular tell people who will ask how your work is coming along. Don't pick other procrastinators like yourself. They will avoid asking you about your progress because they don't want you asking them about theirs.

Use a Step-by-Step Approach

Divide your project into a series of subtasks and give yourself specific deadlines for each one. *Make sure that the first task on your list takes no more than fifteen minutes to accomplish.* Complete that task within twenty-four hours of making your list. After completing that first brief task, cross it off your list and congratulate yourself. Make it a point to tell somebody about your success: "I just started a paper that's due three months from now; I really think I'm getting better at not putting things off."

Maintain Your Momentum

Go on to the next task immediately after completing the first one. Each time you complete a task by its deadline, give yourself some reward.

When you do not finish a task by its deadline, penalize yourself *not by feeling guilty* but by doing something you don't enjoy, such as cleaning your desk or doing the laundry. *Procrastinators need fixed schedules, and they need to reward themselves for sticking to them.* They also need to penalize themselves for failing to follow their time plan.

Look for the Causes of Why You Slack Off

If you find yourself falling back into the old procrastinating ways, investigate why. There may in fact be a legitimate reason. Often it's hard to start writing a paper if you don't have adequate information or to begin an assignment you don't fully understand. In such cases, get yourself back on track by reading for more information or by talking to your instructor.

If you can't find a legitimate cause for postponing your work, write in your journal, answering questions like these: Why am I putting off writing this paper (or preparing for this exam)? Don't I want to succeed? Am I afraid that if I try hard and don't do well, I will prove myself a failure?

Remember the Three R's of Behavior Modification

Once you **recognize** that you are procrastinating, you must flatly **refuse** to do it and **replace** that behavior with a positive action. Complete some task, no matter how small, to advance you one step closer to your goal. To make a beginning on your term paper, make a short informal list of the ideas you need to cover. Although many people are intimidated by the thought of writing a paper, they don't feel concerned about writing a list. In fact, listing potential ideas you plan to develop is a very good way to get started writing a paper.

Don't Get Discouraged by Relapses

It is quite natural to fall back into your old habits when you are trying to create new ones. Don't be surprised or angry if you can't stop procrastinating overnight. No one can. However, when you find yourself reverting to old behaviors, tell yourself that you can kick the habit of procrastination; it's just going to take a little time.

Anytime you feel yourself starting to procrastinate, sit down and list in your journal some of the consequences of this seemingly harmless habit; a constant sense of guilt, a mediocre career, unfulfilled potential, and a life of indecision. Is it really worth it?

> Procrastinators may save their pride, but at a terrible cost to themselves. They never work up to their potential; they let their lives go by without experiencing the satisfaction that real accomplishment brings.

PRACTICE 7

Discover if you, like so many others, are a procrastinator. More than four *yes* answers indicate that you probably need to break the procrastination habit.

	Yes	No
1. When you think about starting a long-term assignment—like writing a research paper—do you often say "I'll do it tomorrow"?	☐	☐
2. Do you think creating your own deadlines is a waste of time?	☐	☐
3. Are you often late for classes or appointments?	☐	☐
4. In the past, have you relied on getting extensions to complete your schoolwork?	☐	☐
5. If you have to do something you dislike, do you put it off until the last minute?	☐	☐
6. Do you often tell yourself you work better under pressure?	☐	☐
7. When you finish a task, do you frequently tell yourself, "I could have done better if I'd only had more time"?	☐	☐
8. Do you think planning your day takes all the fun out of it?	☐	☐
9. Do you think your instructors don't give you enough time to complete your assignments?	☐	☐
10. Do you usually write or type the final draft of a paper, essay, or report the night before it's due?	☐	☐

Working Space

READING ASSIGNMENT

Fear of failure is one key reason why many people procrastinate and do not use their time efficiently. In the following article, Michael LeBoeuf, the author of *Working Smart,* offers some suggestions for combating a fear that haunts us all at one time or another. Read the article and answer the questions that follow.

Fear of Failure

Stop for a moment and think of all the wonderful things in this world that never happened because someone feared failure and hadn't the courage to act. Think of all the books, songs and plays that were never written. Think of all those singers, musicians, painters and sculptors who never developed their talent because they were afraid someone would laugh. Think of all the great labor-saving inventions and cures for presently incurable diseases that were missed because someone was afraid to pursue his far-out theory. And finally, think of all the beautiful relationships that never blossomed because one or both parties feared rejection. This is only a fraction of the price we pay for indulging ourselves in the fear of failure.

The startling fact is that there is no such thing as failure. "Failure" is merely an opinion that a given act wasn't done satisfactorily. As a natural phenomenon it doesn't exist. Imagine, if you will, one honeybee saying to another, "They put me to work in the hive because I got a 'D' in pollination." Better yet; can you imagine one squirrel telling another, "Max, you're a first-class climber, but your nutcracking is inadequate"? How ludicrous can you get? The fact is animals don't know what failure is. They simply do and enjoy. Failure doesn't stop them because it's totally off their map. If Max can't open a nut, he simply tries another. He doesn't wallow in self-pity or swear to subsist on tree bark for the rest of his life.

Like the other immobilizing emotions, choosing to be governed by the fear of failure has definite payoffs. Being ruled by fear of failure lets you take the easy way out. Rather than accepting the challenge of pursuing a meaningful goal, you can scratch it off your list and tell yourself that success is impossible or not worthwhile.

Reacting to a fear of failure also provides a false sense of safety and security. You can't lose a race you don't enter. Thus by not doing, you are spared the seemingly needless humiliation of failure. You'll never be a winner, but you'll never be a failure either.

If you've ever met with less than success in the past (and who hasn't?), the fear of failure gives you a perfect excuse for not trying in the present or future. After all, what's the point in going to all that trouble for nothing?

Finally, by not trying you give yourself the luxury of becoming a critic. You can put your time and effort into being a spectator and ridiculing all those fools who are out there trying to succeed. The most vociferous critics are generally frustrated doers who are ruled by their own fear of failure.

Those who give in to their fears and choose the psychological pay-offs overlook one major point. Failure is not a measure of success. In fact, as we already pointed out, failure isn't anything. In life, it isn't what you lose that counts; it's what you gain and what you have left.

If you find yourself immobilized due to fear of failure, here are some ideas to help you overcome it.

1. Set your own standards of success. Remember that failure is arbitrary. Don't allow your life to be ruled by standards other than your own. You don't have to be president of the company because your father was or your wife wants you to be. It's your choice, not theirs.

2. Don't fall into the trap of success-failure thinking. If you set a goal and pursue it, evaluate your own performance in terms of degrees of success.

3. Don't feel you have to succeed or achieve excellence in everything you do. There's nothing wrong with a mediocre round of golf (at least that's what I keep telling myself) or a poor set of tennis, as long as you're having fun.

4. Meet your fear of failure head-on. Find something you would like to do but fear failure in, and do it. Even if you don't succeed to the degree you hope to, you won't have any regrets. After all, you will be doing what you want to do. It's better to feel sorry for the things you've done than to regret missed opportunities. All ventures involve risk, but not to venture is to waste your life.

5. If you do feel you have failed, recognize it as a learning experience that will make you wiser and contribute to later successes.

Astute young politicians practice this. They join a political race fully realizing they have no chance of winning. However, by throwing their hat in the ring, they get public exposure and learn the ropes of campaigning. All of the exposure and learning can someday contribute to a victorious campaign. We can learn a great deal more from our failures than our successes, provided we avail ourselves of the opportunity.

6. Realize that meaningful success is rarely easy and is usually preceded by a struggle. However, it's those who have the will to see it through that make it. Most of us throw in the towel too soon, when hanging in there a little longer would do the job.

1. According to LeBoeuf, what are some of the benefits of the fear of failure?

2. What did LeBoeuf mean when he wrote, "There is no such thing as failure"? Explain why you agree or disagree with this statement.

3. Does what LeBoeuf wrote apply to you? What would you like to achieve but may not because of your fear of failure?

4. What can you add to LeBoeuf's suggestions for combating the fear of failure?

WRITING ASSIGNMENT

The Latin phrase *carpe diem* means "to seize the day," or to grasp the opportunity while it is available. Describe a time when you did not seize the day and lost out on some opportunity or experience you now regret having missed.

JOURNAL ASSIGNMENTS

1. Make a list of ways in which you waste time, such as talking on the telephone or taking unnecessary breaks. Then make a second list, describing the specific methods you are going to use to stop wasting time.
2. Take the time to evaluate your progress in improving your concentration. In what ways do you think you're improving? In what areas do you still need work?
3. Alec Mackenzie concludes a chapter in his book *The Time Trap* with the following story. Explain why the story is appropriate in a book about managing time.

> There's a story about a man struggling to cut down enough trees to build a fence. An old farmer came by, watched for a while, then quietly said, "Saw's kinda dull, isn't it?"
> "I reckon," said the fence builder.
> "Hadn't ya better sharpen it?"
> "Maybe later. I can't stop now—I got all these trees to cut down."[2]

✔ Checking Out: Review Questions for Chapter 4

1. Explain the principle of divide and conquer.

2. According to the chapter, what's the major benefit of a written schedule?

3. What is a To-Do list?

---

[2]Alec MacKenzie, *The Time Trap,* New York: Amacom, II.

4. What is the purpose of a time log?

5. List three reasons why procrastination is so common.

▶ In Summary

Taking charge of your time means paying attention to how and where you spend it. It means giving up the notion that time manages itself without any help from you. You must take charge of your time and your life. Start by scheduling your daily, weekly, and monthly tasks so that you may eventually achieve your long-term goals. Step by step, hour by hour, you are responsible for planning your days and building your future. No one is going to do it for you.

If procrastination is your problem, try to control this negative habit by using behavior modification on yourself.

When deciding how much time to commit to studying, ask yourself: "What does a college degree mean to me? Am I willing to sacrifice some leisure now for better opportunities all my life?"

2

UNIT

Listening and Remembering

CHAPTER **5**

Becoming a Good Listener

"Listening requires entering actively and imaginatively into the other person's situation and trying to understand a frame of reference different from your own."
—*S. I. Hayakawa, educator and author*

Being a good listener will help you in every aspect of your life. However, good listening skills are particularly valuable in college, where lectures are a primary source of information. Start today to sharpen your listening skills by:

- Distinguishing between *hearing* and *listening*
- Taking steps to improve your listening ability
- Avoiding the mistakes made by poor listeners
- Learning how to pose effective questions

Distinguishing Between *Hearing* and *Listening*

On the surface, effective listening might seem to require little more than an acute sense of hearing. But in fact, there's a big difference between hearing and listening. *Hearing* occurs when sound waves travel through the air, enter your ears, and are transmitted by the auditory nerve to your brain. As long as neither your brain nor your ears are impaired, hearing is involuntary. It occurs spontaneously with little conscious effort on your part.

Listening, in contrast, is a voluntary act that includes attending to, understanding, and evaluating the words or sounds you hear. If you sit through a lecture without making an effort to listen, there's a good chance that the speaker's words will become just so much background noise.

As surprising as it sounds, **listening is hard work** and good listeners are in short supply. Actually, research suggests that the ability to listen begins to decline around the time we leave elementary school. It seems that the more chances we have to speak, the less time we take to listen. But the same research also shows that the ability to listen can be improved by training and practice.[1]

Strategies for Effective Listening

Psychologists and communications experts generally agree that without training most of us are not good listeners. Studies show that for every ten minutes of spoken communication, the untrained listener hears about two and one-half minutes.[2] However, studies also show that listening can be markedly improved by putting the following pointers into practice.

Work with the Speaker

Poor listeners think the lecturer's job is to deliver a message, while their own job is to sit back and receive it. Good listeners, however, know they have to work with the speaker because communication is a two-way process requiring their active participation. Outwardly quiet but inwardly active, good listeners try to (1) determine the purpose of the lecture, (2) identify key points, (3) make connections between ideas, and (4) jot down specific illustrations or reasons. Alert and energetic, good listeners sift and sort information, deciding what's essential and what's not.

---

[1]James J. Floyd, *Listening: A Practical Approach* (Glenview: Scott Foresman, 1985), 1–14.
[2]Ed Kelsay, "Listen Up," *Association Management,* February 1990, 220.

Prepare in Advance

Reading research suggests that the more background knowledge you have about a subject, the easier it is to understand the author's message. Research on listening supports a similar conclusion: **the more you know about a lecture before you hear it, the more easily you will follow the speaker's train of thought.**

If your instructor has assigned a textbook chapter related to an upcoming lecture, read that assignment *before* the day of the lecture. If you can't read the whole assignment, skim all of it and read parts. (For a discussion of skimming, see Chapter 10.) If the instructor hasn't already assigned a chapter, check your syllabus, or look in the table of contents of your textbook for related chapters. Read or skim as much of the material as you can before going to the lecture. While you are waiting for the lecture to begin, review your notes from the previous class. Then if the speaker refers to any points made in that lecture, you'll immediately understand the reference.

Give Yourself an Incentive

Any time you feel your concentration flagging during a lecture, give yourself an incentive for staying focused. Remind yourself that exam questions frequently come from lectures. Therefore, it's in your interest to listen as closely as you can. Your success as a student depends on it.

Always Take Notes

Taking notes is probably the best way to maintain concentration during lectures. In order to **select, condense, and organize information for your notes,** you have to maintain the kind of attentive concentration that is the key to good listening. In addition to improving your listening ability, taking notes during lectures offers an additional bonus: it aids remembering. (For more detailed pointers for taking notes during lectures, see Chapter 6).

Respond to What You Hear

Generally, you can think about four times faster than your instructor can speak. Unfortunately this gap between thought and speech makes it easy for you to drift off into daydreams, particularly if your instructor speaks very slowly. To avoid daydreaming, you need to stay mentally active. Periodically summarize key points in the lecture, anticipate what's coming next, and jot down questions or exceptions you might want to mention once the lecture is over.

Keep an Open Mind

Avoid letting your personal opinions interfere with your willingness to listen to an opposing point of view. Say that your political science instructor, lecturing on the Vietnam War, criticizes the American government's role. Because several members of your family supported the war, you may strongly disagree with her position. However, don't close your mind to the content of the lecture. Instead, listen carefully to her arguments and jot down your responses. When the instructor opens up the class for discussion, you will be ready to express your opinions.

Maintain a Positive Attitude

Don't let negative feelings about a subject interfere with your determination to become an effective listener. If you enter a classroom thinking "I'm not interested in history; this lecture will be deadly," you have given yourself a counterproductive message, one that will inhibit your ability to listen well.

To listen effectively, you need to counteract negative feelings with positive self-talk like the following: "I'm going to find a way to make this subject interesting," or "If I listen closely, maybe I can figure out what questions will be on the exam." When you find yourself uninterested in the topic of a lecture, don't give in to those feelings. Instead double your efforts to concentrate.

Judge Content, Not Delivery

It would be wonderful if every speaker had a dramatic style that compelled you to listen. Unfortunately truly gifted speakers are not all that common, and you can't let an instructor's delivery affect your willingness to listen. If you do, you're the one who will be the loser.

Figure 5–1: Characteristics of Good and Poor Listeners

Good Listeners	Poor Listeners
Sit in the front of the classroom or lecture hall.	Sit in the back of the classroom or lecture hall.
Keep in mind the benefits of listening.	Don't think about listening one way or another.
Work with the speaker to make sure communication takes place.	Sit back and wait for the speaker's message to sink in.
Refuse to let negative thoughts interfere with their concentration.	Give in to negative thinking.
Prepare for lectures in advance by skimming or reading chapters for background.	Never think about the content of lectures in advance.
Listen to opposing points of view.	Refuse to listen when they don't agree with the speaker.
Take notes throughout, always evaluating what are major or minor points.	Doodle instead of taking notes.
Anticipate, summarize, and respond to the speaker's words.	Drift off into daydreams.
Maintain eye contact and sit up straight.	Slump in their chairs, daydream, look out the window.
Ask questions if confused.	Assume the speaker will straighten out any confusion.

Sit in the Front of the Classroom

If you sit in the back of the classroom, you may find it difficult to hear, particularly if you are in a large lecture hall. As a result, you'll find it easier to get distracted, and you may miss something important. By sitting close to the instructor, you'll be able to see his or her facial expressions; this more personal contact will help draw you into the lecture.

Watch Your Body Language

If you usually sit slumped in your chair with your head resting on your hand, you are inviting your mind to wander. Worse, you are telling your instructors you are not particularly interested in what they have to say.

To improve concentration (and maintain your instructors' goodwill), sit with your back fairly straight and your pen poised to take notes. When you're not taking notes, maintain eye contact with the speaker—another way to make sure your mind stays focused on the lecture.

PRACTICE 1 To evaluate your listening behavior during lectures, answer the following questions.

	Yes	No
1. For motivation, do you tell yourself how important listening is to your academic success?	☐	☐
2. Do you arrive early and get a seat near the front of the room or lecture hall?	☐	☐
3. Do you make a conscious effort to give the speaker your full attention?	☐	☐
4. If you catch yourself daydreaming, do you try to stop immediately?	☐	☐
5. Do you think it's your responsibility to work with the lecturer and make sure communication takes place?	☐	☐
6. Do you replace negative thoughts—"I don't know anything about this subject; it's bound to be dull"—with positive ones—"Once I know more, I'll find a way to get interested in this subject"?	☐	☐
7. Whenever possible, do you prepare for lectures in advance?	☐	☐
8. Do you get to lectures on time so as not to miss the speaker's opening comments?	☐	☐
9. As you are waiting for the lecture to begin, do you review your notes on the previous lecture?	☐	☐
10. While listening to the lecture, do you try to predict the speaker's next point?	☐	☐
11. Throughout the lecture, do you mentally review key points?	☐	☐
12. Do you always take notes on the lecture?	☐	☐
13. Do you jot down questions or comments?	☐	☐
14. While you listen to a lecture, do you sit up straight and maintain eye contact when you aren't taking notes?	☐	☐
15. If you get confused, do you ask questions?	☐	☐

As you may have guessed, *yes* should be the answer to every question. Look over those questions you answered with a *no* and figure out what you need to do to transform every *no* into a *yes*.

> * Alert and energetic, good listeners sift and sort information, deciding what's essential and what's not.

Framing Effective Questions

College lectures pack a lot of information into a short period of time. Thus it is a rare student who can grasp every point and detail without posing a question or two. However, there are effective and ineffective ways to ask questions. If you keep the following guidelines in mind, your questions are bound to be effective.

1. Jot down your question before you ask it.

Have you ever had a question in mind but had it fly out of your head when you were called upon? When you're first learning to speak up in class, such sudden amnesia is not uncommon. To avoid this problem, **write down your question before you ask it.** If you get self-conscious while talking, you can look at what you've written.

2. Word your question precisely.

In your question, identify the specific point or detail you didn't grasp. A clear question ("Can you please go over once more the way environment makes cells more or less resistant to disease?") is one that will get you the information you want. A vague question ("What did you say last?") will usually prove less productive.

3. Listen carefully to the questions of your classmates.

Try not to get so caught up in your own question that you don't listen to what others say. If you do not listen to your classmates, you might pose a question already asked and answered.

4. Look for role models.

One or two students in every class usually ask questions without becoming flustered or nervous. Study their behavior and model your techniques on theirs. Do they pause and start over if they feel their question isn't clear? Do they speak slowly and take time to make their questions clear and precise? Do they jot down the instructor's answer and respond to it? These are all characteristics worth imitating.

5. Pose a challenging question politely.

Some questions may directly challenge or oppose your instructor's point of view. There's nothing wrong with expressing your own viewpoint as long as you are polite about how you frame your questions. You can expect a sharp reply if you phrase them like this: "Do you seriously believe that there are stages in personality development even though the latest studies don't support that theory?" Opposing other people's point of view doesn't mean you have to insult their intelligence.

The following question would get much better results: "What do you think of the current research on personality development? Doesn't new research suggesting that major character traits remain stable throughout a person's lifetime undermine theories of predictable stages or passages in a person's life?"

Remember that a willingness to ask questions is a sign of a bright, curious mind. It's also a sign of confidence. People who are really confident aren't afraid to ask questions.

Working Space

READING ASSIGNMENT

In the following article, James Floyd describes a habit that can seriously interfere with good listening. As you read, see if you are a victim of the "entertainment syndrome." Then answer the questions that follow.

The Entertainment Syndrome

A major characteristic of poor listening is the demand that all speeches and speakers be interesting or entertaining before they deserve one's time and attention. It is, therefore, extremely easy to develop the habit of rejecting messages that lack novelty or interest and speakers who do not satisfy our need for entertainment.

One might reasonably argue that an effective speaker has a responsibility to adjust to the audience and to make the subject interesting enough that listeners will be motivated to pay attention. As tempting as it may be to use such reasoning as a justification for not listening, it does not satisfactorily address the problem of ineffective listening. Let us consider two examples of situations in which you might function as a listener. In the first instance the speaker is highly entertaining, telling numerous jokes and entertaining stories. This speaker's delivery is animated, forceful, and varied. While the topic is not developed well and provides little useful information, you leave the presentation feeling that it was interesting and fun. You might not have learned much, or you might have received watered down, overly simplified information, yet you comment on what a good speaker this person was.

In the second instance the speaker is not at all entertaining. Delivery is monotonous and colorless. This speaker's voice is too soft, forcing you to strain in order to hear. Yet this speaker presents solid, useful information. You may not have listened to much of it, but the message was substantive and well-supported. You excuse your poor listening by finding fault with the speaker, commenting on the dull, uninteresting delivery.

One might object to these two examples by pointing out that these speakers are extreme examples. There are, after all, speakers who deliver excellent content in an interesting, entertaining manner. Certainly there are such speakers. They represent an ideal in that they keep us entertained at the same time that they present worthwhile messages. Unfortunately, however, such speakers are probably the exception rather than the rule, and if you demand such excellence before you are willing to listen, you are exemplifying the entertainment syndrome.

The basic issue is this: when it is to your advantage to listen well, can you afford to justify poor listening because your entertainment needs are not met? Perhaps we need to ask whether we are actually serving our own best interests when we daydream, talk to others, sleep, and so forth, simply because the speaker is "dull" or the topic is "boring." It might pay to listen to dull speakers. If your boss is explaining information about new procedures that will directly affect the way you are expected to do your job, failure to listen carefully because he or she is a dull, monotonous speaker will probably prove costly to you. Whether the speaker is interesting or not, it is to your advantage to listen carefully.

1. According to Professor Floyd, what is the entertainment syndrome?

2. Why does the author think it's important for his readers to know about the entertainment syndrome? What does he want to persuade them to do?

WRITING ASSIGNMENT

Describe the kind of person you think could best listen to and understand your problems.

JOURNAL ASSIGNMENTS

1. Make a list of the ways you could benefit from improving your listening behavior.
2. List the specific steps you are going to take in order to become a better listener. Be sure to date your list. Within about a week, look the list over to see which steps you have actually taken and which you have not. If you have taken all the steps you planned, keep up the good work. If you haven't, try to determine what is holding you back.
3. How would you interpret or explain this quotation: "The next best thing to brains is silence"?

✔ Checking Out: Review Questions for Chapter 5

1. Explain the difference between listening and hearing.

2. According to the chapter, when does the ability to listen begin to decline?

3. Identify three characteristics of good listeners.

4. Identify three characteristics of poor listeners.

5. Describe at least three things you can do to improve your ability to ask questions.

▶ In Summary

The ability to hear is only the first and most basic prerequisite for good listening. Good listeners are mentally active and alert. They take notes on lectures and respond to what they hear by identifying key points, making connections, and anticipating shifts in thought. Unlike poor listeners, who sit back and expect the speaker to do all the work, good listeners know that communication is a two-way process that demands their intense concentration *and* participation. Every time they feel their attention drifting, good listeners remind themselves that the ability to learn from lectures is essential to academic achievement.

CHAPTER 6

Taking Notes on Lectures

This chapter explains the steps you need to know in order to take good lecture notes. In Chapter 6, we'll cover:

- Making your lecture notes clear and legible
- Identifying key points
- Adapting your note-taking style to the lecture
- Filling in the gaps
- Learning from lecture notes

Making Your Notes Clear and Legible

"I take notes, but I'm doing something wrong. When I look at them a few hours later, I can't make much sense out of what I wrote."
—Patty Fresa, a freshman returning to school after raising a family

As you know from Chapter 4, you can slow down the rate of forgetting by reviewing new material soon after you have learned it. It makes good sense, therefore, to review your lecture notes on the same day that you take them. However, some students, when they sit down to review their lecture notes, can't decipher them. Either they tried to record too much and wrote too hastily and illegibly, or they abbreviated too much, and left out essential information.

Such problems are common, particularly among freshmen who often haven't had much experience in high school taking lecture notes. But to say that these problems are common is not to say that nothing can be done about them. There is a lot you can do to make sure that once the lecture is over, your notes are easy to read and to understand.

Use a Pen for Lecture Notes

Over time, notes written in pencil are likely to smear and fade. When exams roll around, you don't want to confront a stack of barely legible notes; however, that could happen if you take notes with a pencil instead of a pen.

Experiment with pens to see which ones move across the page quickly. Ballpoint and felt-tip pens are good choices. You don't have to use a lot of pressure to write clearly. Just remember that felt-tip pens can create problems if you write on both sides of the page.

Don't worry about making mistakes you can't erase. You can always cross out errors and continue writing. A few crossed-out letters and words are preferable to pencil-smeared, half-legible notes.

Separate Notes from Different Courses

Use a different notebook for each course, or use colored dividers to create several sections in one notebook. Some students like to use spiral notebooks because pages can't fall out. Others prefer a loose-leaf binder that allows them to group together lecture notes and instructor handouts.

Whatever kind of notebook you prefer, make sure it's large enough. If you try to take notes in a $4'' \times 5''$ spiral notebook, your writing will become cramped and hard to read, creating problems when you review for exams. Generally your best bet is a notebook that holds standard-size paper ($8\frac{1}{2}'' \times 11''$). This will give you enough room to take notes *and* jot down your questions and comments.

Record the Essentials

Instructors usually organize their lectures around a few general points or principles, which they then develop and clarify through *supporting details*—reasons, examples, statistics, studies, and so on that make general statements clear and convincing. Recording the general points or principles introduced in a lecture is absolutely essential. However, if the instructor provides three different examples to illustrate one generalization, think about recording two of those examples in detail, but only briefly summarizing the third. **Good note takers never try to write everything down.** They know they can't write as fast as the lecturer can speak, so they concentrate on listening alertly and recording the essentials.

Write Legibly; Don't Assume You Will Recopy Later

Deciphering and recopying carelessly written notes is a time-consuming, tedious job. Too often time runs out before you can finish, and you are left with pages of barely readable notes. Take notes as clearly as possible during the lecture, rather than assuming you can recopy later.

Don't Rely on a Tape Recorder

Using a tape recorder is not a very effective method for learning from lectures. Once the lecture is over, you have to play back the tape in order to take notes. Usually you have to start and stop the tape to make sure you have heard it correctly. By the time you finish, you have spent two to three hours taking notes on a one-hour lecture.

If you feel you need to *back up* your notes by making a tape, you should certainly do it. You can always use the tape to fill in any gaps in your notes. But don't record a lecture on a tape recorder *instead of taking notes.* This is not an efficient use of your time.

Date Your Notes

Often instructors will tell you that an upcoming exam will cover information presented between two specific lecture dates. If you date your notes, you will know what material you need to review for exams. You'll also find it easier to combine lecture and textbook notes on the same topic.

Create Pictures and Diagrams

Any time you can translate words into pictures, you increase your chances of retaining information. So when you're taking lecture notes, don't rely just on words. If, for example, your instructor is describing the layers of the earth, think about making a drawing like the one shown below.

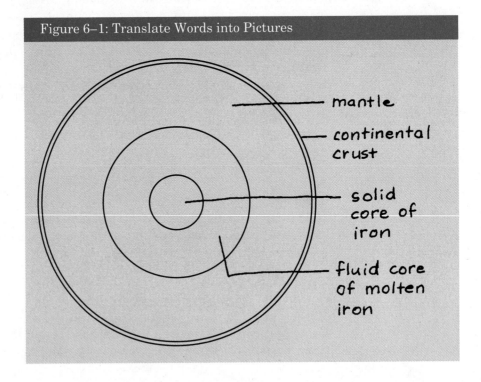

Figure 6–1: Translate Words into Pictures

mantle

continental crust

solid core of iron

fluid core of molten iron

Use Abbreviations and Symbols

To save time, use abbreviations or symbols whenever possible. Thus, if a speaker were to make this point: "A recent survey of executives identified speed and time as the number one competitive issue of the 1990s," your notes should record a briefer version of that same statement: "Recent survey of execs shows speed & time #1 competitive issue for 90s."

You should also develop your own symbols to identify and emphasize key points. The letters Ⓣ︎Ⓠ︎ with a circle around them might identify potential test questions while the letters RP in a box might highlight possible topics for research papers. You can also save yourself some time by creating and consistently using abbreviated forms of specialized terms used repeatedly in your courses. Say you're taking an economics course, and the phrase *national income* comes up constantly. Don't write it out each time; instead use an abbreviation like *n. inc.* Remember, your abbreviations don't have to make sense to anyone but you.

Some Standard Abbreviations and Symbols

Following are some common abbreviations and standard symbols you can use when taking lecture notes.

Common Abbreviations

dept.	department
govt.	government
psych.	psychology
bio.	biology
intro.	introduction
max.	maximum
info.	information
assoc.	association
imp.	important
adv.	advantage
prod.	produces
employ.	employment
pop.	population
indiv.	individual
pres.	president
subj.	subject

Standard Symbols and Abbreviations

vs.	versus
#	number
=	equals
≠	does not equal
+	and
w.	with
w/o	without
cf	compare
e.g.	for example
ex.	example
→	leads to or produces
%	percentage

You can also create your own abbreviations by using these two methods:

1. Use the first syllable and the first or second letter of the second syllable.

musc.	muscle
molec.	molecule
carb.	carbon
gluc.	glucose
reac.	reaction
comm.	communist
cong.	congress
info.	information

2. Use the first and second syllables.

admin.	administration
cosmet.	cosmetics
pharma.	pharmaceutical
accus.	accusation
conseq.	consequence
decis.	decision
inclu.	inclusion

☐ **PRACTICE 1**   Rewrite the following five sentences using abbreviations or symbols whenever possible. Write down only the most essential words.

Example

Original   Hispaniola was the first testing ground of Spain's Indian policy, a policy Samuel Eliot Morrison later called "Hell on Hispaniola."

Abbreviated Form   Hispaniola 1st test of Spain's Indian pol., called by Sam E. Morrison "Hell on Hispaniola."

1. Beginning around 1870, the increasing pace of the Industrial Revolution in Europe stimulated a more rapid change in the Latin American economy and its politics.

_____

_____

_____

_____

2. Shyness is often triggered by novel or unfamiliar situations. For example, a person who does fine with family and friends may become shy when meeting a stranger.

_____

_____

_____

_____

3. The total population of developing countries is approaching 4 billion people. Of this population, 28 percent live in China, 21 percent live in India, and 4 percent live in Indonesia.

—Boyes and Melvin, *Economics*

_____

_____

_____

_____

4. Until recently, the prognosis for schizophrenia was generally unfavorable. But that prognosis improved enormously when schizophrenia began to be treated with the phenothiazine class of drugs.

_____

_____

_____

_____

5. Like numerous groups in Africa and Asia, the social organization of many Native Americans was based on family and clan units.

_____

_____

_____

_____

Note Taking: Deciding What's Important

Students who know the value of taking lecture notes that are complete but concise frequently ask, "How do I decide what's important and what's not?" The question is a good one, but like most good questions, it doesn't have a simple answer. If you are taking notes on a history lecture, dates are usually significant. In a psychology lecture, however, dates are often less important than psychological theories or principles. Your American history instructor, for example, will undoubtedly want you to remember the beginning and ending dates of the Civil War (1861–1865). Your psychology instructor, in contrast, would expect you to know the results of Ivan Pavlov's experiments, but probably not the exact dates when those experiments took place.*

Note taking would be much easier if we could give one or two simple rules for what to include and what to leave out, but no one set of rules applies to all subjects. However, it helps to know a few general guidelines.

Get to Class on Time

Although it's certainly true that most teachers don't appreciate stragglers, getting to class at the beginning of a lecture is not just a matter of politeness. **Instructors frequently open their lectures with a statement of purpose**—a few general remarks about what they hope to accomplish. Here's an example from a marketing course: "Today I want to discuss four different promotional methods and briefly describe how they are used in an organization's marketing campaign. If we have time, I'll compare and contrast the four methods in order to point out their individual strengths and weaknesses." Statements like these can help you decide what to record in your notes and what to leave out.

Link the General to the Specific

When taking lecture notes, you definitely need to record specific facts and figures. But you also need to identify the general theories, ideas, or principles those facts and figures explain. For an example of why it's important to link the general to the specific, imagine you had recorded in your notes these two specific dates and events:

---

*Pavlov investigated the role of conditioned behavior in learning.

1. In 1964, when Harry Truman's public approval was at a low point, the Gallup poll found that the percentage of Americans who called themselves Democrats was down to 39.
2. In 1972, when the very liberal Democratic Senator George McGovern was being trounced by Richard Nixon, the percentage of Americans who called themselves Democrats declined to 43.

Taken by themselves, these two isolated statements don't seem very significant. That's because they have been separated from the generalization that makes them meaningful: "If their candidates are out of favor, Democrats, like Republicans, are less likely to publicly identify themselves as supporters of their party." With the addition of this generalization, the two statistics about voter identification become not isolated tidbits of information but supporting details that illustrate a larger point.

Getting down the facts and figures an instructor provides during a lecture is useful. But be sure to **record the generalizations that interpret or explain the larger meaning of those facts and figures.**

Be Selective About Examples

Instructors frequently offer several different examples to illustrate one general principle or point. If you have time, you can certainly write all of those examples down. But if you are pressed for time or find it hard to keep up with the speaker, be selective. Record one or two of the most pertinent examples in detail, selecting those that illustrate the main point most clearly. For the remaining examples, jot down only a few key words and fill in the specific details right after class or later in the day.

If you understand the instructor's general point and have recorded at least one or two detailed examples, your notes are as complete as they need to be. So don't be concerned if you fail to record every single example. Generally your instructor will not hold you responsible for every example mentioned in the lecture.

Listen for Organizational Patterns

Teachers, like writers, frequently organize their lectures according to a recognizable pattern or patterns. They may, for example, describe the **causes and effects** of global warming or **compare and contrast** the administrations of presidents Harry Truman and Dwight D. Eisenhower.

Recognizing organizational patterns will help you take effective lecture notes. If you can **identify the pattern (or patterns) used to organize a lecture,** you are in a better position to recognize crucial information. Say that the speaker employs a **sequence-of-steps** pattern to describe the development of a human embryo. Once you recognize that a sequence is being introduced, record both the steps and the order in which they occur.

To get a good grasp of some common organizational patterns and their essential elements, study the chart below.

Figure 6–2: Common Organizational Patterns

Identify Patterns	Record Essential Elements
Sequence of dates and events describes the dates and events leading up to some crucial occurrence.	List the individual dates and events: the order in which they occurred.
Sequence of steps describes the individual steps or stages in some larger process.	Record the number of individual steps; any technical terms; and the larger process or sequence being described.
Problem-solution defines a problem and its causes, then offers one or more possible solutions.	Identify the specific problem and cite the individual causes and possible solutions cited.
Comparison and contrast points out the similarities and differences between two people, events, objects, or theories.	Record the two subjects; the specific similarities and/or differences mentioned; and the general statement proved or illustrated through the use of comparison and contrast.
Cause and effect describes how one event (the cause) produces or creates another event (the effect).	List the causes and effects cited.
Classification explains how some larger group can be broken down into smaller subgroups.	Identify the large group being subdivided; the characteristics of each subgroup; the names of each group if names are mentioned.
Definition explains a key term in detail.	Give the definition; the concrete examples used to illustrate and any exceptions cited.

Listen for Transitions

To get the most out of lectures, listen for **transitions.** These are the verbal bridges speakers and writers use to provide emphasis and make connections. To tell students, for example, to pay attention, instructors often precede key points with transitions such as *significantly* and *more importantly*.

Instructors also use transitions to highlight organizational patterns. Words and phrases such as *first, second, third,* and *in the final stages* emphasize a sequence of steps, while transitions like *as a result* and *consequently* suggest cause and effect.

Transitions can also signal a shift or continuation of the speaker's train of thought. Words and phrases like *however, nevertheless,* and *in spite of the fact* tell listeners to expect a contradiction or reversal, whereas words such as *likewise, similarly,* and *furthermore* signal a continuation of the speaker's original line of thought. See Figure 6–3 for a more complete list of transitions.

Become Familiar with Your Instructor's Teaching Style

Most instructors have their own distinctive *teaching style.* They have a particular way of talking, moving, and gesturing while in the classroom. The more attuned you are to a teacher's particular style, the easier it will be to identify essential information in a lecture.

Pay Attention to Body Language   Your instructor's body language can frequently help you identify crucial information. Some instructors point a finger to make an important statement; others may pause and wipe their glasses or tap the chalkboard. Be aware of whatever conscious or unconscious gestures or movements your instructor makes when introducing key points.

Note Changes in Tone of Voice or Speaking Rate   Some instructors become very animated when introducing significant information. Others speak more rapidly or more slowly when they are trying to get a key point across. Here again attentive listeners note any changes in a speaker's tone or speaking rate.

Figure 6–3: Common Transitional Signals

Transitions Used to Signal Significance or Repetition

A key point

It's important to note

It's important to remember

More importantly

What's important here is

Above all

Remember

Of central significance

Crucial to this issue

A crucial point

Of particular importance

Here again

It's worth repeating that

Here in another context

As I mentioned before

Transitions Used to Signal a Sequence of Steps or Events

First . . . Second . . . Third . . .

Meanwhile

Next

In the next step

Then

During

At this stage

At this point

Finally

Eventually

In the final stage

In (plus date)

Transitions Used to Signal Reversal or Contrast

Nevertheless

In contrast

Just the opposite

But

On the other hand

Notwithstanding

Despite

On the contrary

However

Transitions Used to Signal Continuation or Comparison

Similarly

Likewise

In the same vein

In addition

By the same token

Along the same lines

Furthermore

Transitions Used to Signal Cause and Effect

As a product of

Consequently

As a result of

In response to

Therefore

Thus

Watch the Board   Some instructors outline their lectures on the board and point to key statements as they talk. Others emphasize a major point by jotting down a key word or phrase on the board as they come to it. Although instructors vary in the way they use the board, anything they choose to write on it is important and should not be ignored.

Record All the Points in a List   When instructors take the time to enumerate the causes of some event ("There are at least four explanations for Hitler's rise to power") or steps in a process ("Geologists point to five separate stages in the development of coal"), number and record each step.

Get a Sense of Proportion   Say the title of the day's lecture is "The Computer Revolution." If your instructor spends forty minutes illustrating how computers will affect the American work force in the future, and ten minutes describing the way computers already have affected education, you can reasonably assume that the former topic carries more weight. The more time a lecturer spends on a subject, the more complete should be your notes.

Listen for Repetition   To reinforce important ideas, instructors often repeat them; so take notes on any point mentioned more than once. Listening for transitions ("As I said before," and "Here again") will alert you to ideas that are repeated in the lecture.

✱   The more attuned you are to a teacher's lecture style, the easier it will be to identify essential information.

Adapting Your Note-Taking Style to the Lecture

Just as there's no one rule for deciding what's important in a lecture, there's no one way to take lecture notes. The note-taking method you use depends both on the subject of the lecture and your particular learning style. Although you might use informal outlines for psychology lectures, you could switch to diagrams when taking notes in a science course.

In addition, don't assume you have to take the same kind of notes throughout the lecture. In a history course, if you begin by outlining the differences between the Federalists and the anti-Federalists, switch to a time line when the instructor traces the events leading up to the Constitutional Convention.

Several different methods for taking notes on lectures or textbooks follow. Use these different methods alone or in various combinations. Most important, choose the format that best records the subject matter of the lecture.

Informal Outlining

If a lecture has lots of detail and no obvious organizational pattern, consider an informal outline.* With an informal outline, you can show relationships between key points through indentation and various symbols (dashes, letters, abbreviations, and numbers). See Figure 6–4.

Informal outlines are particularly appropriate for lectures that include several main generalizations, each followed by supporting details. But to be effective, **informal outlines must show relationships;** they must distinguish between key points and supporting details. You often can indicate relationships simply by indenting as in this example.

Generalization	Individual branding is the strategy of using a different brand for each product.
Supporting Detail	Procter & Gamble soaps inclu. Ivory, Camay, Safeguard, Coast

But as your notes get longer and more detailed, it helps to include letters, numbers, or labels.

1. Individual branding offers 2 major advantages.

   a. A product with one brand doesn't affect others
   b. Different brands can be directed toward different markets

      ex. Holiday Inns & Hampton Inns directed toward budget minded while Residence Inn toward apartment dwellers

2. Family branding is strategy of using same brand for all or most products.

      ex. Sunbeam, IBM, Xerox

---

*It is considered informal because you can use any symbols you choose and need not worry about following the rules for formal outlining.

Figure 6–4: Informal Outline

American Government 101   9/28

There have been many unsuccessful attempts
to amend the Constitution.

1. Equal Rights Amendment (ERA) reads: "Equality
   of rights under the law shall not be denied
   or abridged by the U.S. or by any state on
   account of sex"

   a. Bitter opposition to amend by conservatives
   b. Congress voted to ext. deadline for
      ratification but couldn't muster more votes —
      3 short of 38 states needed

2. District of Columbia Congressional Representation

   a. Approved by Congress in 1978
   b. Amendment would have granted D.C. full
      Congress representation
   c. Only 10 states willing to ratify

3. Balanced Budget Amendment

   a. 1982 Senate approved amendment to
      require balanced fed. budget
   b. Proposal rejected by House
   c. Prop. would have permitted deficit only in
      time of war or a 3/5 vote by Congress

Block Diagrams

Particularly useful for science courses, block diagrams work well for lectures that outline a sequence of steps. Block diagrams give visual form both to the overall sequence and to the individual steps that comprise it. To make your block diagrams effective, first identify the overall process being described. Then as your instructor introduces each step or stage, create a chain of squares that describes each one. Use arrows to indicate the order in which the steps occur. To illustrate, here's a completed block diagram.

Figure 6–5: Block Diagram

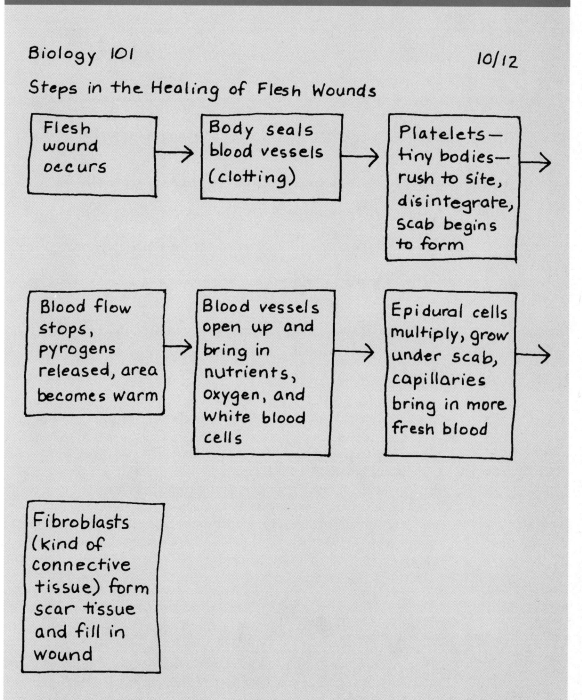

Biology 101   10/12

Steps in the Healing of Flesh Wounds

Flesh wound occurs → Body seals blood vessels (clotting) → Platelets—tiny bodies—rush to site, disintegrate, scab begins to form →

Blood flow stops, pyrogens released, area becomes warm → Blood vessels open up and bring in nutrients, oxygen, and white blood cells → Epidural cells multiply, grow under scab, capillaries bring in more fresh blood →

Fibroblasts (kind of connective tissue) form scar tissue and fill in wound

Figure 6–6: Time Line

History 201   10/18

From 1907 to 1916 Rasputin controlled the czar's
court, discrediting both himself and the czar.

1907	Seeming to heal the czar's son, Rasputin gained influence over Czarina.
1911	Rasputin began to meddle openly in politics.
1916	Aristocrats found him useful at first, but he stood in way of reforms needed to prevent revolution. They assassinated him.
1917	The Russian revolution begins.

Time Lines

In a history class, instructors frequently trace a sequence of dates and events. To record such a lecture, incorporate time lines into your notes. Like block diagrams, time lines make it easier to visualize the information you are hearing.

To make an effective time line, first record the general point or event being explained by a sequence of dates and events. Then divide your notebook page in half so there is room for dates on one side and room to describe events on the other. Figure 6–6 shows a completed time line tracing a portion of a Russian history lecture.

Filling In the Gaps

When you take notes, there frequently will be a definition you can't quite complete or an example you don't have the time to record. That's natural.

Figure 6–7: A Revised Time Line

```
History 201                    Grigory              10/18
From  1907 to 1916, Rasputin controlled the czar's
court, discrediting both himself and the czar.
_____
                                      who had hemophilia,
   1907  │  Seeming to heal the czar's son, Rasputin
         │  gained influence over Czarina. — actually
         │  hypnotized the boy
   1911  │  Rasputin began to meddle openly in politics.
         │   —allowed to make government appointments
         │
   1916  │  Aristocrats found him useful at first, but
         │  he stood in way of reforms needed to
         │  prevent revolution. They assassinated him.
   1917  │  The Russian revolution begins. economic and
                                              social
```

It happens to everyone, and you shouldn't panic. Instead, fill in the gaps when the lecture ends. This is the time to refine definitions, clarify key points, and add the details you couldn't get down during the lecture.

If you can't fill in the gaps right after class, be sure to revise and refine your notes that night. Forgetting takes place most rapidly right after learning. If you wait too long to revise your notes, you're likely to forget the information you wanted to add. Then, too, when you flesh out your original notes, you give your mind another chance to process the material from the lecture. That quick review—if it takes place soon after the lecture—will aid long-term remembering.

Filling in the gaps in your notes shouldn't take more than fifteen or twenty minutes, so don't postpone this very crucial task. For an illustration of what it means to fill in the gaps, look at the sample notes in Figure 6–7 and compare them to those appearing in Figure 6–6.

_____

*Obviously, in your own notes you would abbreviate.

Learning from Your Notes

How well you learn from your notes depends a lot on the format you use for note taking. Here are two different formats. Experiment with both and choose the one that works best for you.

Format 1: The Two-Column System

To create this format, draw a line down the left side of your paper so that you create a two-and-a-half-inch column. During lectures, leave this column blank. Take notes only on the right side of the page.

When you edit your notes, use the left column to jot down key words and potential test questions. Continue to fill in the left column during your first review for exams. However, by the second or third review, begin covering the right-hand column of your notes and using the words and questions in the left-hand column as **recall clues** to jog your memory. See if you can recite the information from your notes without directly looking at them. Look at the column on the right only to test the accuracy of your responses.

Figure 6–8 illustrates lecture notes using format 1.

Format 2: The Three-Column System

The three-column system for taking notes was created by Dr. Walter Pauk of Cornell University. Although you can buy notepads with the three columns already in place, you can just as easily create your own.

Here again, you should start by drawing a vertical line down the left side of the page two-and-a-half inches from the edge. But this time, end the line about two inches from the bottom and draw a horizontal line about two inches up from the bottom of the page. This column is reserved for summarizing your notes.

Summarizing your notes during reviews ensures that you don't focus exclusively on specific facts and lose sight of the larger picture. In order to write a summary, you have to understand the general point or principle illustrated or explained by the more specific supporting details. (For more on how to write summaries, see Chapter 7.)

Figure 6–9 on page 124 illustrates the three-column format for note taking.

Figure 6–8: Two-Column System

Recall Clues	Notes

Sociology 101   **9/20/93**

Bernard Mustein has created a three-stage theory of mate selection.

Mustein

Three-Stage Theory:

1. Stimulus
2. Value
3. Role

Test Questions:

According to B. Mustein, What are the 3 stages of mate selection?

Describe each one.

Stimulus Stage

One ind. drawn to another because of physical or social attributes →

Value Comparison

Decide if they share similar values, interests, attitudes, & beliefs →

Role Stage

Couple decides if they share same view of hus. & wife roles

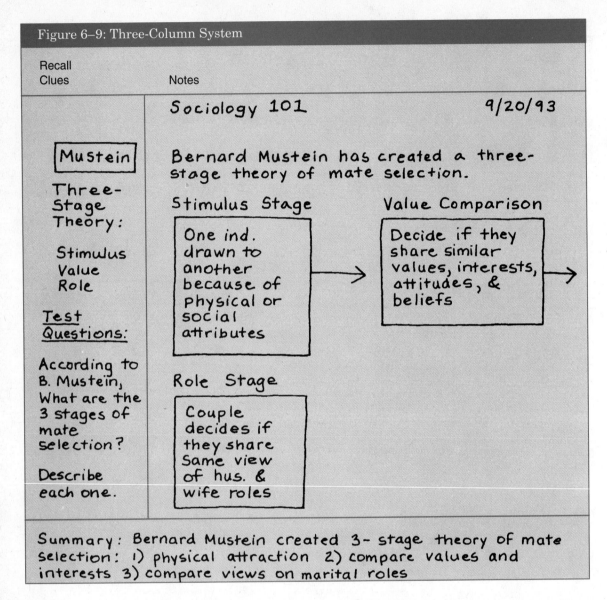

Figure 6–9: Three-Column System

Recall Clues	Notes

Sociology 101   9/20/93

Mustein

Three-Stage Theory:

Stimulus
Value
Role

Test Questions:

According to B. Mustein, What are the 3 stages of mate selection?

Describe each one.

Bernard Mustein has created a three-stage theory of mate selection.

Stimulus Stage

One ind. drawn to another because of physical or social attributes

Value Comparison

Decide if they share similar values, interests, attitudes, & beliefs

Role Stage

Couple decides if they share Same view of hus. & wife roles

Summary: Bernard Mustein created 3-stage theory of mate selection: 1) physical attraction 2) compare values and interests 3) compare views on marital roles

Working Space

READING ASSIGNMENT

Parables are stories that illustrate a moral. Read the following parable and consider the meaning of the prophet's message to the king and the meaning of the story as a whole. Then answer the questions that follow.

The Prophet's Message

Wanting to know the future, an unpopular king and his two wives called a prophet to court. The prophet looked into the future and told the king and his queens this story: "There was a king, and the king had many armed soldiers, all of whom would fight to the death for their sovereign. But the king was despised by his people. When a secret tally was taken, it was found that the people who hated the king greatly outnumbered the soldiers who would die for him. Although the king did not know it, the remaining days of his reign were few."

After hearing the prophet's story, one queen said, "That man has such an odd voice." The other said, "His clothes are so funny." The king himself wasn't listening; he was too busy laughing at the court jester. Although he did not know it, the days of the king and his wives were numbered.[1]

1. What is the moral of the story the prophet told the king and his wives? What does he want the king to realize?

2. What is the moral of the story as a whole? Why would it appear in a book about listening?

WRITING ASSIGNMENT

Create your own version of a parable. Write a brief story that illustrates some point or advice about listening.

JOURNAL ASSIGNMENTS

1. During a class, study your instructor's lecture style, and after class try to answer these questions.

    - Does the instructor emphasize key points with any particular gestures or movements?

---

[1]Adapted from Robert L. Montgomery, *Listening Made Easy* (New York: American Management Association, 1981), 100–101.

- Does the instructor's tone of voice or speaking rate vary in relation to the importance of the material?
- How does the instructor use the chalkboard?

Use your journal to describe the various ways the instructor lets you know what lecture material is particularly important.

2. Describe two specific things you do (or will do) to make sure your lecture notes are easy to read and understand when it comes time to study for exams.

3. Use your journal to interpret or explain the meaning of this statement by the German writer Johann Wolfgang Goethe: "Things which matter most must never be at the mercy of things which matter least."

4. Based on your most recent study session, evaluate your ability to concentrate. Are you finding it easier or harder to shut out distractions? What techniques for improved concentration have you put into practice? How are they working? To help you get started, here's a sample entry.

I've started taking notes in the margins while I read, and it really makes a difference. I seem to concentrate better. What doesn't seem to help is working with Malcolm. He complains constantly about studying. From now on, I have to work alone. I only hope I don't lose my best friend.

✔ Checking Out: Review Questions for Chapter 6

1. According to the chapter, what are three things you can do to make your notes easy to read and understand?

2. Why is getting to class on time important?

3. In addition to specific facts and figures, what do you need to include in your notes?

4. How can recognizing the organizational pattern or patterns in a lecture be of use to you?

5. List three common patterns and their essential elements.

6. What can you learn from transitions?

7. Name three transitions that signal reversal.

8. Why is it important to be aware of your instructor's teaching style?

9. To make informal outlines effective, what do you need to remember?

10. Explain the purpose of each column in the three-column format.

▶ In Summary

Good lecture notes are clear, complete, and concise. To take good notes, you don't have to write down your instructor's every word; that's not humanly possible. Instead identify and summarize the lecture's key points. Include enough specific supporting details so that you can explain those same points on your exams. Make sure to show relationships between ideas, indicating which are major and which are minor.

Remember, too, that you don't have to rely on just one method of note taking. You can change methods to suit the material. Outlines might be fine to record a series of generalizations, but diagrams might prove more useful for recording a sequence of steps. Whatever method you choose, don't forget to fill in the gaps as soon as you possibly can.

Keep in mind that your ability to learn from your notes depends a good deal on the format you use. Some students like to use a two-column format; others prefer a three-column format. It's up to you to experiment with both and decide which one works best for you.

CHAPTER 7

Remembering What You Learn

Far too many students believe that the ability to remember is some special gift bestowed on only a select few. This chapter was written in the hopes of dispelling that belief. Read it to discover how you can conquer memory problems by:

- Defeating the forces of forgetting
- Understanding the relationship between short-term and long-term memory
- Learning selectively
- Chunking information
- Learning in depth
- Combining reading with reciting
- Memorizing efficiently
- Remembering new vocabulary

Defeating the Forces of Forgetting

No one single theory adequately accounts for or explains the troubling phenomenon of forgetting. Researchers have formulated various theories, each one offering at least a partial explanation. The more you know about these theories, the easier it will be for you to remember what you learn.

Without Reinforcement, Memory Traces Decay

According to one theory, **memory traces** (changes in nerve cells or brain activity) fade or weaken over time if the original trace is not reinforced. Even information that has made its way into your long-term memory may fade if you don't strengthen or reinforce the memory trace. Researchers who support this theory believe that periodic **rehearsals** or reviews of material already learned can actually reproduce changes in nerve cells and strengthen the original memory.

Putting Theory into Practice   Let's say that you want to remember the terms and consequences of the Versailles Treaty that brought World War I to an end. To accomplish your goal, review the terms of the treaty shortly after you learn them. Forgetting occurs most rapidly right after learning but a brief rehearsal as soon as possible after the material is learned can noticeably reduce the rate of forgetting.

From that point on, plan on several spaced or **distributed reviews** over the period of a few weeks to reinforce the original memory. A good deal of research suggests that a series of brief reviews extended over time is more effective than **massed practice** or one long marathon review.

Interference

Although researchers don't know exactly why it happens, they do know that new learning interferes with previous learning. In one experiment, two groups of students learned a list of nonsense syllables. One group went to sleep after learning the list while the other group continued to work on a different list. When both groups were tested, the group that slept right after learning had a better memory of the original list.[1] No new

---

[1]M. K. Johnson and L. Hasher, "Human Learning and Memory," *Annual Review of Psychology* 38 (1987): 631–668.

material had interfered with or inhibited their retrieval of information already learned.

Putting Theory into Practice   Knowing the role interference can play in forgetting doesn't mean you have to lock yourself in a darkened room once you finish studying. However, to ensure long-term remembering, you should seriously consider the following advice:

1. If you work on two courses in one study session, make sure they are very different from one another, say, history and math.
2. If you can't go to sleep right after studying, do something to help you unwind and avoid any task that takes a lot of mental effort. Go for a walk or watch television.
3. New material is bound to interfere with the old. But if you take accurate notes, you can review them and quickly jog your memory into retrieving what you previously learned.

Lack of Intention

We also forget because we never *consciously* intended to remember. In one experiment, a group of students were asked if they could accurately draw a penny. Most believed they could, but in the end only a few produced anything near an accurate drawing. However, the students in this experiment hadn't *forgotten* what a penny looked like. They had mistakenly assumed that repeated exposure to the face of a penny had ensured their ability to remember it clearly.[2] They didn't realize that a **conscious intention is essential to stave off the forces of forgetting.**

Putting Theory into Practice   Both learning and remembering would be far easier if we could absorb what we read or hear without a conscious effort. But, unfortunately, human memory doesn't work that way. To remember new information, first reduce it to the most essential points. Then **tell yourself explicitly, "This is the information I need to remember."**

Understanding How Memory Works

"Memory is an active system that receives, stores, organizes, alters, and recovers information."

—Dennis Coon, psychologist

---

[2]R. S. Nickerson and M. J. Adams, "Long-Term Memory for a Common Object," *Cognitive Psychology* 11 (1979): 287–307.

Many students are unduly concerned about their ability to remember, in part because they don't have a clear understanding of how memory works. When they talk about their supposed inability to remember, they speak as if human memory were a single entity or action. "I have a memory like a sieve." "My memory is useless." "I don't know what's the matter with my memory." But actually humans possess three different kinds of memory: *sensory, short-term,* and *long-term.* If you learn how these three different memories work together, you can make them work in your favor.

Sensory Memory

All incoming verbal or visual information enters your sensory memory, which holds an exact copy of everything you see or hear for several seconds. Generally, your sensory memory will retain information just long enough so that your short-term memory can register it.

Short-Term Memory

Think of short-term memory as a storehouse in which information is briefly held. If your brain does not identify that information as *meaningful* or important, it quickly disappears. In this way, short-term memory lets you think about the task at hand—reading a paragraph, dialing a phone number, or making a shopping list—but prevents your mind from collecting too much useless trivia.

To understand how short-term memory works, imagine that the radio is playing a familiar song while your best friend tells you he is moving out of the state. Chances are you would not recognize what's playing on the radio because your attention is totally focused on your friend's words. What's happened is this: your selective attention has canceled out competing information that was registered in sensory memory. In effect, your mind has made a decision about what's important enough to remember and has transferred only your friend's news to short-term memory.

Long-Term Memory

Information that your mind identifies as significant or meaningful makes its way into long-term memory, which can store information for much longer periods of time. In fact, some researchers believe we never lose any fact or idea that has made its way into long-term memory. We only forget how to *access* or recall it.

Unlike sensory memory or short-term memory, long-term memory appears to have a limitless storage capacity. However, information is stored in long-term memory on the basis of meaning or importance. Any information you don't really understand or consider significant is unlikely to find its way into your long-term memory.

Putting Theory into Practice   In practical terms, then, your ability to remember what you study depends primarily on you, on your willingness to make sure you thoroughly understand the material and can relate it to your existing store of knowledge and experience.

☐   PRACTICE 1   Use your understanding of how human memory works to explain the following situation:

Your instructor is reviewing the material on which the final exam is based. During the first ten minutes, you are having trouble concentrating because people in back of you are whispering and you can't help overhearing their conversation. But after a while, you stop being distracted, and once the lecture is over, you don't even remember what they were talking about. Explain why this is possible.

_____

_____

_____

Learning Selectively

"A good memory is like a fishnet. It should keep all the big fish and let the little ones escape."

—Dennis Coon

If you bombard your short-term memory with insistent demands to remember everything you hear or read, you will probably forget most of it. Your short-term memory, like everyone else's, has its limitations. To deal with those limitations, **evaluate incoming information and select only what is essential.** To evaluate what you hear in a lecture or read in a text, stay mentally active and pose questions like the following: (1) Which ideas in the text or lecture receive the most emphasis, development, or explanation? (2) What are the important new concepts? (3) What information elaborates on material we have already learned?

Chunking Information

To **chunk** separate pieces of information, *classify* or combine them into larger groups or categories. Say you were reading an article describing the causes and effects of organizational conflict. Rather than trying to remember each cause and effect separately (six in all), ensure remembering by creating two chunks of information:

<u>Causes of Organizational Conflict</u>
1. Competition
2. Differences between groups
3. Differences in goals

<u>Effects of Organizational Conflict</u>
1. Hostility
2. Withdrawal
3. Increased motivation

When you chunk or collect individual bits of information into broader, more general categories, you make that information easier to retrieve later. The headings or names of the larger categories function as **memory pegs** and help you recall the individual pieces of information to which they refer.

Authors or lecturers frequently introduce words that can function as memory pegs, such as *benefits* and *drawbacks; similarities* and *differences; causes* and *effects;* and *advantages* and *disadvantages.* However, don't assume that it's up to others to group and classify information for you. If the text or lecture does not supply you with the appropriate memory pegs, create them for yourself.

PRACTICE 2   Use the blanks that follow to chunk information from the passage below. Fill in the first blank with the heading you would use as a memory peg. Fill in the remaining blanks with the individual pieces of information that come under that heading.

Telemarketing: A Tool for the 1990s

Telemarketing is defined as selling on the telephone; it does not include customer service provided on the phone. Direct marketing by telephone was the fastest-growing sales medium of the 1980s; it now employs nine million telemarketers. Annoying as the calls are to most people, telemarketing does sell, and it is used by both large and small companies to control costs and maximize sales. A combination of telemarketing, traditional advertising, and sales promotions allows companies to almost immediately increase sales volume.

- Telemarketing can help firms reduce their overall marketing costs while allowing them to gauge results with greater precision. Companies that have successfully supplemented personal selling with telemarketing include IBM, MCI Communications, Chrysler, and General Electric.
- Telemarketing speeds up order taking and shipping. Integrated services digital network (ISDN) technology is already making the telemarketer's job much easier and faster. ISDN automatic number identification (ANI) helps the telemarketer process calls, increase productivity, and improve call handling.
- Telemarketing is flexible. Scripts can be adapted to the responses of the listener, and entire campaigns can be adjusted midway, if necessary.
- Telemarketing provides immediate, measurable results, unlike other sales strategies.
- Telemarketing boosts the effectiveness of print, radio, and television ads.

—William Pride et al., *Business,* Houghton Mifflin, 330

Heading: _____

Consolidating Old and New Knowledge

Consolidation is a remarkable mental process in which the mind reflects on new information and makes connections to its preexisting store of knowledge. If you take a brief break right after studying and mentally review what you have covered, you give your mind a chance to consolidate new information with old.

Say that you have been reading about the nineteenth-century Latin-American movement for independence. Just to unwind and think over what you have learned, you take a quick walk after studying. While you are walking, it may suddenly strike you that the Latin American struggle and the American Revolutionary War were similar in many ways. Given a little time, your mind has spontaneously begun to consolidate what you have just learned with what you already know.

Distributing Your Study Sessions

Some students don't worry about procrastinating because they have their excuse ready: "One of these days I'm going to study all night and put in the same eight hours I would have if I'd studied on four different days."

As convincing as that explanation sounds, it has a serious weakness. Research on learning suggests that spaced or **distributed practice is superior to massed practice.**[3] In fact, a good deal of evidence suggests that three twenty-minute study sessions can produce more learning than an hour of continuous study.[4]

When you distribute several review sessions over time, you automatically benefit from your mind's ability to consolidate information. It's also true that during a marathon study session, you are likely to get fatigued. Without your realizing it, your concentration flags and the quality of your work suffers.

The Value of Overlearning

A number of different studies suggest that **overlearning** improves remembering.[5] Once you have reached the point of being able to explain, for example, the complex causes of the Civil War, don't stop there. Instead **review the material until you have internalized it,** until you know it so well you could, if necessary, teach it to someone else.

---

[3]C. P. Rea and V. Modigliani, "Educational Implications of the Spacing Effect," in *Practical Aspects of Memory,* (Chinchester, England: Wiley, 1987), 402–406.
[4]Dennis Coon, "Memory," in *Introduction to Psychology* (St. Paul: West, 1989), 246–247.
[5]Dennis Coon, "Memory," 247.

In these additional reviews, take different approaches; first start with what you believe is the most significant social cause. The next time around, begin by explaining the most important economic or political cause of the war. If you have extra time available, read a biography of Abraham Lincoln, skim his writings on the war, or go to an exhibit of Civil War memorabilia. In short, immerse yourself in the material.

In-Depth Learning Ensures Remembering

To ensure in-depth learning and long-term remembering, use the following strategies.

Paraphrase

When you paraphrase, feel free to add or delete words. You can also change the length and order of sentences. But do not change the author's original point or insight. We'll use the following passages to illustrate.

> Original text: Speech and sex are linked in obvious ways. Let the reader, if he doubts this, start talking like a member of the opposite sex for a while and see how long people let him get away with it.
> —EDWARD HALL, *THE SILENT LANGUAGE*

> Paraphrased version: Your gender noticeably affects how you speak. Anyone who doesn't agree should try speaking like a member of the opposite sex for a time and see people's reactions.

Compare the original text with the paraphrased version. The language differs and so does the length, but the meaning is approximately the same.

Summarize

Your ability to paraphase comes in handy when you need to **summarize** or condense a text into its briefest possible form. When you summarize, don't evaluate or judge an author's ideas. Concentrate on reducing the original text to the barest essentials.

To create an effective summary, look at each sentence and decide how important it is for the larger point of the text. Be ruthless about eliminating all but the most essential details. Not surprisingly, this focused attention to the material aids remembering. For a more detailed explanation of how to summarize, see Chapter 9.

Analyze

On the most basic level, **analyzing** means breaking a whole into parts. To analyze a text, look at the problem or point discussed from various perspectives. Ask questions that force you to probe the meaning and explore the larger context.

1. **To what larger group does the topic belong?**
   If the topic is "special-interest groups in government," ask yourself what other groups participate in the government. What is the relationship between these groups and special-interest groups?

2. **Does the idea or problem explained in the passage have a long history or is it a recent phenomenon?**
   For example, have we always had special-interest groups in politics or is this a relatively new development?

3. **Can you find useful points of comparison or contrast between this idea or event and similar ones?**
   In the past, were special-interest groups less open about their determination to influence government?

4. **Are there any causes or effects the author does not mention that you think should appear?**
   If, for example, the passage focuses on the negative effects of special-interest groups, are there positive effects you think should be mentioned?

5. **Is the author's primary purpose to inform or to persuade?**
   Although the primary goal of most textbooks is to inform rather than persuade, authors of textbooks are only human. Their particular **biases** or personal leanings can find their way into the text. In analyzing a text, study the language. Look for words that reveal an author's personal point of view. For example, how do you think the author of the following sentence views special-interest groups? "Despite efforts to control their effect on government, special-interest groups continue to exert an extraordinary—and perhaps excessive—amount of influence on our legislators."

   Through raising and answering questions like the ones above, you engage in the kind of deep, analytical thinking that fosters good comprehension and long-term remembering. For more on thinking analytically, see Chapters 13 and 14.

Associate

"The extent to which we remember a new experience has more to do with how it relates to existing memories than with how many times or how recently we have experienced it."

—Morton Hunt

As you study, try to create conscious links between what you are learning and what you already know. Look for ways in which the new material is similar to or different from your personal experience and knowledge. These associations don't have to mean anything to someone else. What's important is that they **forge a link between you and the material you are studying.**

If you learn, for example, that an extra twenty-first chromosome causes Down's syndrome, connect that information to your neighbor's child, a lovable little girl born with this condition. Later on, when trying to remember the cause of Down's syndrome, you will think first of the little girl and then of the genetic abnormality that caused her condition.

Studying to Achieve In-Depth Learning and Long-Term Remembering

Janice Chen is a good student, well organized and efficient. Here is her personal system for learning and remembering.

1. Read the passage carefully to get a sense of the author's message.
2. Then read it again carefully, looking for connections between ideas.
3. Write a label or title beside each paragraph in the text, saying what it covers.
4. List the key terms and ideas in a notebook.
5. Jot down personal connections: "Birds have temperatures in limited range. So do I: my temp ranges between 96 and 99."
6. Identify any spot where meaning is murky; mark for rereading.
7. Mentally review key ideas and how they connect; ask:
   • Can I identify key points and the connections between them?
   • Can I explain this passage clearly to a classmate?

After going through this process, Janice has thoroughly understood the material and all but guaranteed long-term remembering.

☐   PRACTICE 3   Paraphrase each of the following statements.

1. Words often fall short of accurately depicting someone's intentions and
    we can't really guess at times what someone else really means. In the
    long term, behavior is what gives evidence of our true intentions.

    —*Psychology Today,* February 1993, 49

    _____

    _____

    _____

    _____

2. Part of the population would like the island of Puerto Rico to become
    independent, another part wants statehood, and a third group favors
    continued status as a commonwealth.

    —Earl Shorris, *Latinos,* Norton, 27

    _____

    _____

    _____

    _____

3. Although the idea that pieces of the Earth are in constant motion and
    that the continents had once been attached to each other goes back
    hundreds of years, it was formally put forward first by Alfred Wegner in
    his 1915 book, *The Origins of the Continents and Oceans.*

    —Kenneth C. Davis, *Don't Know Much About Geography,*
    Morrow, 18

    _____

    _____

    _____

    _____

4. *Mediation* is the use of a neutral third party to assist management and the union during their negotiations. This third party (the mediator) listens to both sides, trying to find ground for agreement.

—William M. Pride, et al., *Business,* Houghton Mifflin, 307

_____

_____

_____

_____

Reading and Reciting

When you are reading a textbook, your short-term memory retains the individual words of a sentence long enough for you to understand the sentence and relate it to what came before. But as you know, your short-term memory is only a *very temporary* storehouse for information. If you don't actively work to retain that information, it disappears. In many cases, **reciting** or saying aloud what you've read is a good way to capture it in memory.

Recitation aids remembering because it forces you to search for and retrieve information recently stored in your short-term memory. During that time of search and retrieval, you consciously rethink what you have just read and give your long-term memory a chance to store this new information. In addition, recitation provides your sensory memory with another avenue for learning, bringing into play hearing as well as seeing.

Visualizing

"To everything we wish to remember, we should give an image."

—Matteo Ricci

Unaccustomed to doing so, many students don't use visualization as a strategy for remembering, yet several studies suggest **visualization is a powerful tool for learning.** When you combine words with pictures, you double your chances for long-term remembering. Imagine that you wanted to learn the difference between a convex and a concave lens. In addition to reading about the two kinds of lenses, you could draw a picture like the one in Figure 7–1.

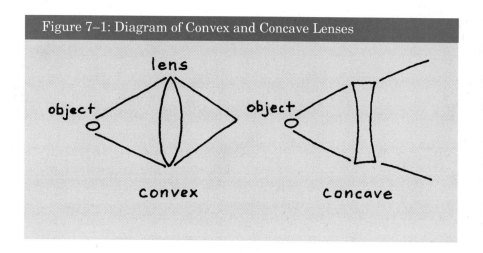

Figure 7–1: Diagram of Convex and Concave Lenses

Later on, should words momentarily fail you, you could recall the picture you had created to help jog your memory.

PRACTICE 4   Read this passage. Then follow the directions for creating a mental image that matches this verbal description.

> Nimbostratus clouds are thick grayish or white clouds that appear in the form of a patchy series of sheetlike masses in the sky. They are usually composed of water droplets, occasionally of ice crystals. When you see nimbostratus clouds, rain—or some other form of precipitation—is likely.
> —Joseph S. Weisberg, *Meteorology,* Houghton Mifflin, 42

Create your mental image step by step. Begin by imagining one thick gray or white cloud. Then imagine several that form "sheetlike masses." Next make your mind's eye zoom in on one cloud in particular and see its composition of "water droplets." Once you can visualize the clouds, get a pencil and some paper and create from memory a description of nimbostratus clouds.

Enlarging Your Store of Personal Knowledge

The larger and more varied your store of personal knowledge, the more readily you will understand the various allusions and references in your reading. However, developing a rich store of knowledge does not happen overnight. It takes persistent effort and a willingness to do all of the following:

1. Take basic introductory courses seriously. They lay the groundwork for the more specialized courses you take later on when you are sure of your major.
2. Start or join a study group in which you and two or three other students share information about your courses and discuss your ideas.
3. Read widely. When you take a course, do not rely solely on the textbook or lecture for information. Ask your instructor or check your textbook for titles of additional books or articles that might enrich your understanding of the subject.
4. Take as many courses in the humanities as you possibly can. History, architecture, drama, and literature courses will give you the kind of *cultural literacy* or background knowledge most writers expect their readers to possess.

Memorizing

Verbatim or word-for-word memorization is necessary if you are studying unrelated names, terms, or dates that have no internal logic or organization of their own. In a language course, for example, you'll need to memorize lists of nouns and verbs; in a physiology course, you'll need to know the exact names of the bones in the human body.

For those times when you need to memorize, keep in mind the following pointers.

Combine Anticipation with Repetition

Most students know that memorization requires some form of repetition. If given a list of names or dates to learn, they dutifully look at it over and over again. But there is a better, more active way to memorize that combines anticipation with repetition and that decreases the time needed for learning. The trick is to arrange the items you want to memorize so that

gene	the unit of heredity
allele	one or two alternative forms of a gene
gene frequency	the proportion of an allele in a population relative to the proportions of other alleles
chromosomes	the cellular structure that contains the genes
DNA	deoxyribonucleic acid, the chemical of the gene
gene pool	the entire genetic makeup of a population
cytosine	a pyrimidine base, important to the structure of DNA

you can **first anticipate** the correct answer and **then check** to see if you were correct.

With a list like the one above, you can cover the right column, anticipate what each term means, and then check to see if you were correct. This **self-testing** is a more active method of memorization; it forces you to search your memory for the right answer *before* you confirm or correct it. Although self-testing may increase the time you spend on individual memorizing sessions, it will decrease the overall number of sessions. See for yourself if combining anticipation with repetition doesn't anchor the information more firmly in your memory.

Create Mnemonic Devices

Mnemonic devices are jingles, rhymes, sayings, or names designed to help you recall information you have committed to memory. Although you might not realize it, you probably have been using mnemonic devices for years. In the spring or fall, for example, many people use the mnemonic device "Spring forward, fall backward" as a way of remembering how they should set their clocks. Likewise many young music students memorize the notes of a musical staff by using two different mnemonic devices, one for lines, "Every good boy deserves favor"; the other for spaces, "Face."

For years zoology students have used the sentence "King Philip came over from Greece singing" in order to remember the categories into which all living things are divided: kingdom, phylum, class, order, family, genus, and species.

Although many mnemonic devices are passed from generation to generation, you should certainly think about creating your own. One ingenious student invented the sentence "Sam Marlowe hated Ernest Owen" in order to remember the names of the Great Lakes: Superior, Michigan, Huron, Erie, and Ontario.

While mnemonic devices can take many forms, their function is always the same; they help you memorize separate bits of information that cannot be linked in any meaningful way.

Focus on the Middle

If you have to memorize material in order—for example, a chronological list of dates and events—you are more likely to forget the dates in the middle of your list. This is called the **serial position effect.** You will remember the first items on your list because they enter a relatively empty short-term memory. You'll probably remember the last ones because they tend to interfere with and cancel out some of the preceding dates. Thus you are most at risk of forgetting the dates and events in the middle. To combat the serial position effect, give a little more time and attention to those items in the middle of your list.

Learn in Parts

When you memorize the lines of a poem or a long speech, the best method is to divide the text into short parts or pieces. Study part A until you have memorized it. Then, learn the remaining parts until you have mastered the whole and can say it all several times without errors.

☐   **PRACTICE 5**   For each column, invent a mnemonic device to help you memorize the names of the planets and the elements of the periodic table.

Planets	Elements
	Hydrogen
Mercury	Helium
Venus	Lithium
Earth	Beryllium
Mars	Boron
Jupiter	Carbon
Saturn	Nitrogen
Uranus	Oxygen
Neptune	Fluorine
Pluto	Neon

Remembering New Vocabulary

Throughout college, you constantly will be adding new words to your vocabulary. In addition to learning the **specialized terms** of each new discipline or subject, you will need to expand your general vocabulary so that you can speak and write with greater vividness and precision.

Learning new words is one of the best ways to put into practice all that you have just learned about remembering. To help you expand your vocabulary and make you think about strategies for remembering, here are some tips for learning new words.

1. Take an active role in reviews.

Put the words you want to learn on index cards. Write the word on one side and the definition on the other. Test yourself by trying to recall the definitions before actually turning the cards over to check your response. Here again, self-testing is the key to remembering. Unlike passive repetition—repeatedly looking at the word and definition—searching your memory for the meaning forces you to take an active role in reviews.

2. Reword the definition you find in your textbook or in the dictionary.

In addition to writing down the formal definitions from the dictionary or your textbook, paraphrase those definitions by translating them into your own words.

To learn *peremptory,* for example, certainly record the dictionary definition, "dictatorial." But also jot down a more familiar definition like "bossy."

3. Create associations between the words and your experience.

To remember the phrase *persona non grata,* meaning a person who is "unacceptable or unwelcome," think of how you might feel about a houseguest who stayed too long, complained about your hospitality, and played loud music late into the night.

4. Create a visual image of the word in action.

If you want to learn the word *surreptitiously,* which means "in a secret or underhanded fashion," visualize a burglar tiptoeing up carpeted stairs, or a child passing a note in class.

5. Give words a context as well as a definition.

Whenever possible, record the sentence in which a new word appears. Try to collect examples of the same word in different contexts and note the effect context has on meaning. In many cases, you will record additional definitions on the back of your index cards because a change in the context of a word can change the meaning as well.

Word	Example	Definition
sanguine	1. The professor pulled his sanguine sword from the vampire's chest.	1. bloodstained
	2. As a child, I was more sanguine, I always assumed the world would treat me well.	2. optimistic, cheerful

6. Look for antonyms and synonyms.

To learn the word *imperious,* for example, compare and contrast it with words like *arrogant* and *humble.* When learning the word *dorsal,* meaning "back," learn the word *ventral,* meaning "front."

7. Create your own comparisons or analogies.
To learn the word *osmosis,* an essential term in biology, create an analogy like the following.

> In the process of osmosis, the cell membrane functions like a gate-keeper. It lets in the appropriate visitors and keeps out the inappropriate ones.

8. Make maps of words with common roots.
Periodically go through your index cards looking for words with common roots. Use mapping to highlight their common origins.

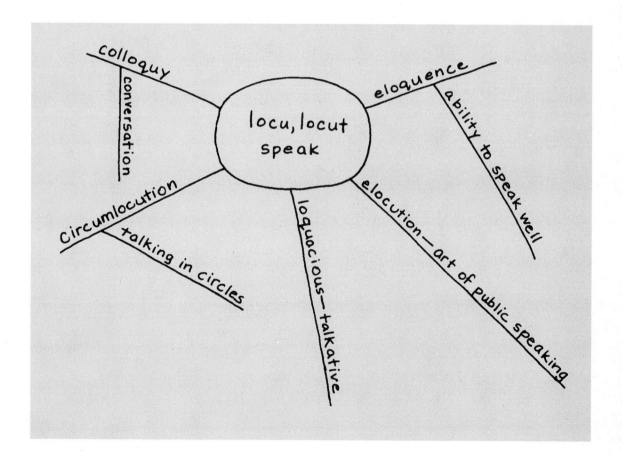

PRACTICE 6   In the first column are five words used to describe people, their personalities and temperaments. In the second column are definitions. In the third column write down some of the associations or images you might use to remember what they mean.

WORD	DEFINITION	ASSOCIATION
diffident	shy	
gregarious	sociable	
loquacious	talkative	
vivacious	lively	
avaricious	greedy	

Useful Strategies for Learning and Remembering

1. Translate the author's or speaker's words into your own language.
2. After finishing a chapter section, see if you can recite the key points.
3. Create a mental image of what you read. If possible, turn that image into a moving picture.
4. Make your own diagrams, charts, or time lines.

5. Even if you agree with what you read or hear, think of possible objections that someone with a different perspective might raise.
6. Create your own concrete examples of important generalizations.
7. Consider how the author's words might apply to your own life.
8. Think of exceptions to the ideas being discussed.
9. Compare and contrast one idea with another.
10. Analyze the author's arguments or explanations.
11. Use the margins of your textbook to keep a running dialogue with the author.
12. Start a discussion group in which you informally discuss what you are learning.
13. Create a condensed version or summary of the original text.
14. Overlearn the material until you can teach it to someone else.
15. Space or distribute your reviews.

Working Space

READING ASSIGNMENT

The following essay by John Niemand briefly describes nineteenth-century experiments in memory performed by the German psychologist Hermann Ebbinghaus. As you read the essay, think about how you can apply Ebbinghaus's findings to your own work. Then answer the questions that follow.

The Ebbinghaus Experiments

At the end of the nineteenth century a German psychologist named Hermann Ebbinghaus became interested in the carefully controlled laboratory experiments being used to do research in the fields of physiology and physics. He was so impressed with the results of these experiments that he decided to introduce similar methods into the study of human memory.

Using only himself as a subject, Ebbinghaus devoted six years of research to his experiments. During that time he memorized lists of nonsense syllables, put them aside for specified intervals of time, and then relearned them. By comparing the time taken to learn the lists with the time taken to relearn them, Ebbinghaus was able to come to several important conclusions about the role of memory in learning;

and these conclusions, after nearly a century of research, have been repeatedly confirmed.

One important conclusion concerned the rate of forgetting. As a result of his research, Ebbinghaus maintained that the rate of forgetting is rapid right after learning and becomes progressively slower over time. A list of nonsense syllables that Ebbinghaus had learned and then put aside for an hour required more than half the original study time to be relearned; but a list that had been put aside for more than twice that time (9 hours) was not, as one would expect, totally forgotten. The rate of forgetting had slowed down, and only two-thirds of the original study time was required to relearn the nonsense syllables.

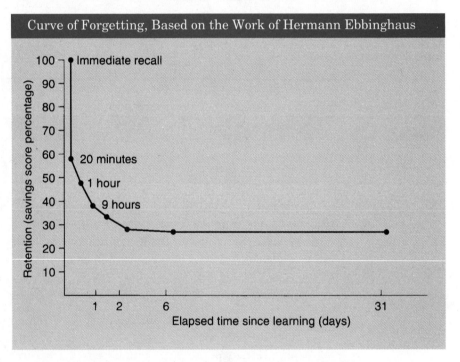

Curve of Forgetting, Based on the Work of Hermann Ebbinghaus

Since 1885 when Ebbinghaus first published his work, investigators have studied the rate of forgetting. They have used not only nonsense syllables but also passages of prose, lists of facts, and excerpts from poetry. Like Ebbinghaus, they have almost always discovered that the rate of forgetting slows down over time; it is rapid at first but becomes slower as the amount of time between learning and relearning increases.

Modern researchers have, however, pointed out that the rate of forgetting depends on various circumstances. It depends, for example, on the kind of remembering involved. If two people are given the same passage to learn, but one is told to remember the exact words, while the other is told to remember only the general idea of the passage, the one told to remember the exact words will forget more rapidly. Researchers have also found that the rate of forgetting depends on how meaningful the material is.

Another of Ebbinghaus's conclusions, which modern research has confirmed, but again with certain modifications, is that overlearning during the initial learning period makes relearning at a later time easier. Based on his experiments, Ebbinghaus maintained that the more repetitions involved in the original learning, the fewer repetitions needed for relearning. Investigators who followed have come to similar conclusions but have also concluded that each and every repetition will not produce an equal return in time saved during the relearning period.

Research that followed the Ebbinghaus experiments by more than half a century has also confirmed Ebbinghaus's belief that learning sessions are more effective if they are distributed over a period of time. In 1940 an American psychologist, A. P. Bumstead, decided to do a series of experiments to determine whether it was better to have several short learning sessions spaced out over a period of time or one long unbroken learning session. Using only himself as a subject, Bumstead memorized several different poetry selections, spacing his learning sessions at intervals that varied from one hour to eight days. After finishing the experiment, Bumstead concluded that increasing the time between learning sessions actually decreased the overall amount of time needed to memorize the material.

1. What did Hermann Ebbinghaus's experiments prove about the rate of forgetting?

2. What did Ebbinghaus discover about overlearning?

3. How did later experiments modify his findings?

4. The research of A. P. Bumstead supports what piece of advice of-
    fered in this chapter?

WRITING ASSIGNMENT

Describe a childhood experience that you did not consciously try to remember but that has stayed with you all your life. Begin by describing the experience in as much detail as possible. In the final paragraphs, explain what it
was about the experience that etched it so deeply in your memory. What
made it so meaningful?

JOURNAL ASSIGNMENTS

1. Write down three things you intend to do to improve your ability to re-
    member.
2. According to the poet and writer Samuel Johnson, "The true art of mem-
    ory is the art of attention." Explain what you think Johnson meant by this
    statement.
3. Ask yourself if you have been making progress in the management of
    your time. If your answer is yes, write a paragraph explaining how you
    know that you have made progress. If your answer is no, write a para-
    graph defining the specific problems that are keeping you from efficiently
    managing your time.
4. Review the list of motivation techniques offered on pages 34–38 in Chap-
    ter 2. Check off the techniques you have used. If you haven't used any,
    select at least two and put them into practice—not tomorrow but today.

✔ Checking Out: Review Questions for Chapter 7

1. Describe the relationship between short-term and long-term
    memory.

2. What does it mean to *chunk* information?

3. Explain what it means to paraphrase.

4. What does research suggest is the key to long-term remembering?

5. List three questions you can ask to analyze a text.

6. What is overlearning?

7. Why does recitation work to ensure remembering?

8. Describe two theories of forgetting.

9. What are *mnemonics?*

10. Describe the serial position effect.

▶ In Summary

To remember what you learn from your lectures and textbooks, you have to make sure your short-term memory registers the information and transfers it to your long-term memory. Fortunately, there are many different strategies you can use to make sure the transfer occurs.

Be selective. Decide what is essential to remember and what can safely be forgotten. Whenever possible, chunk information into larger categories that function as memory pegs. By recalling the headings, you'll remember the separate terms or ideas clustered around them.

Distributing your study sessions over time will also help you retain what you learn. Periodic reviews allow your mind to consolidate new information with what you already know. Overlearning, or reviewing a text until you can teach it to someone else, is another key strategy.

Like overlearning, learning in depth also aids remembering. The more deeply you can think about a text, the more likely you are to remember its contents. Paraphrasing, summarizing, analyzing, and associating are all forms of in-depth learning that will help you remember what you read. Useful too are strategies like reciting and visualizing.

All in all, there is no such thing as a poor memory. However, if you don't *work* at remembering you will be more likely to forget.

3

UNIT

Learning from Textbooks

CHAPTER 8

Three Strategies for Reading Textbooks

In Chapter 8, we'll describe three different strategies for reading textbooks: *prereading, intensive reading,* and *analytical reading.* Some chapters will require all three kinds of reading. Others will become clear with only two—a brief prereading followed by a more intensive one. Occasionally, if the material is familiar, you might rely solely on a careful intensive reading. It's up to you to decide which reading strategies best fit your assignments.

- *Prereading* to get advance knowledge about chapter length, content, and structure
- *Intensive* reading to determine what each individual section of the chapter contributes to your understanding of the whole
- *Analytical* reading to decipher particularly difficult passages

Prereading to Get Advance Knowledge

Unless the material in a textbook chapter is very familiar, skillful readers usually **preread** or preview *selected portions* in order to get advance knowledge about chapter length, content, and organization. Prereading can take anywhere from five to twenty minutes, depending on the length and difficulty of the material. The selected portions or sections of text that you'll preread can vary, depending on (1) your **purpose** or reason for reading; (2) your familiarity with the **topic** or subject under discussion; and (3) the **organization** or structure of the text. It's up to you to decide how many of the following steps you need to include in a prereading.

Read the Title and Subtitle

The title of a chapter is a crucial clue to the chapter's topic. The subtitle usually identifies the author's particular approach or emphasis.

Read the Introduction

Many textbook authors open their chapters with a brief introduction outlining the **controlling idea** or focus of the chapter. Often there is an explicit **statement of purpose** that defines exactly what the chapter should accomplish. The statement of purpose that follows opens a chapter titled "From Boom to Depression": "In the previous chapter, we characterized American society in times of economic prosperity. In this chapter, we will expand that explanation to explore the aftermath of an economic boom—a downturn or depression."

Look for Lists of Questions, Chapter Objectives, or Topics

Textbook authors frequently use the opening page of a chapter to list the key concepts, questions, or topics they will cover in the chapter. For an illustration, look at the opening page of the chapter you are now reading.

Read Chapter Headings and Turn Them into Questions

Major headings open chapter sections and identify the key topics or issues to be addressed. **Minor headings** appear under the major headings and divide the larger topics into more specific *subtopics* or points.

Major Heading	**THE MAJOR PARTIES IN AMERICA**
Minor Headings	A History of the Parties
	Why Two Parties?
	Third Parties

By reading just the major and minor headings of a chapter, you can learn what topics the chapter will cover and how thoroughly the author will explore each one. However, you should also use the headings to raise questions about the chapter. Headings such as "Learning While Asleep" or "Learning on the Right Side of the Brain" can be turned into questions: "Can we learn while asleep?" and "What kind of learning is controlled by the right side of the brain?" These questions will give your reading a purpose and help you maintain your concentration.

Read One or Two Sentences Following the Major Headings

The first sentence or two immediately following a major heading frequently introduces the central point or generalization to be developed in that section. Often you can get useful information by reading the first sentence or paragraph of each major section.

Look at All the Visual Aids

Don't ignore pictures, diagrams, or graphs. Whatever form they take, visual aids serve an important function; they highlight and clarify key points in the chapter.

Read End-of-Chapter Questions, Summaries, or Reviews

Textbook authors know that their readers often need help identifying key points in a chapter. Usually they provide some guidance in final sections called *Summary, Review, Questions,* or *Conclusions.* These sections sum up the chapter; they are the author's way of saying "These are the key points of this chapter; make sure you know them."

Map the Chapter's Content

By making an organizational map, you can help yourself understand a chapter's content and structure. **Organizational maps** will help you grasp the relationships among chapter sections. Once you understand those relationships, it will be easier to reconstruct the author's line of thought.

To make an organizational map as you preread, follow these steps.

1. Put the main topic of the chapter either in the middle or at the top of the page.
2. To make the topic stand out, put it in a circle or in a box. Or just underline it.
3. Attach a series of spokes or lines to the topic and write a major heading on each one.
4. Whether to add minor headings to your map will depend on the chapter. If there are only a few under each major heading, add them. Otherwise, leave them out.

Figure 8–1 on page 160 shows that the author divided the chapter into six major sections, each one exploring some aspect of mate selection. One of those sections is further divided into two minor **subsections,** each one clarifying some facet of "International Mate Selection."

Once you have created an organizational map, you can use it to **monitor your comprehension** after completing an intensive reading of a complete chapter. Look at each heading on the map and review or recite the key points introduced in that section. If you can't remember the key points, mark the heading to indicate the need for rereading.

Make Personal Connections

During prereading, consider what you already know about the topics or ideas discussed in the chapter. As you learned in Chapter 7, connecting new information with what you already know helps both learning and re-membering. Say you are prereading a chapter on how the media shapes public opinion. Think about how television, radio, film, and newspapers have personally affected you. Has your opinion of a political candidate ever changed because of a campaign commercial? Has an advertisement ever persuaded you to buy anything?

To be sure, you may not have personal knowledge about some topics. But this will happen less often once you make a concentrated effort to connect what you are about to read with what you already know.

Figure 8–1: Organizational Map

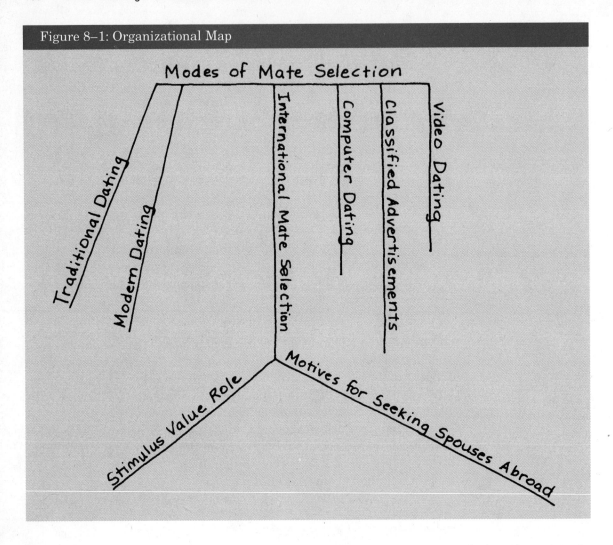

PRACTICE 1   Preread the sample chapter on pages 172–178. Then answer the following questions.

1. After reading the opening page of the sample chapter, check the statement that best paraphrases the chapter's controlling idea or point.

_____ a. Many different factors influence the choice of a mate, and surprisingly, those factors have undergone relatively little change over the last few decades. Now, as in the past, our choice of a mate is circumscribed by many of the same criteria.

_____ b. A few decades ago, dating was the main source of mate se-lection, but today that has changed. Many Americans are using a variety of different methods to locate and choose a mate.

Explain why you chose the answer you did.

_____

_____

2. Based on the headings, develop three questions you could use to guide your actual reading of the sample chapter.

_____

_____

_____

3. What does the table on page 173 suggest to you about the chapter's content? What point does the author want to make about dating?

_____

_____

_____

Intensive Reading

After prereading, you might understand one or two key points in a chapter, but you probably couldn't explain how those points are developed or how they relate to one another. For that deeper level of comprehension, you need to do an **intensive reading.** You need to go through the entire chapter, pulling out the essential elements of every chapter section to discover what each one contributes to the whole. Like prereading, intensive reading involves several steps.

Make Predictions Based on the Headings

During prereading, you should turn chapter headings into questions. During an intensive reading, you should use those same headings to **make predictions about chapter content and organization.** A heading like "Kennedy and Nixon: A Study in Contrasts," for example, suggests a comparison-and-contrast pattern of organization in which the author focuses on the differences between the two presidents.

Once you make your predictions, read to confirm, reject, or modify them. Like the questions based on your prereading, predictions focus your attention on the text and help you maintain concentration.

Sift Out the Essentials

The goal of intensive reading is to analyze each section of a chapter by reducing it to its essential elements, the **main point** or general thought being explained and the **supporting details** used to develop it.

In the following excerpt from our sample chapter, the authors offer three different examples of what dating was like in the 1950s and 1960s. These three examples are supporting details that clarify their main point: "Although there is some disagreement about when dating in America started, it was in full bloom between World War I and World War II. By the 1950s and 1960s, certain recognizable patterns could be discerned."

Traditional Dating

Main point
Example 1

Although there is some disagreement about when dating in America started, it was in full bloom by the period between World War I and World War II. By the 1950s and 1960s, certain recognizable patterns could be discerned. For one thing, young people seemed to start dating at an earlier and earlier age. (At the present time it is quite common for young people of both sexes to have their first date before they are fourteen.)

Example 2

Another pattern that emerged was the tendency for dating to assume a competitive quality. Boys could achieve status by dating the prettiest girls, while girls set their sights on the most popular or best-looking boys. Because good looks are always in short supply, some young people felt left out.

Example 3

Still another development in the dating game was the parrying involved in the dating situation itself. There were all kinds of dating arrangements, but in one common game plan the boy would call for the girl (preferably in a car) and take her out for an evening's entertainment. Depending on the boy's economic resources, the "entertainment" might range from a local movie to a full-course dinner and show. Throughout the evening the boy would use his "line," while the girl—with equal skill—would employ various counterplays. For the boy, of course, the whole idea was to obtain demonstrable favors from the girl. For the girl, the idea was to remain in control of the situation without appearing to be too standoffish.

Recite

Each time you finish a chapter section, test your comprehension by covering up the text and reciting the essential elements. Don't worry about recalling the author's exact words. Just paraphrase the main point and supporting details. If you can't paraphrase the essential elements, mark the text for rereading (RR).

Whenever you feel that recitation takes too much time, remind yourself that **reciting ensures remembering.** In fact, in one study, the best memory score was earned by students who spent a good portion of their time reciting as well as reading.

Make Connections

Keep in mind that each chapter section is part of a larger whole. Once you finish a major section, ask yourself two key questions:

1. What does the point made in this chapter contribute to the chapter as a whole?
2. How does this section connect to the previous one?

PRACTICE 2   Do an intensive reading of the sample chapter on pages 172–178. Then answer the following questions. If you need to, refer to the chapter to answer the questions.

1. Which generalization is developed in the chapter section titled "Modern Dating"?

✳
    The goal of intensive reading is to analyze each section of a chapter by reducing it to its essential elements, the main point and the details.

    a. Although dating nowadays has a lot in common with that of yester-year, there are some significant differences.
    b. The main difference between modern and traditional dating is that not all young people adhere to the same scripts.

Explain why you chose the answer you did.

_____

_____

_____

2. In the sample chapter, what is the main point of the section titled "International Mate Selection"?

_____

_____

_____

3. Identify two supporting details used to develop this point.

_____

_____

_____

_____

4. Why does the author include this section on international mate selection? What does it contribute to the chapter as a whole?

_____

_____

_____

5. The section titled "Video Dating" offers a specific example of a general point appearing in the chapter introduction. What is that point?

_____

_____

Analytical Reading

The amount of **analytical reading** you need to do will vary from text to text. Your psychology textbook may contain only an occasional passage requiring a slow, almost word-for-word reading. However, every page on your chemistry text may contain one or two passages so dense and difficult they need a close and careful reading. No matter how much analytical reading you do, the steps are as follows.

Read Slowly; Read Difficult Passages Aloud

If you are having trouble with a difficult passage, it usually helps to read it very slowly, sentence by sentence, practically word for word. By reading slowly, you can consciously consider the meaning of each sentence and figure out what it contributes to the larger point of the passage.

Reading aloud also helps. Sometimes _hearing_ the words, in addition to seeing them, can help you to make sense of the text.

Look Up Unfamiliar Words

If they are central to the text's meaning, just two or three unfamiliar words can cause confusion. If you keep losing the author's line of thought each time you encounter a particular word, that word is essential to understanding the passage. Before you go any further, look it up. The **glossary,** or list of specialized terms in the back of the book, defines those words essential for understanding the subject of the text. If the glossary doesn't help, turn to the dictionary.

Analyze Individual Sentences

If particular sentences are stumbling blocks to comprehension, you will need to analyze or break them down into their core or essential parts. All sentences consist of two core parts: subjects and predicates.

The **subject** is the person, place, object, or event that performs or receives the action described by the verb. The **predicate** includes the verb and any word or words needed to complete the action of the verb. The following sentences have been analyzed into their core parts.

The Iroquois / have many sacred rituals.
　　　S　　　　　　　　　P

The East Germans / tore down the Berlin Wall.
　　　S　　　　　　　　　P

Sometimes a sentence has more than one subject and predicate. If a writer uses a semicolon (;) or linking words such as *and, but, or, nor, for,* and *yet* to combine two complete and closely related ideas, you will need to identify two subjects and two predicates.

Many Americans / did not want to enter World War II, but
　　　S　　　　　　　　　P

Pearl Harbor / changed their minds.
　　　S　　　　　　P

The decision / was not in the interests of workers; it / was in the
　　　S　　　　　　　　P　　　　　　　　　S　　　P

interests of management.

Once you can identify subjects and predicates, look for **modifiers.** These are words or groups of words that provide additional information about *time, place, condition,* or *causes.* The following sentences all include modifiers:

The Iroquois, <u>who are a very religious people,</u> have many sacred
M
rituals.

<u>To symbolize their new-found freedom,</u> the East Germans tore down
M
the Berlin Wall.

<u>Because they were committed to a policy of isolationism,</u> many Amer-
M
cans did not want to enter World War II, but Pearl Harbor changed their minds.

The decision, <u>which was supposed to be a breakthrough,</u> was not in
M
the interest of workers; it was in the interest of management.

Words Introducing Modifiers

under	because	since
after	during	although
in	whoever	according
if	before	due to
that	while	without
who	when	by
whose	whenever	to
which		

Paraphrase Each Part

Once you have analyzed a sentence into its core parts, translate each element into your own words. Whenever possible, make abstract language more concrete. See Figure 8–2 on page 169.

It also helps to break long sentences into two or even three shorter ones. To illustrate, we will use a rather complicated passage from Bruno Bettelheim's essay, "The Ignored Lesson of Anne Frank."

The ideas, that in our day a people's personalities might be changed against their will by the state, and that other populations might be wholly or partially exterminated, are so fearful that one tries to free oneself of them and their impact by defensive denial or by repression.
—Bruno Bettelheim, *Surviving and Other Essays,* Knopf, 62

Step 1: Locate the core parts.

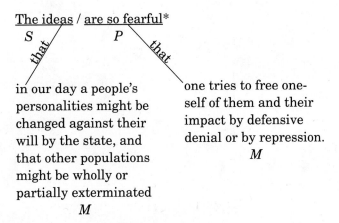

Step 2: Determine the meaning of each part and paraphrase the sentence.

It's scary to think that in our time, the state could be powerful enough to forcibly alter a people's way of thinking and behaving or that a whole population could be destroyed. The thought is so scary that we try to deny or forget it.

Check Your Comprehension

Make sure that your paraphrase of the passage fits the larger context. If it makes sense by itself but doesn't follow from the rest of the text, you might be on the wrong track and need to start over.

---

*You would not necessarily be creating a diagram on paper. We have done so only for purposes of illustration.

Figure 8–2: Concrete Words for Abstract Terms

Abstract Phrase	Concrete Paraphrase
Achievement in sports	Winning a gold medal in the Olympics
Capacity for personal affiliation	The ability to make and keep friends
Scholastic achievement	Getting good grades
It is reasoned that	People think
Marital problems	Quarrels over in-laws
The ambiguity of language	Words can have several meanings
The scientific method	Developing a hypothesis or theory and testing it to prove its accuracy
Social problems	Homelessness in America, unwed mothers, abused kids
Residential propinquity	Living close by in the neighborhood
Weak familial ties	No family feeling

If Necessary, Ask for Help

If you do an analytical reading and still cannot make sense out of the passage, ask for help from your instructor. You might be having trouble because your definition of a key term is not appropriate. Or it might be that a portion of the text is not written clearly enough for student readers and requires more explanation.

*

   If you are having trouble with a difficult passage, it usually helps to read it very slowly, sentence by sentence, practically word for word.

☐   PRACTICE 3   Read the following sentences. Put a circle around the subject and underline the predicate. Put a double line under all modifiers. Here's an example.

> <u>Because the land was rich in artifacts,</u> (the anthropologist) hoped to
>
> <u>make a spectacular discovery</u>.

1. Fifty years ago the Chinese rejected all foreign influence, but recently they have begun to seek out foreign investment.
2. Because of a lack of funds, research on the language of chimpanzees has ceased.
3. Central America, an area that for years has been in political turmoil, shows no sign of becoming peaceful in the near future.
4. The right to vote is a privilege that many people in other countries do not have, yet Americans do not always take advantage of that privilege.
5. The American Medical Association deems hypnosis a valid therapy, but it does not consider hypnosis a reliable means of refreshing memory.

☐   PRACTICE 4   Do an analytical reading of the following passage. Write a paraphrased version in the accompanying blanks.

There is room for skepticism about the socializing functions of the extended family. While proximity and contact appear relatively high, we know little about the quality of interactions between older people and their families. Existing patterns of interaction do not necessarily imply emotional closeness, and contacts may be largely ritualistic. . . .

The grandparent role offers a case in point. Studies of grandparenthood suggest that it carries limited significance and is primarily symbolic, with little meaningful involvement in the lives of grandchildren.

—Russell Ward, *The Family Coordinator,* 368

_____

_____

_____

_____

Figure 8–3: Three Strategies for Reading Textbooks

Prereading

How to Do It

- force yourself to turn pages quickly
- read title and introduction
- read lists of questions, objectives, or topics
- read all headings, captions, tables, boxes
- read any summaries or lists of final questions

Purpose

- to get a sense of chapter's overall point before an intensive reading
- to help you raise questions about chapter
- to help you anticipate what is to come

Intensive Reading

How to Do It

- read at a comfortable rate
- read to answer questions and confirm predictions
- do regular comprehension checks by reciting or reviewing after reading

Purpose

- to figure out what each individual section contributes to the chapter as a whole
- to identify difficult or confusing passages that need analysis
- to re-create author's message

Ans Reading

How to Do It

- read slowly, word for word
- break sentences down into core parts
- paraphrase
- check to see if your paraphrase fits the context

Purpose

- to decipher dense passages from chemistry or philosophy texts
- to understand passages that were confusing the first time around
- to understand poetry

Sample Chapter

Modes of Mate Selection

Sometimes overlooked by students of the family is the following truism. To a considerable degree, who marries whom depends on the *mode of mate selection*. A decade or two ago, for example, chance encounter followed by dating was the only mode of mate selection that young people really considered. Today, however, the picture may be changing.

In the 1990s, hundreds of thousands of Americans are trying innovative modes of mate selection. These include the use of modern technology, personal advertisements, agents, singles' groups, and social networks. Those eligible for marriage have thus expanded the field of eligibles far beyond schools, neighborhoods, and the usual chance encounters. In effect, they have overcome distance and culture as barriers to love and marriage. Dating, of course—however initiated—remains the most popular form of mate selection, especially on college campuses.

TRADITIONAL DATING

Although there is some disagreement about when dating in America started, it was in full bloom by the period between World War I and World War II. By the 1950s and 1960s, certain recognizable patterns could be discerned. For one thing, young people seemed to start dating at an earlier and earlier age. (At the present time it is quite common for young people of both sexes to have their first date before they are fourteen.)

Another pattern that emerged was the tendency for dating to assume a competitive quality. Boys could achieve status by dating the prettiest girls, while girls set their sights on the most popular or best-looking boys. Because good looks are always in short supply, some young people felt left out.

Still another development in the dating game was the parrying involved in the dating situation itself. There were all kinds of dating arrangements, but in one common game plan the boy would call for the girl (preferably in a car) and take her out for an evening's entertainment. Depending on the boy's economic resources, the "entertainment" might range from a local movie to a full-course dinner and show. Throughout the evening the boy would use his "line," while the girl—with equal skill—would employ various counterplays. For the boy, of course,

Table 10–1   First-Date Scripts

A woman's first date	A man's first date
Tell friends and family.	Ask for a date.
Groom and dress.	Decide what to do.
Be nervous.	Groom and dress.
Worry about or change appearance.	Be nervous.
Check appearance.	Worry about or change appearance.
Wait for date.	Prepare car, apartment.
Welcome date to home.	Check money.
Introduce parents or roommates.	Go to date's house.
Leave.	Meet parents or roommates.
Confirm plans.	Leave.
Get to know date.	Open car door.
Compliment date.	Confirm plans.
Joke, laugh and talk.	Get to know date.
Try to impress date.	Compliment date.
Go to movies, show, or party.	Joke, laugh, and talk.
Eat.	Try to impress date.
Go home.	Go to movies, show, or party.
Tell date she had a good time.	Eat.
Kiss goodnight.	Pay.
	Be polite.
	Initiate physical contact.
	Take date home.
	Tell date will be in touch.
	Kiss goodnight.
	Go home.

Source: Suzana Rose and Irene Hanson Frieze, "Young Singles' Scripts for a First Date," *Gender and Society*, June 1989, 258.

the whole idea was to obtain demonstrable favors from the girl. For the girl, the idea was to remain in control of the situation without appearing to be too standoffish.

MODERN DATING

Some of the negative aspects of dating still remain. Rose and Frieze, for example, found that in the late 1980s women were still significantly more likely than men to wait to be asked for a date and to worry about their appearance.[1] In addition, as Table 10–1 shows, dating scripts for men include more action, more leadership, and more initiative. Today's dating script seems to have much in common with that of yesteryear.

The main difference between modern and traditional dating is that not all young people adhere to the same scripts. Many find dating much less formal than in the past. Dress is more casual; so are the occasions. Instead of being planned a week or more in

---

[1]Suzana Rose and Irene Hanson Frieze. "Young Singles' Scripts for a First Date. "Gender and Society, June 1989, 258–268.

advance, with the evening's entertainment carefully mapped out, today's dates are much more likely to be spontaneous, spur-of-the-moment affairs. The man is still more likely to pay for the entertainment and food, though this practice is no longer invariable.

Perhaps the most important change in the dating system is that young men and young women can talk to one another as equals. Traditionally, women on dates often "played dumb" to make the man appear more important and more intelligent. This demeaning experience is less likely to occur now because of the equalization of gender roles.

Sex, we should add quickly, is frequently a part of modern dating. In fact, the scenario shown in Table 10–1 includes initiation of physical contact by the male even on the first date.

Table 10–2   Number and Percentage of Immigrants Admitted into the United States Through Marriage to U.S. Citizens, 1982–1987

Year	Number of immigrant spouses[a]	Percentage of all marriages[b]
1982	104,218	4.1
1983	112,666	4.4
1984	116,596	4.5
1985	129,790	5.1
1986	137,597	5.2
1987	132,452	—

[a]U.S. Bureau of the Census, Statistical Abstract of the United States, 1989, Washington, DC, 1989, 11.

[b]Calculated on the basis of recorded marriages in the United States. See U.S. Department of Health and Human Services, "Advance Report of Final Marriage Statistics, 1986," Monthly Vital Statistics Reports, National Center for Health Statistics, July 1989, 9.

INTERNATIONAL MATE SELECTION

Table 10–2 shows that well over 100,000 Americans are finding their spouses in other countries *every year*. This figure is by no means negligible: in fact, it is higher than the number of marriages in all but a handful of states. And while there is some fluctuation from year to year, it is safe to say that international mate selection has become a major component of marriage in the United States.

Most American-international marriages take place between persons of the same race and ethnicity, although in recent years tens of thousands have involved Caucasian men and Asian women. For some reason, these marriages have attracted an inordinate amount of media coverage. Americans seem to be curious about the men and women who cross oceans and ignore boundaries in pursuit of marriage and happiness.

Who are these individuals? What is their background, and what is their motivation? In our ongoing study, we tried to answer these and other questions by applying Murstein's stimulus-value-role theory. Interestingly, we found that the theory applies even when the initial contacts are not face-to-face!

Stimulus-Value-Role

In our survey we conducted personal interviews and examined the advertisements of many foreign participants. Findings indicate that physical appearance is valued highly in these relationships. Participants decide whom to contact by viewing photographs. In this respect the stimulus stage depends as heavily on appearance in international mate-selection networks as in ordinary dating.

We found that the exchange of photographs was an important part of the stimulus stage. Participants began serious correspondence only after they found each other's appearance acceptable. We never read their letters, but we were told that the letters tend to be long and frequent. Correspondents discuss mutual idiosyncrasies, attitudes, values, hobbies, likes, dislikes, and plans for the future. They thoroughly explore their values and, in more serious cases, their role expectations in marriage.

The role stage of the relationship, of course, is the most serious. At that point a pair decides whether or not to marry. This decision gains significance when long distances, travel, and money are involved. Before this commitment is made, according to an agent in California, most Americans go abroad to continue their courtship face-to-face. For some, the courtship abroad may take weeks or months. If young people are involved, the courtship rules are followed to the parents' satisfaction. If everything goes well, the couple marries before coming to the United States.

Until January 1987, it was also possible for thousands of individuals to come to the United States and marry a person whom they had never met. The marriage-fraud provision of the 1986 Immigration Act, however, now prohibits this practice.

Motives for Seeking Spouses Abroad

The best clue to why Americans seek spouses abroad comes from the data on marital histories. More than 57 percent of the American participants were divorced. Most of the others had had unpleasant experiences during courtship and engagement. Frequently they revealed that they had been victims of deceit, unfaithfulness, loss of wealth due to divorce, and even fraud. A full 75 percent of the American participants had experienced some kind of trauma. As a result, many were trying to avoid repeating the experience by finding someone geographically removed and culturally different.

Twenty-five percent, however, were simply interested in expanding their cross-cultural experiences. They used this mode of selection in addition to ordinary dating at home. Actually, more than 90 percent of the American participants feel comfortable with any mode of mate selection, including face-to-face chance encounters. Only 10 percent use agencies and correspondence because they feel that their temperament, personality, or lifestyle is better suited for this mode of mate selection.

One can only guess about the motives of foreign participants. Yet in view of the fact that in many Third World countries women are more likely than men to graduate from college, we believe that the educational imbalance is a major reason. This imbalance would explain why so many foreign participants are college students or college graduates.

One benefit for all participants is the expansion of their field of eligibles. Whether abroad or at home, innovative modes of mate selection can bring into contact people who otherwise would never have a chance to meet.

COMPUTER DATING

In 1977, the National Science Foundation sponsored a study on computer applications in information exchange. About 500 scientists in various disciplines throughout the United States and Canada participated. Using their computer terminals, these scientists dispatched messages, research findings, and answers to inquiries. As the experiment progressed, those with common interests formed alliances and strengthened their professional ties. For the sociologists among them this experience led to the next logical question: could similar procedures be applied to people interested in the search for love and marriage?

This question led to a study titled "Automated Go-Betweens: Mate Selection of Tomorrow?"[2] A few years later that "tomorrow" had arrived. Computers are now matching hundreds of people every day. Regardless of place of residence or availability of partners in one's locality, anyone with access to a personal computer can get in touch with others through computer-dating networks called "dial-your-mate."

"Dial-your-mate" refers to mate selection with the aid of personal computers. Unlike other innovative modes of mate selection, dial-your-mate is gaining acceptance rapidly. Because tens of thousands of people are experimenting with it, let us examine how it works.

To participate, one must have a telephone, a personal computer, and a *modem*—a unit that connects the computer to the telephone. The cost of this equipment can vary from around $300 to more than $3,000. (If there is no dial-your-mate service available locally, long-distance telephone charges could be a substantial part of the searching cost.) There are no membership fees, because the system is operated by hobbyists and computer clubs throughout the country.

To use this service the participant must have a telephone number to reach one of the computers in the dial-your-mate network. These numbers are available from local computer clubs anywhere in the United States. Because the demand for these services is so high, it may take several hours to reach a

number, but sooner or later everyone gets through.

Once the participant is on the line, there is no need for any knowledge of computer programming. Each caller is prompted step by step to provide the information necessary for mate searching. The questions appear on the screen with instructions for answering. Although the questions vary from network to network, our perusal of various services indicated that they are based on popular notions of what is important to people looking for dates.

The most frequently asked questions assess one's appearance, as follows:

What is the color of your hair?
What is your height?
How would others rate your appearance?
A. Very attractive B. Good looking C. Average D. Nothing special.

There are also questions about personal characteristics such as age, race, educational level, marital status, occupation, religious preference, and political affiliation.

Other questions probe personal hobbies, racial preferences, level of commitment sought, musical preferences, and so on. Once all the questions are answered, the computer compares the answers with those of all opposite-sex participants and ranks them on percentage of agreement. If two people gave similar answers to every question, they would agree 100 percent. On the opposite end of the scale, 0 percent would show that they have no answers in common. As soon as these comparisons are completed, the participant is provided with the code numbers of those with the highest percentages of agreement.

[2]Davor Jedlicka. "Automated Go-Betweens: Mate Selection of Tomorrow?" *Family Relations,* July 1961, 373–376.

The recipients' responses have not been studied. Those involved can ignore the messages, exchange more messages, or terminate interactions for any reason. Both senders and recipients are spared the unpleasantness of face-to-face rejections because communications remain anonymous until the individual decides otherwise.

CLASSIFIED ADVERTISEMENTS

Any person, whether single or married, can find a mate through personal advertisements. Bookstores, grocery stores, and newsstands across America sell newspapers that carry personal advertisements for mate selection. Although it may seem strange or unusual for people to advertise themselves, this mode of mate selection dates back to the frontier days. As the men in the nineteenth century moved west, they advertised in newspapers for brides. In his 1867 book on marriage in America, Carlier was among the first to note this frontier American innovation:

> Circumstances sometimes prevent the immigration of women and the gloom and languor which pervade these sections can scarcely be imagined. Thus, in some of the rapidly formed territories, we may perhaps find only men—it having chanced that women had not thought to go in this direction. We soon find appearing in the papers positive supplications from those unfortunate men to the young women of the other states, entreating them their choice, and promising dowries quite comfortable and well assured.[3]

There is evidence that personal advertisements in newspapers appeared even in colonial times. On the frontier, however, this became a common mode of mate selection. Ever since that time, specialized magazines and newspapers have carried matrimonial advertisements. Until the mid-1970s such publications were sold nationally. Today they are increasingly local or regional.

VIDEO DATING

Video dating, a relatively recent innovation, is restricted to walk-in clients who seek assistance from an agent. Part of the agent's responsibility is to prepare an audio and a video presentation for the clients. This service usually costs $600 or more. Some agencies minimize the cost of taped videos by charging viewing fees and by selling addresses on request. This procedure minimizes third-person involvement and lowers the cost for participants, but it appeals only to those for whom identity protection is not important.

Most agencies, though, guard their clients' identities by restricting participation to paid-up members. To be a member, one must have prepared a videotaped presentation, which then is viewed by other members in consultation with the agent. In this capacity the agents act as counselors. They give advice, answer questions, and suggest good matches.

If we may judge by the number of agencies emerging throughout the country, it seems that the clientele for video dating is increasing despite the high cost of membership. Some agencies have grown so fast that they need computers to keep track of their clients

---

[3]August Carlier. *Marriage in the United States*. 44–45. New York: Arno Press, 1972.

and to help them with the matching process. They administer computerized questionnaires similar to those found in dial-your-mate networks. This information is used together with the video as an aid in choosing a mate.

SUMMARY

Mate selection is one of the most important factors in the development of family relationships. Dating initiated by chance encounter is the most prevalent mode used by young Americans, but other modes are increasing in popularity. For reasons ranging from lack of time to geographic isolation, significant numbers of Americans rely on innovative methods of mate selection, including participation in international networks, computer dating, video dating, and personal advertisements. Not all of these methods work for everyone, but for many people the innovative methods lead to love, romance, and marriage.

Romantic love is the basis of mate selection whether conventional or less conventional methods are used. Romantic love, although difficult to define, has been classified into *six styles:* eros, ludus, storge, mania, pragma, and agape. These styles may be present in various degrees in each individual, and they may also vary with each individual over time. Some differences in love styles between the sexes also have been discovered.

QUESTIONS

1. What is meant by the "adversarial aspects" of the American dating system? Are some of these aspects still with us, or are they a thing of the past? Discuss on the basis of your own observations and experiences.
2. What are some of the differences between modern dating and traditional dating? What would you say is the most important difference?
3. Is the usual search for dating partners suited for everyone? Explain.
4. What are some theoretical reasons for international mate selection? Are the reasons the same for American participants as for their foreign partners?
5. Some people fear computers as a dehumanizing influence on society. Do you share that sentiment with respect to computer applications in mate selection? Explain in detail.
6. Consider a person's age, marital history, social status, and geographic location; which mode of mate selection do you think may be best suited for various categories of eligibles?
7. Classified personal advertisements have a long history in the United States. Explain how this mode of mate selection originated, why it exists today, and whether you think it will be useful in the future.

Working Space

READING ASSIGNMENT

Read the following passage, in which David Bartholomae and Anthony Petrosky describe the process of reading. Then answer the questions that follow.

Reading involves a fair measure of push and shove. You make your mark on a book and it makes its mark on you. Reading is not simply a matter of hanging back and waiting for a piece, or its author, to tell you what the writing has to say. In fact, one of the difficult things about reading is that the pages before you will begin to speak only when the authors are silent and you begin to speak in their place, sometimes for them—doing their work, continuing their projects—and sometimes for yourself, following your own agenda.

—David Bartholomae and Anthony Petrosky, *Ways of Reading*
St. Martin's Press, 1

1. What do you think the authors mean when they say, "You make your mark on a book and it makes its mark on you"?

2. Explain what the authors mean when they say, "the pages before you will begin to speak only when the authors are silent and you begin to speak in their place."

WRITING ASSIGNMENT

Having read the sample chapter, you now know a lot about the many different methods of mate selection. Write a short paper in which you identify the best method and explain what makes it particularly effective.

JOURNAL ASSIGNMENTS

1. Which of your textbooks will require an analytical reading? Which ones will not?

2. What do you think the American philosopher Ralph Waldo Emerson meant when he said, "One must be an inventor to read well"?

3. Evaluate your progress in improving your listening ability. In what areas have you made great strides? What aspects of your listening still need some work?

✔ Checking Out: Review Questions for Chapter 8

1. What is the purpose or goal of prereading?

2. What portions of a chapter should you look at during prereading?

3. Explain the difference between major and minor headings.

4. What is the purpose of making an organizational map?

5. What is the goal of an intensive reading?

6. During an intensive reading, what should you do once you finish a chapter section?

7. When should you do an analytical reading?

8. Describe the first four steps of an analytical reading.

9. Name and define the *core parts* in a sentence.

10. When paraphrasing core parts of sentences, you should try to do what?

▶ In Summary

During prereading, look over selected portions of the text to get advance knowledge about chapter content, organization, and length. Use that advance knowledge to pose questions about the chapter and give your reading a focus. Do an intensive reading to determine the essential elements of each chapter section and test your understanding of the material. Save your analytical reading for those portions of text that are particularly dense and difficult. Don't be afraid to read very slowly, almost word for word. There are times when a slow, painstaking reading is absolutely essential for good comprehension.

Although your philosophy or chemistry texts may require all three types of reading—prereading, intensive, and analytical—some psychology texts may need only one good intensive reading. You're the only one who can make that decision. You have to consider (1) your purpose in reading, (2) your knowledge of the subject matter, and (3) the author's style and method of organization.

Taking Notes from Your Textbooks

In Chapter 9, we offer you several different methods for recording what you learn from textbooks. We introduced two of the methods in previous chapters; two are brand new. Vary or combine these methods, using whichever works best with each of your textbooks.

- Taking notes directly on the pages of your textbook
- Writing summaries of each major section in a chapter
- Outlining informally to produce a concise blueprint of the author's ideas
- Using organizational maps to give visual form to the underlying pattern of the text

Marking Your Texts Effectively

For subjects that are not dense with new and unfamiliar information, consider taking notes directly in the pages of your textbook. You can underline and mark to highlight content and structure. You can also **annotate,** or jot notes in the margins. When review time rolls around, simply reread your marginal notes and study only marked passages. With this approach, you won't waste time rereading entire pages.

Underlining

Indiscriminate or thoughtless underlining of unnecessary words is the most common mistake inexperienced students make. Either afraid of leaving out something important, or just not paying close attention, they underline everything and end up reviewing entire chapters rather than selected portions.

1. **Be selective.**
   When you underline, you should **concentrate on key sentences,** the sentences that introduce the main points and supporting details. Since these are the most important sentences in the text, they deserve the most attention.

   However, rather than underlining every word in these sentences, underline only the key words necessary to communicate the meaning. To select key words, **imagine you are sending a telegram.** What are the fewest words you need to make your meaning clear? Underline only those words.

   Here is a sample passage in which only the key words are underlined. Read just the underlined words, and see how they convey the message of the paragraph.

   > In the <u>two decades after</u> the <u>Civil War</u> (1861–1865), <u>U.S.</u> policy makers focused their concerns on territorial expansion and increased trade in Latin America, finding little success in either. The <u>major diplomatic triumph</u> of the era <u>came in 1866</u> when <u>Secretary of State</u> William H. <u>Seward</u>, belatedly <u>invoking</u> the <u>Monroe Doctrine</u>, de<u>manded</u> that <u>France remove</u> its <u>troops</u> from <u>Mexico</u> where they propped up the rule of the Emperor Maximilian, the Austrian Archduke.
   >
   > —Benjamin Keen and Mark Wasserman, *A History of Latin America*
   > Houghton Mifflin, 512

The selective underlining shown in the passage takes more time, but in the long run, it pays off. As you think about which words to underline, you are mentally sifting and sorting information, picking only the most essential. The kind of in-depth thinking required for efficient underlining may explain why research shows students are more likely to remember information they underline.[1]

2. In the beginning, underline only after a complete reading.

While you are still learning how to underline selectively, wait until you begin a second reading before underlining anything. What you think is important during your first reading may change by the time you start your second.

As you become more experienced, consider underlining during your first reading. Just remember that you need to slow down your reading rate in order to be selective. Underlining at high rates of speed usually produces carelessly marked pages. For more on varying your reading rate, see Chapter 10.

3. Use pencil rather than pen.

While you are still learning how to underline efficiently, use a pencil rather than a pen or a felt-tip marker. Then if you change your mind, you can always erase your underlining. When you review and further refine your understanding of what's essential, go back and underline again with a pen or felt-tip marker.

4. Test the accuracy of your underlining.

Test your underlining periodically to see if it makes sense. When you read over the underlined words, see if you can fill in the gaps and re-create the meaning of the passage. If reading the underlined words produces a completely different message, erase and start over.

Of these two passages, which one do you think has been effectively underlined and why?

A

The attitudes and expectations <u>teachers have</u> about male and female students have been called <u>a "hidden curriculum"</u> that reinforces tradi-

---

[1]Sarah Peterson, "The Cognitive Function of Underlining as a Study Technique," *Reading Research and Instruction*, 31, 2 (1992), 54.

tional gender-role stereotypes (<u>Chafetz, 1978; Clarricoates, 1978</u>). Because teachers <u>expect boys to be</u> more <u>active</u> and <u>difficult to control</u> than girls, much <u>classroom time</u> is often <u>spent catering to boys' interests</u> and trying to subdue them. When girls do better than <u>boys academically</u>—which they usually do at least until high school—<u>teachers</u> may <u>regard</u> them merely <u>as</u> conscientious and <u>diligent,</u> in conformity to the female stereotype. In contrast, <u>boys who achieve</u> are thought to <u>have "real" creativity</u> and to be more interesting than girls (Clarricoates, 1978). Thus, if a girl does what is expected of her, she is not given the same recognition as a boy (Chafetz, 1978).

B

The <u>attitudes</u> and <u>expectations teachers have</u> about <u>male</u> and <u>female students</u> have been called <u>a "hidden curriculum"</u> that <u>reinforces</u> traditional gender-role <u>stereotypes</u> (Chafetz, 1978; Clarricoates, 1978). Because <u>teachers expect boys</u> to be <u>more active</u> and <u>difficult to control than girls,</u> much classroom time is often spent catering to boys' interests and trying to subdue them. <u>When girls do better</u> than boys academically—which they usually do at least until high school—<u>teachers</u> may <u>regard</u> them merely <u>as conscientious</u> and diligent, <u>in conformity to the</u> <u>female stereotype.</u> <u>In contrast,</u> <u>boys who achieve</u> are thought to <u>have "real" creativity</u> and to be more interesting than girls (Clarricoates, 1978). Thus, if a girl does what is expected of her, she is not given the same recognition as a boy (Chafetz, 1978).

—David Poponoe, *Sociology,* Prentice Hall 336

If you said passage B, you are absolutely correct. Reading only the underlined material in passage A, you might assume the paragraph is strictly about the treatment of boys. What gets lost in the underlining is the comparison and contrast of boys and girls that is central to the author's message. This comparison comes through quite clearly in passage B.

❑ PRACTICE 1   Read each underlined passage. Indicate whether passage A, B, or C best fits our guidelines for effective underlining. Then explain why the other two passages are less effectively underlined.

A

Janice Morse and Caroline Park studied differences in perceptions of pain of childbirth among four different cultural groups living in western Canada: English-speaking Canadians, Ukrainians, Hutterites, and East Indians (Morse & Park, 1988). Parents who were about to have hospital deliveries were asked to compare the pain of childbirth with eight other painful events: heart attack, kidney stone, severe burn, toothache, gallstones, eye injury, broken bone, and migraine.

The Canadian sample had the highest mean rating for childbirth pain of 11.15 (12.9 for females and 10.55 for males). The views surrounding birth for this group were similar to those of most middle-class Americans. They expected it to be painful and used a variety of methods to prepare for it, but they also knew that if labor became too uncomfortable, they would be offered or given medications to relieve the pain.

B

Janice Morse and Caroline Park studied differences in perceptions of pain of childbirth among four different cultural groups living in western Canada: English-speaking Canadians, Ukrainians, Hutterites, and East Indians (Morse & Park, 1988). Parents who were about to have hospital deliveries were asked to compare the pain of childbirth with eight other painful events: heart attack, kidney stone, severe burn, toothache, gallstones, eye injury, broken bone, and migraine.

The Canadian sample had the highest mean rating for childbirth pain of 11.15 (12.9 for females and 10.55 for males). The views surrounding birth for this group were similar to those of most middle-class Americans. They expected it to be painful and used a variety of methods to prepare for it, but they also knew that if labor became too uncomfortable, they would be offered or given medications to relieve the pain.

C

Janice Morse and Caroline Park studied differences in perceptions of pain of childbirth among four different cultural groups living in western Canada: English-speaking Canadians, Ukrainians, Hutterites, and East Indians (Morse & Park, 1988). Parents who were about to have hospital deliveries were asked to compare the pain of childbirth with eight other painful events: heart attack, kidney stone, severe burn, toothache, gallstones, eye injury, broken bone, and migraine.

The Canadian sample had the highest mean rating for childbirth pain of 11.15 (12.9 for females and 10.55 for males). The views surrounding birth for this group were similar to those of most middle-class Americans. They expected it to be painful and used a variety of methods to prepare for it, but they also knew that if labor became too uncomfortable, they would be offered or given medications to relieve the pain.

—Kelvin L. Seifert and Robert J. Hoffnung,
Child and Adolescent Development, Houghton Mifflin, 134.

Developing a Code of Symbols for Marking Pages

There are limits to what you can express with underlining. You can't really use it to identify potential test questions, indicate confusing passages, or show relationships among ideas. So in addition to underlining, you need to **develop and consistently use a code of symbols for marking pages.**

For example, use the letters *TQ* to identify the source of a potential test question and the letters *RR* to set off passages that need a second reading.[2] Consider using stars to label key points and circles to highlight important names or dates. You can also mark to identify relationships, for example, boxing transitions that introduce a numbered sequence—*first, second, third*—or a shift in meaning—*however, but, nevertheless.*

The chart on page 188 lists some of the common symbols that are available to you. Experiment with them and adapt them for your own personal use. If you want to circle instead of boxing transitional words, go ahead. It's a good idea to develop your own distinctive code of symbols, such as squiggly lines for confusing passages. Just make sure to use those symbols *consistently.* If you change your symbols with every reading, you are likely to find that marking pages confuses rather than clarifies.

Look over this sample passage to see how symbols can be used in combination with underlining.

Cherokee Nation v. Georgia

In 1829, the Cherokees turned to the federal courts to defend their treaty with the United States and prevent Georgia's seizure of their land. In *Cherokee Nation* v. *Georgia* (1831), Chief Justice John

---

[2]The source of this suggestion is Michele L. Simpson and Sherrie L. Nist, "Textbook Annotation: An Effective and Efficient Study Strategy for College Students," *Journal of Reading,* October 1990, 123.

Common Symbols for Marking Pages

═══	Use **double underlining** (sparingly) to highlight a key generalization or principle.
✱ ✱ ✱ ✱	Use **asterisks** to identify points emphasized in lectures.
1, 2, 3, 4	Use **numbers** to identify a series of supporting details or to itemize a list of characteristics.
ex., ill., res., f, stdy., stat., exc.	Use **abbreviations** to identify the kinds of supporting details used by the author: examples, illustrations, reasons, facts, studies, statistics, exceptions.
(1830)	Use **circles** to highlight specialized vocabulary, key terms, statistics, and dates.
?	Use **question marks** to indicate unclear points.
!	Use **exclamation points** to register your surprise at the author's statements.
～～～	Use a **squiggly line** under words you need to look up.
see p. 27 or compare p. 27	Use **cross-references** to encourage the habit of comparing closely related statements in the text.
first	Draw **boxes** around transitional words and phrases (like *first, second, third, next, similarly, likewise, for example, for illustration*) to help you recognize supporting details.
→	Use **arrows** to highlight cause-and-effect relationships.
‖	Use **vertical lines** to emphasize a key passage.
RR	Use this symbol to indicate passages in need of a second reading.
RP	Use to identify ideas for research papers.
TQ	Use this symbol to identify the possible source of a test question.

Marshall ruled that under the federal Constitution an Indian tribe was neither a foreign nation nor a state and therefore had no standing in federal courts. Nonetheless, said Marshall, the Indians had an unquestioned right to their lands; they could lose title only by voluntarily giving it up. A year later in *Worcester* v. *Georgia,* Marshall defined the Cherokee position more clearly. The Indian nation was, he declared, a distinct political community in which "the laws of Georgia can have no force" and into which Georgians could not enter without permission or treaty privilege.

President Andrew Jackson had little sympathy for the Indians and ignored the Supreme Court's ruling. Keen to open up new lands for settlement, he was determined to remove the Cherokees at all costs. In the Removal Act of 1830, Congress provided Jackson with the funds he needed to negotiate new treaties and resettle the resistant tribes west of the Mississippi.

—Mary Beth Norton et al., *A People and a Nation,* 211

☐   PRACTICE 2   Here is the conclusion of the sample passage shown above. After reading it, underline and mark the passage to effectively highlight key points.

The infamous Trail of Tears had begun. The Choctaws in the winter of 1831 and 1832 were the first to go. Soon other tribes joined the trail: the Creeks in Alabama in 1836 and the Chickasaws in 1837. The Cherokees, having fought through the courts to stay, found themselves divided. Some recognized the hopelessness of further resistance and accepted removal as the only chance to preserve their civilization. The leaders of this minority signed a treaty in 1835, in which they agreed to exchange their southern home for western land. But when the time for evacuation came in 1838, most Cherokees refused to move. President Martin Van Buren then sent federal troops to round up the Indians. About twenty thousand Cherokees were evicted, held in detention camps, and marched to present-day Oklahoma under military escort. Nearly one-quarter died of disease and exhaustion on the Trail of Tears. When the forced march to the West ended, the Indians had traded about 100 million acres of land east of the Mississippi for 32 million acres west of the river, plus $68 million. Only a few scattered remnants of the tribes, among them the Seminoles, remained in the East and South.

What was the impact of removal? Change had been thrust on these tribes so suddenly and drastically that they had to transform much of their culture. In the West, they occupied an alien environment; they had no generational ties with the new land. Many could not be at peace with the land or get used to the strange animals and plants they found there. Many Indians became dependent on government payments for survival. Finally, removal brought new internal conflicts that would ultimately shatter Cherokee tribal unity.

—Mary Beth Norton et al, *A People and a Nation,* 212

Annotating in the Margins

The annotations or jottings you make in the margins can take several different forms. Decide which of the following types of annotation are appropriate to the texts you are currently reading.

Outline the essential elements   Whatever text you are reading, use your marginal jottings to outline the essential elements very briefly. Indicate the main point of each chapter section and list one or two key supporting details. When it comes time to review, you'll be able to reread only the essential elements of the text and avoid wasting time.

Jot down key terms to use as recall clues   Use the margins to jot down key terms and words. Later when preparing for exams, use these words as **recall clues** to test your ability to remember important information *without looking at the original text.*

Raise questions and argue with the author   If you disagree with a point in the text or question the author's interpretation, use the margins to formulate your questions and explain your point of view. "This doesn't make sense; where's the author's evidence?" "This program can't be put into practice given the current federal guidelines."

Identify any source of confusion   In addition to marking a passage for a second reading (*RR*), try to pinpoint what troubles you: "I don't understand the way the author uses the word *personality.*" "The author assumes a lot of background knowledge here."

Whenever possible, offer a personal response   As much as you can, jot down your personal reactions or responses to the author's message. The more you interact with a text on a personal level, the more readily you will absorb and remember what you read.

   Here is a sample to illustrate how underlining, marking, and annotating combine to create effective notes.

Marriage

[margin notes:]
Colonial times
marriage an
obligation
1. unmarried
   women held in
   disfavor
2. men taxed and
   watched
3. widows
   expected to
   remarry and
   fast

TQ: Compare and
contrast the
modern attitude
toward marriage
with that of
colonial times

In the <u>colonial</u> period, <u>marriage</u> was <u>considered</u> an <u>obligation</u> as well as a privilege. People were expected to marry, and they normally did so at a moderately young age. There was <u>little place for</u> the <u>unmarried</u>, who were generally looked upon with <u>disfavor</u>. For a <u>woman, marriage</u> was deemed to be the <u>only honorable state.</u> <u>Bachelors</u> were suspect and in most of the colonies were heavily <u>taxed</u> and kept under close <u>surveillance.</u> *— Sounds like it was official. Who did the watching?*

Widows and <u>widowers</u> were <u>expected to remarry</u>—and they generally did, usually without much time elapsing. "The first marriage in Plymouth was that of Edward Winslow, a widower for seven weeks, and Susanna White, a widow for 12 weeks. One governor of New Hampshire married a widow of only ten days standing, and the amazing case is cited of Isaac Winslow, who proposed to Ben Davis' daughter the same day he buried his wife."   *Not very romantic!!*

Widows, incidentally, were considered to be excellent marital choices because of the property inherited from their previous marriages. They also would have had valuable experience as homemakers, a qualification that was lacking in the younger, unmarried girls. Of course, remarriages did not always work out as anticipated, a colonial epigram reading as follows:

> Colonel Williams married his first wife, Miss Miriam Tyler, for good sense, and got it: his second wife, Miss Wells, for love and beauty, and had it: and his third wife, Aunt Hannah Dickinson, for good qualities, and got horribly cheated.

—William M. Kephart and Davor Jedlicka,
Family, Society and the Individual

☐   PRACTICE 3   Now try your hand at underlining, marking, and annotating the following passage.

Marriage Rituals

Historians report that no uniform marriage ritual existed in the early colonial period. Weddings were apparently performed at the bride's home. The wording of the ceremony—whether civil or religious—does not appear to have been standardized. It is likely that in the trying days of the seventeenth century there was neither time nor inclination to make marriage a festive occasion. At the same time, Americans have always had a proclivity for celebrations of all kinds, and before long the "quiet American wedding" had mushroomed into a panorama of relatively large dimensions. Prayers, psalm singing, music, bridal processions, and feasting became commonplace. By the eighteenth century, weddings had become recognized occasions for revelry and merrymaking. Gifts were given, drinking and dancing were on the wild side, muskets were fired, and pranks such as bride stealing were practiced. For better or worse, the American wedding had come of age.

Common-Law Marriage

Not all colonial marriages were celebrated in the foregoing fashion. Some couples dispensed with all formalities, both social *and* legal. Such marriages were referred to by a variety of terms, such as "hand-fasting," "self-gifta," "clandestine contracts," and later "common-law marriage." Historically, these unions have always been a legal and judicial headache. In the colonial period, matrimonial laws generally provided for consent, banns, officiant, and registration. But what to do with violators? What should, or could, be done when banns were not posted, or when the marriage ceremony was performed by an unauthorized person?

In general, the colonists chose to recognize such marriages as valid, even though a fine might be imposed on the violators. Common-law marriages were treated in the same manner: they were recognized as valid even though the offenders were often fined. Some colonies attempted to invalidate such unions, but the efforts proved ineffective.

It can be argued that, in view of the sanctity attributed to marriage, the colonies should have imposed heavier penalties on the violators. Actually, it was *because* matrimony was held in such high esteem that common-law marriages were accepted. After all, once a common-law wife became pregnant, what was to be gained by having the marriage invalidated? Moreover, during colonial times and throughout much of the nineteenth century, the frontier was being pushed westward. Members of the clergy or authorized civil officials were frequently unavailable in sparsely settled areas, and common-law marriage was often the only recourse.

Whether or not such marriages serve a worthwhile purpose today is debatable, but in this earlier period the recognition of common-law unions was a functional necessity.

—Kephart and Jedlicka, *Family, Society, and The Individual*

Writing Summaries

Sociology, business, and psychology texts place less emphasis on facts and figures and more emphasis on concepts and generalizations. For these texts, summaries that reduce each major section of the chapter to a few paragraphs are often the ideal vehicle for taking notes. But they are obviously less appropriate for textbooks in which specific facts and figures play a more significant role. Scientific writing does not lend itself to the drastic reduction of material that summarizing requires.

If you decide that chapter summaries are appropriate for some of your textbooks, the following pointers will help you write concise and complete summaries.

Be Selective About Supporting Details

Each summary should reduce a chapter section to about a quarter of its original length. Naturally you need to include the main point of a chapter section. In fact, it's a good idea to open your summary with a paraphrased statement of the main idea. But since summaries need to be very concise, be extremely selective about the supporting details you record. In a summary, one or two examples should be sufficient. Yes, do include the names of those experts or researchers who have made unique contributions, but be wary of including the name of anyone who is not a major figure. Similarly, record the results of crucial studies but avoid detailed explanations of how those studies were conducted.

Underline and Annotate Before You Summarize

Underlining and annotating the text before you write your summary will help you decide what is essential information. You'll be more likely to create a lean and tight summary.

Be Guided by Organizational Patterns

If you detect any underlying patterns (say, *comparison and contrast* or *cause and effect*), use them to decide what points to include in your summary. You know, for example, that citing similarities and differences is essential to the comparison-and-contrast pattern. Any summary of a text using comparison and contrast to organize information should include several of the similarities or differences mentioned.

Use Transitions to Connect Ideas

In writing your summary, you often will bring together ideas that originally appeared paragraphs apart. To avoid producing a choppy and confusing version of the original text, include appropriate transitions to indicate relationships between ideas.

Rely on Your Own Words

In writing summaries, paraphrase whenever possible. Although you need to record verbatim any specialized terminology, the rest of the text should be translated into your own words.

To illustrate how the above suggestions should be applied, here is a summary of one section of the sample chapter from pages 175–176.

Computer Dating

Hobbyists and computer clubs have set up a system called *dial-your-mate,* and anyone with access to a personal computer connected to a modem can use the computerized dating service. Participants are given a number to call, at which point; the computer asks them a series of questions like "What are your hobbies?" and "What color hair do you have?" Once the questions are answered, the computer is programmed to match the caller responses with those of potential mates. Callers can then contact those people who seem to fit their interests and requirements. Because initial contacts are made without any face-to-face encounters, values seem to play an important role in the first stage of mate selection.

Even if summarizing is not appropriate for any of your current textbooks, be sure to add summary writing to your repertoire of note-taking strategies. College instructors often require students to summarize outside readings. Then, too, you'll need to summarize articles that might be useful for your research papers. In addition, exam questions often ask for summaries of key works or theories.

PRACTICE 4   Following this excerpt are three different summaries. Choose the one you think most effectively summarizes the passage and explain your choice.

Hypnosis, Imagination, and Memory

In 1976, near Chowchilla, California, 26 children were abducted from a school bus and held captive for a ransom. Under hypnosis, the bus driver recalled the license plate number of the kidnappers' van. This memory helped break the case and led to the children's rescue. Such successes seem to imply that hypnosis can improve memory. But does it? Read on, and judge for yourself.

Research has shown that a hypnotized person is more likely than normal to use imagination to fill in gaps in memory. Also, when hypnotized subjects are given false information, they tend to weave it into their memories (Sheehan et al., 1984). It has been shown that "leading" questions asked during hypnosis can alter memories (Sanders & Simmons, 1983). And even when a memory is completely false, the hypnotized person's confidence in it can be unshakable (Laurence & Perry, 1983). Most telling of all is the fact that hypnosis increases false memories more than it does true ones. Eighty percent of the new memories produced by hypnotized subjects in one experiment were *incorrect* (Dywan & Bowers, 1983).

Overall, it can be concluded that hypnosis does not greatly improve memory (Kihlstrom, 1985). Even when hypnosis uncovers more information, there is no way to tell which memories are true and which are false. Clearly, hypnosis is not the "magic bullet" against forgetting that some police investigators hoped it would be.

—Dennis Coon, *Introduction to Psychology*, 234

A

In 1976 in Chowchilla, California, 26 children were kidnapped and held for ransom. Under hypnosis the bus driver recalled the kidnappers' license plate. This memory helped break the case and led to the children's rescue. This incident poses an intriguing question: Does hypnosis improve our ability to remember?

Actually research has shown that a person under hypnosis is more likely to use imagination to fill in gaps in memory. In addition, when hypnotized subjects are given false information, they tend to add it to their memories. Even questions asked during hypnosis can change the content of memory. In one study 80 percent of the memories produced under hypnosis were false. In general, it appears that hypnosis does not improve remembering. It is not the "magic bullet" some police investigators had hoped for.

B

Although in some cases hypnosis can aid remembering, a good deal of research suggests that the memories produced under hypnosis are frequently inaccurate. Studies have shown, for example, that subjects under hypnosis will use their imagination to fill in memory gaps, include false information, and even change what they remember because of questions asked during hypnosis. In fact, in one study 80 percent of the memories produced by people under hypnosis were inaccurate.

C

Research has shown that the ability to remember is not aided by hypnosis. In one study 80 percent of the memories produced under hypnosis were not accurate.

Which of these three summaries do you think is the best? _____

What made you *not* select the other two? _____

_____

_____

PRACTICE 5   Read, annotate, and summarize the following selection.

The Need Hierarchy

Although several different theories about needs have been advanced, the one most familiar to managers is Maslow's **need hierarchy.** Maslow argued that humans have a variety of different needs that can be classified into five specific groups and then arranged in a hierarchy of importance.

At the bottom are the **physiological needs**—the things we need to survive, such as food, air, and sufficient warmth. In the workplace, adequate wages for food and clothing, reasonable working conditions, and so forth are generally thought to satisfy these needs.

Next are **security needs,** which reflect the desire to have a safe physical and emotional environment. Job security, grievance procedures, and health insurance and retirement plans are used to satisfy security needs.

Third in the hierarchy are the needs for **belongingness.** These include the desire for love and affection and the need to be accepted by our peers. Making friends at work and being a part of the team are common ways in which people satisfy these needs.

Esteem needs come next. These actually comprise two different sets: the needs for recognition and respect from others and the needs for self-respect and a positive self-image. Job titles, spacious offices, awards, and other symbols of success help satisfy the externally focused needs, and accomplishing goals and doing a good job help satisfy the internally focused ones.

Finally, at the top of the hierarchy are the **self-actualization needs**—the needs to continue to grow, develop, and expand our capabilities. Opportunities to participate, to take on increasingly important tasks, and to learn new skills may all lead to satisfaction of these needs. As described more fully in *Management Today: Small Business and Entrepreneurship,* many people who break away from jobs in large corporations to start their own business may be looking for a way to satisfy their self-actualization needs.

—David D. Van Fleet, *Contemporary Management,* 356–357

Making Informal Outlines

Informal outlining is an excellent method of organizing information for exam reviews, particularly if the material is very detailed. Because it forces you to sort ideas and see relationships, outlining will improve your comprehension.

Although you are already familiar with informal outlining from our discussion of lecture notes in Chapter 6, the following suggestions apply more specifically to textbooks.

Begin with the Chapter's Controlling Idea or Purpose

The chapter's overall purpose should be the first item in your outline. It should appear flush against the left margin of the paper. Everything else in the outline will be **subordinate** to or function to explain this first statement or question.

Use Indentation to Reflect Relationships

Beneath the controlling idea, sentences or phrases representing the main points in each major section of the chapter should be indented and aligned. This alignment shows the points are **coordinate** or equal in importance. Examples, reasons, studies, or statistics used as supporting details in the chapter sections should be further indented and placed beneath the general point they explain. Here again the use of indentation highlights the subordinate status of the material. Numbers or letters also help show relationships.

Controlling Idea
1. Main point
    a. example
    b. example
2. Main point
    a. example
    b. example
    c. example

Include the Chapter's Major Headings

Using the headings to divide your outline into sections is a good way to make sure that you are accurately recording the author's train of thought. See Figure 9–1.

Select the Most Essential Details

If an author provides four different illustrations to explain one key generalization, decide which one (or two) best conveys the author's point. Mention the others only by the briefest reference, if at all.

Use Your Own Words

Aside from specialized vocabulary words or a few direct quotations, **paraphrase the author's original language** to ensure that you have truly understood and internalized what you have read. If possible, condense whole sentences into brief phrases.

Here to illustrate how these pointers should be put into practice is an outline based on a portion of our sample chapter (pages 172–175).

Figure 9–1: Informal Outline Showing Indentations and Alignment

Modes of Mate Selection

Controlling Idea: Dating remains popular, but there are now lots of other ways to find a mate.

1. <u>Traditional Dating</u>: By the 50s and 60s, dating, in full bloom, had definite patterns.
   a. people dating at an early age
   b. competitive quality to dating
      — who's got the best-looking date
   c. a lot of game playing involved

2. <u>Modern Dating</u>: Some negative aspects remain, but there have been some changes.
   a. women still wait to be asked
   b. not everybody follows the same script
      1. less formal, more spontaneous
      2. men don't always pay
      3. males and females treat one another as equals
      4. sex plays a significant role

3. <u>International Mate Selection</u>: Over 100,000 Americans find spouses in other countries.
   a. most between people of same race and ethnicity
   b. but thousands involve Caucasian men and Asian women
   c. physical appearance plays key role
      — photographs exchanged
   d. since 1987 you can no longer marry somebody you have never met

Using Organizational Maps After Reading

Organizational maps are excellent for prereading, and they are also valuable when you have finished reading and need to take notes. If a textbook chapter does not include numerous minor headings and is not particularly detailed, use an organizational map like the one shown in Figure 9–2.

Figure 9–2: Organizational Map of a Chapter Containing Few Minor Headings

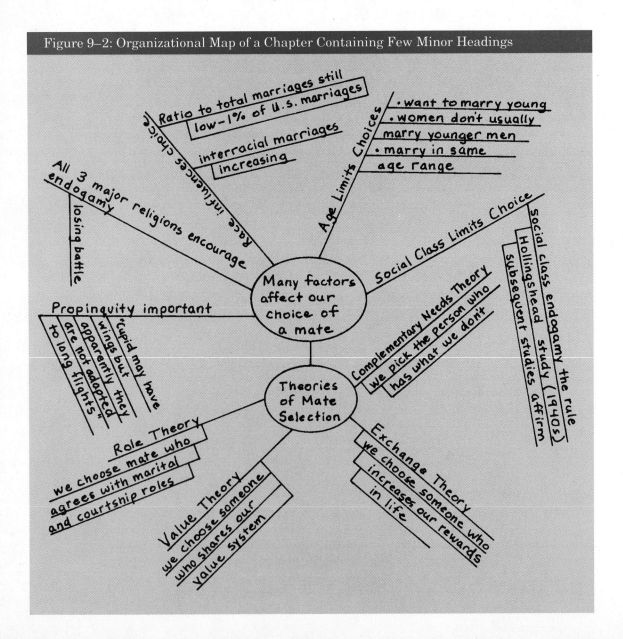

Generally speaking, however, organizational maps lend themselves more readily to taking notes on sections of chapters rather than entire chapters.

Organizational maps work for chapter sections that rely on comparison and contrast. With an organizational map, you can highlight individual

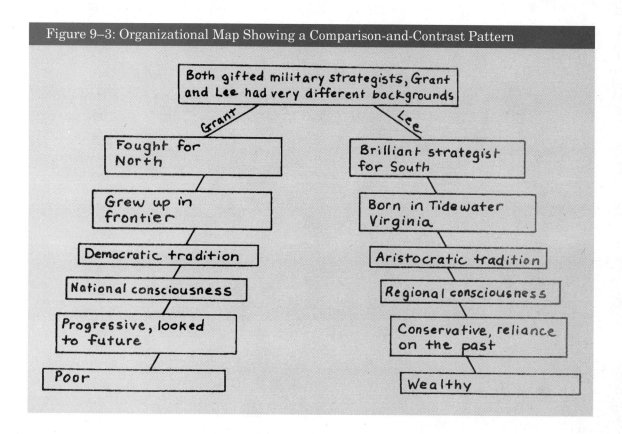

Figure 9–3: Organizational Map Showing a Comparison-and-Contrast Pattern

differences or similarities between two topics. Figure 9–3 illustrates an organizational map based on a passage that compares and contrasts the backgrounds of Robert E. Lee and Ulysses S. Grant.

Textbooks on business and government frequently provide detailed descriptions of how large institutions or groups are organized. Such descriptions are often hard to comprehend, not because the material is inherently difficult but because there is so much detail. Organizational maps are excellent devices for understanding and taking notes on such descriptions. They give visual form to the individual people or offices in an organization, making them easier to remember and relate to one another. Figure 9–4 shows an example.

Figure 9–4: Organizational Map Showing Who Reports to Whom in the State Department

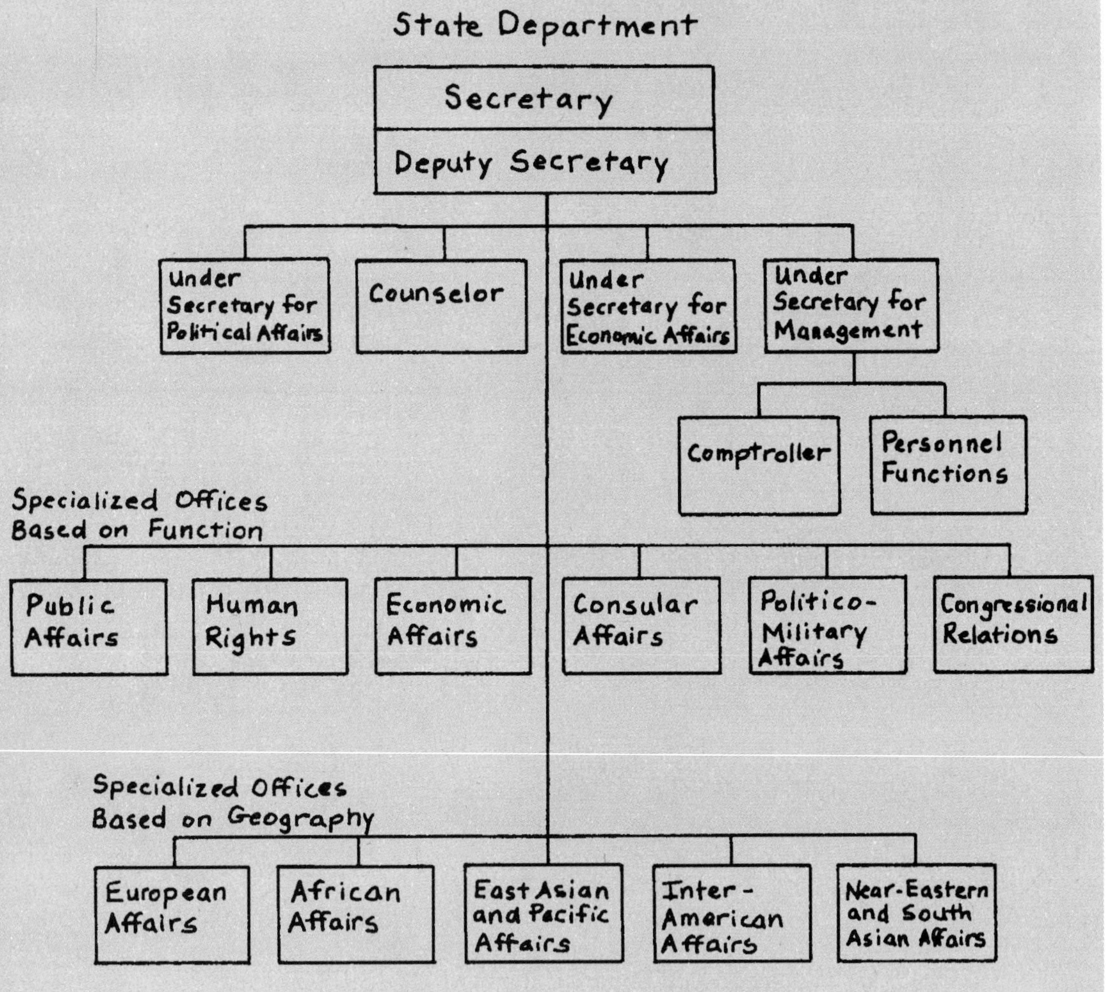

State Department

```
                    ┌─────────────────────┐
                    │     Secretary       │
                    ├─────────────────────┤
                    │  Deputy Secretary   │
                    └─────────────────────┘
```

Under Secretary for Political Affairs   Counselor   Under Secretary for Economic Affairs   Under Secretary for Management

Comptroller   Personnel Functions

Specialized Offices Based on Function

Public Affairs   Human Rights   Economic Affairs   Consular Affairs   Politico-Military Affairs   Congressional Relations

Specialized Offices Based on Geography

European Affairs   African Affairs   East Asian and Pacific Affairs   Inter-American Affairs   Near-Eastern and South Asian Affairs

☐ PRACTICE 6   Create an organizational map that records the essential elements of the following textbook selection.

Physical Properties of Minerals

Minerals are solids formed by inorganic processes. Each mineral has an orderly arrangement of atoms (crystalline structure) and a definite chemical composition which give it a unique set of physical properties. Since the internal structure and chemical composition of a mineral are difficult to determine without the aid of sophisticated tests and apparatus, the more easily recognized physical properties are frequently used in identification. A discussion of some diagnostic physical properties follows.

Luster

Luster is the appearance or quality of light reflected from the surface of a mineral. Minerals that have the appearance of metals, regardless of color, are said to have a *metallic luster*. Minerals with a *nonmetallic luster* are described by various adjectives, including vitreous (glassy), pearly, silky, resinous, and earthy (dull). Some minerals appear partially metallic in luster and are said to be *submetallic*.

Color

Although **color** is the most obvious feature of a mineral, it is often an unreliable diagnostic property. Slight impurities in the common mineral quartz, for example, give it a variety of colors, including pink, purple (amethyst), white, and even black. When a mineral, such as quartz, exhibits a variety of colors, it is said to possess *exotic coloration*. Other minerals, for example, sulfur, which is generally yellow, and malachite, which is bright green, are said to have *inherent coloration* because their color does not vary significantly.

Streak

Streak is the color of a mineral in its powdered form and is obtained by rubbing the mineral across a piece of unglazed porcelain termed a *streak plate*. Although the color of a mineral may vary from sample to sample, the streak usually does not, and is therefore the more reliable property. Streak can also be an aid in distinguishing minerals with metallic lusters from those having nonmetallic lusters. Metallic minerals generally have a dense, dark streak, whereas minerals with nonmetallic lusters do not.

Hardness

One of the more useful diagnostic properties is **hardness,** the resistance of a mineral to abrasion or scratching. This is a relative property that is determined by rubbing a mineral of unknown hardness against one of known hardness, or vice versa. A numerical value can be obtained by using **Mohs scale** of hardness, which consists of ten minerals arranged in order from 1 (softest) to 10 (hardest) as follows:

Hardness	Mineral
1	Talc
2	Gypsum
3	Calcite
4	Fluorite
5	Apatite
6	Orthoclase
7	Quartz
8	Topaz
9	Corundum
10	Diamond

—F. K. E. Lutgens and Charles Tarbuck, *Essentials of Geology*, 192

Working Space

READING ASSIGNMENT

The following section of a textbook focuses on self-esteem. Then make an informal outline to sum up the key points and answer the questions that follow.

Self-Esteem

Awareness of self and self-esteem are particularly relevant parts of the human personality. Coopersmith (1968) has noted the
relationship between self-esteem and psychological health and asserted it is important that we devote more attention to
building up the positive aspects of human
personality. For Coopersmith, the most important factor for effective behavior is self-
esteem.

Research on Self-Esteem

In their research Coopersmith (1968) and
his co-workers found that youngsters with a
high degree of self-esteem are active, expres-
sive individuals who tend to be successful
both academically and socially. They lead
rather than merely listen in discussions.
They are eager to express opinions, do not
avoid disagreement, and are not particularly
sensitive to criticism. In addition, they are
highly interested in public affairs, show little destructiveness in early childhood, and
are little troubled by feelings of anxiety.
They appear to trust their own perceptions
and reactions and have confidence that their
efforts will be successful. They approach
other persons with the expectation that they
will be well received. Their general optimism
stems not from fantasies but rather from a
well-founded assessment of their abilities,
social skills, and personal qualities. They

are not self-conscious or preoccupied with
personal difficulties. They are much less frequently afflicted with psychosomatic troubles such as insomnia, fatigue, headaches, or
intestinal upset than are persons of low self-
esteem.

Boys with low self-esteem present a picture of discouragement and depression. They
feel isolated, unlovable, incapable of expressing or defending themselves, and too weak to
confront or overcome their deficiencies. They
are fearful of angering others and shrink
from exposing themselves to notice in any
way. In the presence of a social group, they
remain in the shadows, listening rather than
participating. They are sensitive to criticism,
self-conscious, and preoccupied with inner
problems. This dwelling on their own difficulties not only intensifies their feelings of
defeat but also isolates them from opportunities for friendly, supporting relationships.
In the words of Epstein and Komorita
(1971): "It is likely that the low self-esteem
person will 'externalize' responsibility for his
actions and attribute the consequences of his
behavior to factors beyond his control. On
the other hand, the high self-esteem individual presumably views himself as determining the outcome of his behavior" (p. 2). Thus,
one's confidence that life can be gratifying
may rest squarely on the self-concept, which
may decide whether one succeeds or fails in
life.

When Coopersmith looked into the backgrounds of boys who possessed high self-esteem, he found that close relationships existed between the boys and their parents. The mothers and fathers showed interest in the boys' welfare, were available for discussion of problems, and encouraged mutual activities. They clearly indicated that they regarded the boy as a significant person worthy of their deep interest. The boys came to regard themselves in a similar, favorable light.

The parents of the high-self-esteem children also proved to be less permissive than the parents of children with low-self-esteem. Though the less permissive parents demanded high standards of behavior and were strict and consistent in enforcing rules, their discipline was not harsh or punitive. By comparison, the parents of the low-self-esteem boys tended to be exceptionally permissive, yet used harsh punishment when their children gave them trouble.

Buss on Self-Esteem

In the words of Buss (1973):

There are two kinds of self-judgments, one temporary and the other enduring. Temporary self-evaluation refers to specific behaviors [in] particular situations: "That was stupid of me," "I played very well today," or "I really out-maneuvered them this time." These transient reactions, limited in time and place, are of less interest to the student of personality than are the more generalized and enduring evaluations each person makes of himself. The latter evaluations are more central to the self and represent the residuals of some of the most fundamental life experiences: affection from others and one's own achievements. [p. 495]

Buss has designed a *model of self-esteem*

to account for the ups-and-downs we all experience in our feelings about ourselves.

The core of self-esteem is formed by the unconditional love of the parents. They love the child simply because he is theirs. They make no demands and place no conditions on their affection. Thus, the infant learns that the most important figures in his life think he is valuable merely because he exists. Love without limits or conditions forms a major part of the core of self-esteem. It creates a permanent feeling of self-love and the expectation that others will offer affection. There is also a peripheral self-esteem that consists of (1) the continued affection of the parents (now with conditions laid down—more love when the child is good, less when he is bad) and (2) the affection of other members of the family and a wider circle of friends. This second part of peripheral self-esteem depends on accomplishments. At first the child performs to please his parents, but gradually his goals are based more and more on group norms.

According to Buss, by middle childhood the core of self-esteem has been established. If the core is sufficient, the person will always be able to fall back on a reserve of self-love. If the core is insufficient, the person will always be driven to seek affection or to demand respect for achievement. "The person who seems *driven* to appeal for love or *driven* to accomplish requires inordinate esteem from others to compensate for his lack of self-esteem. Without a sufficient core of self-esteem, he needs continual assurance of his own worth" (Buss, 1973, p. 497).

Together, the work of Coopersmith and the theorizing of Buss underscore the importance of self-esteem as a core facet of the personality. We may each have personalities composed of differing traits in differing degrees, but these combinations are not very significant compared to the degree to which we are able to esteem ourselves and behave accordingly.

—Elton McNeil,
The Psychology of Being Human

1. What main point does the author make about self-esteem?

2. What connection can you make between this article and the discussion of self-image in Chapter 2 (pages 38–39)?

3. What two kinds of self-judgment are described in the article?

4. Self-esteem can vary with the context or the setting. Evaluate your self-esteem in each of the following roles: as a student, as a son or daughter, as a wage earner, and as a social success.

WRITING ASSIGNMENT

Describe an incident from your past that you feel powerfully affected your sense of self-esteem. Then explain how that incident influences your current behavior.

JOURNAL ASSIGNMENTS

1. Over the next two weeks, experiment with various note-taking methods. Evaluate each one. Does one method work especially well for a particular textbook? If so, why?

   To get started, read what Susan Pettorini wrote in response to this assignment:

No matter what I was reading, I used to make outlines. But then I started writing summaries for sociology and psychology. For these courses, writing summaries seems even better than outlining. I really think about which details I need to include, where before I would just write down examples without thinking about them. I still use outlines for my biology course though. That's because so many of the details are crucial; the summary would be as long as the text. What I am doing differently is drawing more pictures in my notes. I think it's true that visualizing helps you remember.

2. Think about how you are progressing with time management. Are you making a regular To-Do list? If not, why not? What method of managing and monitoring your time are you using instead?
3. In what areas covered so far—concentration, time management, listening—have you made the most progress? How can you tell you've made progress? In what areas have you made the least progress? How can you tell you haven't made much progress?
4. Explain the meaning of this Native American saying: "Tell me, and I'll forget. Show me, and I may not remember. Involve me, and I'll understand."

✔ Checking Out: Review Questions for Chapter 9

1. What is the most common mistake students make when learning how to underline?

2. When selecting keys words to underline, what should you imagine?

3. What are the benefits of *selective* underlining?

4. In addition to underlining, why should you also annotate passages?

5. What forms can marginal annotations take?

6. Outlining is particularly good for what kind of text?

7. Why is indenting crucial to making an outline?

8. In an outline, when you align statements underneath one another, what do you indicate?

9. List at least four pointers for creating a summary.

10. Organizational maps work well for what types of text?

▶ In Summary

You now have at your disposal several different methods for taking notes from textbooks. As with lecture notes, you can use the methods alone or combine them. What's most important is that you choose a method or methods that are appropriate to your textbooks and your own purpose in taking notes. Whichever method you choose, be selective and make decisions about which information is essential and which is not.

Remember to paraphrase whenever possible. Paraphrasing is a first-rate way of checking your comprehension and ensuring that you are not just copying down the author's words without really understanding them. Finally, whether you are using indentation in outlines or transitions in summaries, remember to show relationships among ideas and to indicate any underlying patterns of organization.

CHAPTER 10

Improving Your Reading Rate

The ability to read at high rates of speed is a helpful tool for certain tasks. This chapter will provide pointers on how to increase your reading rate.

- Defining speed reading
- Picking up the pace of your reading
- Creating your own speed-reading course
- Increasing reading rate while maintaining acceptable levels of comprehension

Defining Speed Reading

"Speed-reading training is really skimming training in disguise."

—Ronald P. Carver

Because they have so much reading to do, many college students express an interest in "speed reading." Some even take expensive courses that will supposedly teach them how to read everything—textbooks, newspapers, and novels—at no less than 1,200 words per minute.

Students who take such courses usually are disappointed. For while they do learn to read at high rates of speed, they also discover that this kind of reading—what we would call **skimming**—is not appropriate for most textbook assignments. At 800 to 900 words per minute, readers can get a very general idea of what a chapter will cover, but they cannot register, comprehend, and evaluate an author's words. To do that kind of reading, most people have two fairly fixed rates: 100 to 200 words per minute for a close, analytical reading of material that is difficult and unfamiliar; or 200 to 400 words per minute for understanding material that is new but not necessarily difficult to comprehend. At 1,200 words per minute, even the most experienced readers can absorb only limited portions of text. Consequently, their comprehension drops, and they retain only a general notion of what the author intended to communicate.

Disappointed? Don't be. Skimming—for that's what speed-reading courses are really advertising—is a valuable skill, and you should add it to your repertoire of reading strategies. Skimming is ideal for prereading textbook chapters. Without spending a lot of time, you can get an overview of the author's content and organization. If a chapter is long and complex, a rapid prereading will help you decide how to break it up into more manageable portions for study. Then, too, if you're doing research, it's useful to skim the contents of potentially worthwhile articles or books to decide if they are useful.

Since the ability to read or skim at high rates of speed has definite value, make every effort to increase your reading rate. However, it's important to recognize when it is appropriate to read at high rates of speed and when it is not. The chart on page 212 should help you decide when to speed up and when to slow down.

Picking Up the Pace of Your Reading

"He has only half learned the art of reading who has not added to it the more refined art of . . . skimming."

Arthur, Lord Balfour

Reading Rates and Purpose Appropriate to Each Rate

Reading Rate (Words per Minute)	Your Purpose in Reading
100–200	To do an analytical reading; to reread complex material; to read poetry or a foreign language you have not yet mastered; to read material you intend to memorize or learn in depth
200–400	To read, understand, and remember material with which you have some degree of familiarity or which is new but still not too difficult
400–500	To get a general understanding of easy-to-read newspapers, novels, and magazine articles
500–1000	To skim newspapers, novels, and magazines
1000–1500	To glance down a page and find a specific piece of information

Knowing how to skim is a crucial part of knowing how to read. President John F. Kennedy, for example, was famous for his ability to skim several newspapers in less than one hour. But the ability to skim at high rates of speed usually doesn't happen by chance. You need to work at it.

Schedule Fifteen Minutes a Day

Devote at least fifteen minutes a day to increasing your reading rate. In those fifteen minutes, push yourself to read as fast as you can. Avoid **regressing**—or looking back to reread. And don't worry about what you are missing. During this time, your primary goal is to read for speed.

Establish Your Purpose

While you are working on increasing your reading rate, tell yourself explicitly what you can and cannot accomplish: "I want to increase my reading rate by at least fifty words today, and to do so, I cannot read every word." By explicitly defining your purpose, you can avoid the trap of trying both to read every word *and* to increase your reading rate at the same time. These are simply incompatible goals; attempting to combine them will lead to frustration.

Develop Your Own Reading Materials

Lots of speed-reading texts are available in bookstores, but you don't need to buy one in order to improve your reading rate. Instead develop your own material geared strictly to your interests and your current reading level.

To start, select a novel or an article that particularly interests you. The novel can be any length, but the article should be at least several pages long. Initially, select texts that are relatively easy to read. In time, you can practice on more complicated material in preparation for tackling textbooks or research sources, but at first avoid texts that are too difficult. Since you'll have to struggle initially to make yourself read faster, a difficult book will only make your task harder.

To get an approximate word count for the texts you've selected, count the number of words on three complete lines of text and divide that number by three to get an average number of words per line. Multiply the average number of words per line by the number of lines on one whole page—no half-pages allowed. The number you arrive at is the approximate number of words per page. Now you are ready to use those figures during your timed readings.

Practicing Faster Reading

In your first practice session, don't expect to skim at 600 to 700 words per minute. Reaching that rate will take some practice. Instead tell yourself that you're going to start slow—say, 300 words per minute—and build up speed as time goes on. Before you begin, figure out how many pages you need to cover in five minutes in order to reach your desired reading rate. (You certainly can read for longer if you wish, but you will get results with just five minutes a day.) Then start reading those pages as fast as you can, looking at the clock only when you start and when you finish your allotted number of pages. Jot down both your starting and ending times so you know exactly how much time you spent reading.

When you finish reading, figure out your reading rate by multiplying the number of words per page times the number of pages you've read.

$$390 \text{ words per page} \times 4 \text{ pages} = 1560 \text{ words}$$

Then divide that number by the amount of time spent reading.

$$1560 \div 4.5 \text{ minutes} = 346 \text{ words per minute}$$

A starting figure of 346 words per minute is excellent. But if your comprehension checks out, you should plan on reading around 400 words per minute during the next session.

Getting a Word Count

1. Count the number of words in three complete lines of text: 30
2. Divide that number by 3 to get the average number of words per line: 10
3. Multiply that number by the number of lines on a whole page: $50 \times 10 = 500$

Approximate number of words per page: 500

Check Your Comprehension at Faster Rates

Pushing yourself to read faster is crucial to improving your reading rate. However, as you try to increase your reading rate, do a general comprehension check to be sure you're not missing too much. When reading a novel, see if you can describe any significant changes in plot or character. When reading a magazine article, try to recall the author's main point and one or two supporting details. If you can generally summarize what you've read, you've passed your comprehension test, and you can continue to increase your reading rate by around 100 words per minute.

If after one of these checks, you cannot remember anything about the text, don't increase your rate during the next practice session. Instead, read at the same rate and again test your comprehension. If you still cannot generally summarize what you've read, it's time to slow down. Reduce your reading rate by at least 100 words per minute. Speed up again only when your comprehension improves.

Reading at high rates of speed will decrease your level of comprehension. That's to be expected. The best you'll be able to do at 900 words per minute is get a very general idea of a story or article. Anytime you cannot remember even the general plot or the main point, it's time to slow down.

Push Beyond Your Comfortable Speed

In the beginning, not reading (or for that matter not really seeing) every word is bound to cause you some discomfort. But don't let discomfort slow you down. When you are building up speed, read at a slightly uncomfortable rate because this will discourage *regressions* (backward looks to reread). Natural and necessary during an analytical reading, regressions are obstacles when you are working to increase your reading rate. Maintaining a faster-than-comfortable speed will help you eliminate them.

Additional Tips for Faster Reading

When you want to skim at high rates of speed, not worrying about in-depth comprehension is important. However, to really refine your skimming ability, take these additional steps.

Reread for Speed

If you are having a problem reading more for speed than for comprehension, try reading the same material twice. On the first reading, time yourself but read at a comfortable rate, letting yourself slow down to reread any passages you don't immediately understand. When you are finished, figure out your reading rate (number of words divided by minutes spent reading), and take a five-minute break.

After your break, reread the same material. But this time read more for speed than for comprehension. Strictly limit your reading time, so that you are forced to skim at double or triple your original reading rate.

Having already understood the material, you won't be so tempted to slow down or let your eyes regress. That's the benefit of doing a double reading.

In your early weeks of rate training, do several of these double readings until you feel more confident about skimming at high rates of speed.

Use the Author's Organizational Pattern as a Guide

The ability to recognize and respond to organizational patterns is especially valuable when reading for speed is your goal. Say you begin reading and immediately realize that the author is comparing and contrasting two different topics. Once you recognize this pattern, continue to skim at high rates of speed, slowing down only to identify key points of similarity or difference. In that way, you will maintain your forward momentum but still grasp the author's main points.

Slow Down for the Opening and Closing Paragraphs

If you are skimming articles or essays, try reading the first few and the last few paragraphs at a comfortable rate of speed. Writers frequently use the opening and closing paragraphs to introduce and comment on their central message. If you have grasped that core message, you are in a better position to skim the remaining paragraphs at high rates of speed.

Follow the Pointer

In grammar school, you probably learned that using your finger or pen to keep your place on a line of print was a bad habit. And it's true, children do need to learn how to control their eye movements without the aid of a pen or a pencil. But when you're learning to skim, a conscious variation on this old childhood trait can come in handy.

To keep your skimming rate high, imagine that your pen or pencil is an automatic pointer moving at high rates of speed across the page. As you read, keep the pointer going back and forth in a zigzag fashion and follow it from left to right with your eyes. If you feel yourself slowing down, speed up the pointer and keep it moving at a steady pace down the page.

Work on Vocabulary

If you want to speed up your reading rate, regular work on vocabulary is essential. Your goal should be to **enlarge the number of words to which you can respond automatically.** Responding automatically means that, rather than pausing to search for it in your memory, you can retrieve the appropriate meaning from memory almost instantaneously.

Although the learning strategies described on pages 145–147 will help increase your automatic responses to words, include some reviews that emphasize speed of recognition. *Flash cards,* for example, with the word on one side and the meaning on the other, are an ideal device. Don't give yourself more than a second or two to retrieve a meaning from memory. Review the cards regularly until you can match words and meanings without skipping a beat.

Watch for Typographical Devices

Typographical devices—**boldface,** *italics,* <u>underlining,</u> headings, and colored ink—are all clues to significance. They announce that an author is introducing a key point, term, or topic. Like organizational patterns, typographical devices can help you decide when to speed up or slow down. If you wish, you can skim an entire article at 1,000 words per minute. But slow down to read all headings, boldfaced terms, or statements highlighted in different colored ink.

Use Transitions as Signposts to Speed Up or Slow Down

Some transitions, such as *moreover, also, likewise,* and *in the same vein,* signal alert readers to expect a continuation of the author's original thought and therefore to read faster. Others, such as *however, on the other hand, but,* and *from an opposing point of view,* signal a change of direction in the writer's train of thought and warn readers to slow down.

In particular, keep an eye open for transitions signaling a reversal at the *beginning* of articles or essays. Writers often open with a statement they immediately revise or contradict, as in this example.

An increasing number of educators in the United States are committed to making high school curricula more multicultural. *However,* despite that general commitment, there seems to be no general agreement about how far the schools should go in changing or revising the more traditional curriculum. While some educators want to scrap the traditional curriculum altogether, considering it outmoded or out of touch, others believe only a bit of tinkering is necessary, for example, the addition of more material drawn from other cultures.

In this excerpt, the author opens by saying that there is a general commitment to multicultural education in the high schools. But before speeding off in pursuit of that idea, experienced readers would slow down at the sight of the transitional word *however*. They would not speed up again until they discovered exactly how the author modified or revised the opening statement.

The following chart classifies a number of transitional words to help you know when to speed up or slow down. Familiarize yourself with these words; then use them to pace yourself while skimming at high rates of speed.

Transitions Telling You to Speed Up

Also	In addition
As has been pointed out before	In the same vein
As stated earlier	Likewise
By the same token	Moreover
Furthermore	Similarly
Here again	To reiterate

Transitions Telling You to Slow Down

But	In opposition
Conversely	Nevertheless
Despite that fact	Notwithstanding
From another perspective	On the other hand
However	Yet
In contradiction to	

Working Space

READING ASSIGNMENT

Read the following selection twice. First read it at a comfortable rate, one that will allow you to understand not just the general point of the selection but the specific point of every paragraph. When you finish, answer the four accompanying questions and then take a ten-minute break. After your break, reread the selection, but this time skim it as fast as you can. When you're through skimming, figure out your reading rate.

'White Male Writers' Is the Title of English 112

The reading list for English 112 is familiar: Hawthorne, Melville, James Fenimore Cooper, Twain. But for many students and faculty members at Georgetown University, the appearance of a course titled "White Male Writers" this semester is as surprising as it is revealing.

"This is just one small group within a large body of literature, so let's title it that," said Valerie Babb, the assistant professor of English who originated the course. "Just as we say native American writers, just as we say black women writers, these are white male writers."

At a time when many universities, like Georgetown, have revised survey literature courses to include less familiar but equally important works of minorities and women and have added courses devoted to those authors, Professor Babb's focus on the traditional canon is unusual.

But Lucy Maddox, chairwoman of the English department, said the new course had effectively placed the books of white men on the same academic level as books by minority or female writers, which are being taught both in specific courses and in more general courses, like 19th-century American literature.

As a group, white male authors are often treated as if their sex or race had no influence on their works, Professor Maddox said, but added that in reality "white men are as defined by their race and gender as black women are."

Professor Babb said the course distinguished the way that sex and race affect the writers' strategies, "such as ambivalence, voice, tone and diction." Students also examine how each man changed American perceptions of minority groups.

Professor Babb noted, for example, that Cooper helped define the way that America thought about Indians. He had very little contact with Indians, she said, but felt free to write about them and to place them low in his hierarchy of American races. Because his books were so popular, those perceptions pervaded the culture.

Professor Maddox said the title of the new course drew considerable attention from students and faculty members, many of whom asked "whether it was real." Their reaction, Professor Maddox said, was itself a statement about the English curriculum. "That title should be no more unexpected than 'black women writers,' " she said.

But their surprise was understandable, Professor Maddox said, since white male writers are usually studied under the generic heading of "literature," while works by minority groups have been "tagged" by the race or sex of the author.

Fear of Attack

The first class of 35 students in English 112 was almost evenly divided between men and women—"a very nice mix," Professor Babb said.

But some of her male students say they have been reluctant to contribute to class discussions.

"I feel like if I were to say something in defense of a white male writer, I would have a hard time defending that position because it would be attacked from a lot of different points of view," said Tim Delaune, a sophomore from Titusville, Florida, majoring in government.

Mr. Delaune said he was initially afraid that the class would be "white male writer bashing." Although Professor Babb has not taken that approach, he said, some women in the class have made what he called attacks on the works.

But students like Eric Hayot, a second-year junior in English from Cleveland, said there was often little to defend. "Cooper is obviously an unbelievable racist," Mr. Hayot said, referring to the introduction of *The Last of the Mohicans* in which Cooper ranks the races according to their pre-eminence in American society.

Professor Babb, who concentrated on American 19th-century literature in graduate school, said she did not think it was unusual that she, a black woman, would teach a class on white male writers.

"Who would know white men better than a black woman?" she asked. "I've got a legacy of great-grandmothers and grandmothers who cleaned house, washed clothes, diapered babies for white males; I've got a rich store of information. My entire education has come from what might be called a white male culture."

— *New York Times,* March 3, 1991, 47.

1. According to the article, what does the title of English 112 suggest about the authors who have been included in the course?

_____

_____

_____

_____

2. How have people responded to the title?

_____

_____

3. How have they responded to the course itself?

_____

_____

4. Who is Valerie Babb?

_____

_____

WRITING ASSIGNMENT

Explain why you think it is or is not important for college students to read more literature written by people from minority groups.

JOURNAL ASSIGNMENTS

1. Several hundred years ago, Sir Francis Bacon wrote, "Some books are to be nibbled at or tasted, some are to be swallowed whole, and a few need to be thoroughly chewed and digested." How would you interpret this quotation? What is the relationship between the quotation and the chapter you just read?

2. Are you going to schedule time to work on skimming? Why or why not?

✔ Checking Out: Review Questions for Chapter 10

1. When you read at high rates of speed, what should you expect to happen?

2. According to the chapter, what are some of the ways skimming can be used?

3. What are regressions?

4. If you don't feel comfortable reading at high rates of speed, what should you do?

5. When you are trying to improve your reading rate, what is the value of reading the same selection twice?

6. When reading at high rates of speed, why is it helpful to slow down to read the opening and closing paragraphs?

7. What does it mean to respond automatically to words?

8. Name three kinds of typographical devices.

9. List three transitions that signal change or reversal.

10. List three transitions that signal continuation of the same or a similar point.

▶ In Summary

Reading at high rates of speed and maintaining a high level of comprehension are, by and large, incompatible goals. However, that does not mean you should give up on improving your reading rate. A number of reading tasks can and should be done at high rates of speed—prereading textbooks, making decisions about research materials, or deciding how to manage a lengthy assignment. So it's in your interest to develop your own reading materials and consistently work on improving your reading rate.

Just remember to establish a clear purpose, use any typographical or organizational clues that signal importance, and force yourself to read as fast as you can without letting a little discomfort slow you down. As long as you retain a general sense of what you've read, continue to increase your reading rate. Fifteen minutes a day devoted to increasing your reading speed should bring results in a month or two.

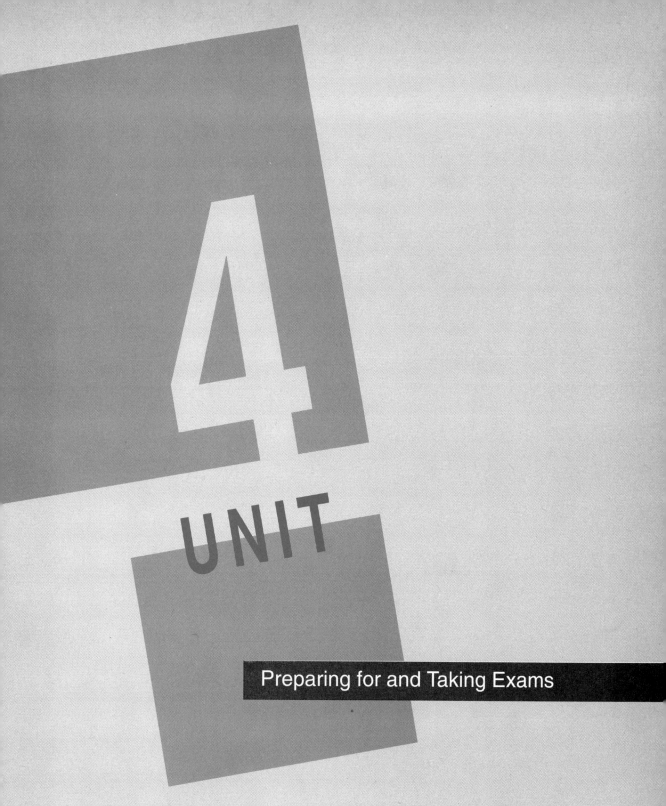

4
UNIT

Preparing for and Taking Exams

CHAPTER 11

How to Do Well on Exams: Preparing

*"Remember that you will take many tests in your life.
No one test can seal your fate or change your future."*
—*Alice Ellis, student*

If you are determined to do well in your courses, you will look at an exam review as a time to double your efforts to prove yourself. Reviewing prepares you to demonstrate what you have learned during the semester. It is no secret that good students prepare carefully for exams.

In this chapter, learn about:

- Studying efficiently for exams
- Scheduling your review sessions
- Taking a constructive attitude toward reviewing
- Learning the most effective review methods
- Overcoming test anxiety

Gearing Up for Exams

All your efforts thus far—attending lectures and keeping up with assignments—have been geared to preparing you to take exams. Ideally, you should simply learn the material of the course for its own sake—so that you can know and make use of it. But in a practical world, the midterm and the final exam are where you prove to others that *you have learned the material*.

To prepare for exams, good students apply three general rules. First, since college students often are given more to read and learn than they can possibly absorb, good students are *selective* about what they learn. Second, as they review for exams, they constantly monitor their pace to ensure that they will cover all the critical topics before the exam.

Finally, they schedule review time according to the difficulty of each course. They spend more time reviewing for their harder courses than for their more manageable courses.

Exams are the means commonly taken by professors to determine how well you have mastered the course and whether you are ready to go on to a higher-level course. All your earlier work is rehearsal; the exam is your performance.

Studying Efficiently for Exams

The key to doing well on exams is not so much what you do on the day of the exam, but the preparations you make beforehand.

To do well on your exams and to cut down on test anxiety, felt by all students to a certain extent, we have one foolproof suggestion: nothing works as well as knowing the material of your course inside and out. To be well prepared for the exam, you should master all the major concepts and be very familiar with most of the minor ones. By the time you take the final exam, you should be ready and able to teach the course yourself. In fact, preparing for the exam is the time you pull together and internalize all the material, and as far as learning the coursework, reviewing is more important than taking the exam.

Plan Your Exam Review as Early as Possible

Plan what to study in your review sessions at least a week prior to a short test or quiz. Before a final exam, start planning your review sessions several weeks or even a month ahead. Why? Planning your exam review is a matter of *estimating* how long the review will take to ensure that you cover all the essentials. And since estimating is at best a rough method, it is far better to have extra time for studying and to overlearn rather than to run out of time and not finish your review. Especially if you have ongoing work and childcare responsibilities, plan early.

Find Out What the Test or Final Exam Will Cover

Your instructor usually will outline in class what you are responsible for on the upcoming test (in some cases, the syllabus will give this information). If not, a legitimate question to ask is "What material will be covered on the test?" You want to find out which lectures, chapters, handouts, and homework problems you should review. (Instructors, however, do *not* want to be asked about the specific questions that will appear on the test.)

You may also ask if the test will contain *objective* questions (multiple choice, true-or-false, numerical problems), *essay* questions, or some of each.

Keep Attending Classes

Don't cut classes; go to lectures right up until the day of your exam. Pick up any final tips on what to review, what the exam will cover, and any hints about what kinds of questions will be asked. The more you know about the test, the better you can prepare for it.

Scheduling Your Review Sessions

For major exams or finals, allow an hour or more to make your review plan because **planning how to use your review time efficiently is critical.**

One student spent all her time reviewing her notes for Chapters 1 and 2 and knew them well, but she had no time for the next ten chapters. She clearly did not plan wisely. But many students make similar, if less glaring, mistakes and run out of time before completing their review of all the essential topics.

How do you figure out a schedule for exam review? As we explain below, determine how long your review will take by quickly surveying what was covered in the course and then estimating how long it will take you to review the essentials carefully. Since you will be guessing how much you can cover in each review session, you must monitor your schedule daily to make sure you are not falling behind.

Make a Quick Survey of What Needs Reviewing

Gather together on your desk all the materials covering each course so that you can scan them quickly.

1. **Use the syllabus or table of contents to develop a concise list of the major topics covered in the course.**
   As you scan your lecture and reading notes to plan your review, use this list to identify significant topics and to give yourself an overview of the subject. If it will help you later, quickly jot down on the list where you will find a given topic, discussed, say in your lecture notes or in a handout.

   To make sure your list of key topics is complete, *use both the syllabus and the table of contents* (or use the contents by itself if you have no syllabus).

2. **Approximate how many lecture notes you can review per study session.**
   Except for math and science courses, the questions found on most exams come from the lecture notes and the text; in math and science courses, they come mainly from the assigned numerical problems.

   One student, now a psychologist, studied his lecture notes very hard—and reviewed little else. Although this method is a risky tactic, it worked for him, and we can learn something from his approach.

   Lecture notes often indicate what professors consider important and what they have pinpointed for you to learn. So when planning your exam review, *make a quick survey of all your lecture notes.* See how many pages they consist of and approximate how much time it will take to review several lectures at once. Depending on your familiarity with them and on the complexity of the topic, some lecture notes will require intensive effort; others will need only a brief review. Then estimate roughly how many review sessions you will need for a thorough review of your lecture notes.

   As a rough guide, figure that you can cover three lectures in one study session.

It often is helpful to **let the lecture notes guide the rest of your review.** Let them indicate what pages of the text, what sets of problems, and what themes you should focus on.

3. Organize your notes on the assigned reading.

Guided by the syllabus and the lecture notes, identify the essential chapters and topics in the text that you should review. Scan the reading notes you have taken on these chapters, and, again, estimate how much time you will need to cover them in a review. If, instead of taking notes, you have annotated or underlined the text, focus on these highlighted passages when reviewing.

Do not reread chapters word for word in your review, unless the topic or passage is very critical or unless you are studying science or math where the information is tightly compressed.

4. Plan how to review problem sets or other homework assignments.

For a science or problem-based course, decide how many homework problems you want to rework. Perhaps rework one-third or one-half of the problems. Divide the problem sets by how many study sessions you have available for your review. Build in extra time for reviewing especially difficult concepts. After a few days, adjust your schedule if it is not realistic. **As a guiding principle, overlearn;** understand these problems deeply rather than superficially so that, if asked, you can work out a slight variation on a problem. Get some reliable help on any problems you don't understand; first identify and then ask about the exact place where you get confused.

5. Look at old tests or earlier quizzes.

In some schools, professors or libraries have copies of earlier exams. Check to see if any exams are available; they will give you some idea of what to expect on the test. Use them to identify major topics to emphasize in your review.

For each course, review any quizzes you have already taken; the same questions might appear on the final in a new form. In particular, learn how to solve any numerical problems you missed earlier.

6. Look over any essential handouts, maps, photocopies, or extra readings.

Be highly discriminating when reviewing these materials. For instance, in an outside reading, look for any good concrete examples that you might use in answering essay questions. However, always give lecture notes, your assigned text, and homework assignments higher priority than extra reading.

Slot Study Times on Your Review Schedule

After you complete your survey, work out your exam review schedule. Take a calendar and count how many days you have until exams; assess how many hours you have available to study each day. Then divide up the materials you need to review into the days you have left to study (adding any remaining assignments you still need to cover). **Schedule a specific number of lecture notes or text pages for each review session.** Use pencil so that you can adjust your schedule.

Revise Your Schedule Daily or as Necessary

See how far you get in your first study sessions. If you see you are falling behind, rethink your schedule. Devise a new strategy; perhaps move faster by postponing the less vital topics until you are back on schedule.

Throughout your review period, spend a few minutes each day evaluating how well your review schedule is working.

Look Over What You Have Reviewed

Every few days, **quickly review what you have already reviewed** to make sure the information remains fresh in your mind.

PRACTICE 1   Decide which of the suggestions for organizing your review sessions seem reasonable to you, and explain why. Explain why one or more of the suggestions might *not* work for you.

Catching Up If You've Fallen Behind

If you've fallen behind during the semester, you will have to complete late assignments and final papers as well as begin your review—not an ideal situation, but it can be done. Above all, resolve to work your hardest until exams are over.

First, concentrate on catching up; make a list of your remaining assignments and rank them according to importance. Assign a priority to each task, ranking it A, B, or C, and complete all A-priority matters first. Then move on to first B and then C tasks. Don't be a perfectionist on B and C tasks. Finish your overdue assignments as soon as possible so you can focus on your review.

Even if you are pressed for time, make a review schedule. Estimate how many days and how many hours you have available to **review the essential core** of lecture notes, reading assignments, or problem sets. If you run out of time, you will at least know the core material well enough to pass all your courses.

Monitor your review plan at each review session to see if you are on target; if not, rework your schedule. Don't allow yourself to lose momentum; if you are confused by some point, force yourself to go around it until you can ask for help from your instructor.

All through this intense period of study, motivate yourself by focusing on one very special thing you want to do as soon as exams are over.

Taking a Constructive Attitude Toward Studying for Exams

Keep a positive and healthy attitude through the days of your exam review. Remind yourself that this intensive study will help you **consolidate and pull together the work of the course.** Realizing how all these pieces fit together can be an invigorating experience as you begin to master a large and complicated body of knowledge.

If you are taking a course to further your professional career (physiology, say, for one of the health professions), your review sessions will help make the course a part of your permanent working knowledge.

Even if you think the course—perhaps a requirement—offers you no direct future benefits, remember that you are learning basic skills—how to set priorities, how to schedule tasks, how to evaluate material. Chances are that you will put these to use at some future point.

Go into Training

Before each big game, the coach of the football team recommends to athletes a sensible combination of diet, sleep, and practice workouts. This total concentration on the game ahead is accepted by team members as a way of getting the best results.

Set up a similar regime of good diet, sleep, exercise, and study sessions during your exam review. To keep yourself alert, exercise briefly several times a day to get your blood moving around and get oxygen to your brain. Avoid cutting down on your sleep. Over time, lack of sleep will make you sluggish, and you won't be able to study attentively.

Be sure to schedule some change of pace. During the exam review period, give yourself short mini-vacations each day—a thirty-minute or hour-long break—and do something enjoyable. Then get right back to the business of reviewing. The exam period will be over soon and then you can celebrate at length.

Put Exams in Perspective

Being underprepared for a test is a legitimate cause for worry. But even well-prepared students feel anxiety: there is far too much for you to remember; the question might be on the one topic you skipped; you might run out of time before finishing your exam review.

To reverse your negative thinking, always think of the overall picture. If you have prepared thoroughly, you should at least pass the exam, and you probably will do well. To ward off last-minute panic, our recommended technique of overlearning the material will help you settle down and do a good job once the test begins. See pages 246–248 for stress-relief techniques that have helped many students.

If you feel chronic, intolerable anxiety at the thought of tests, see a school counselor or psychologist for some personal guidance.

☐   PRACTICE 2

1. Give some reasons why exam review sessions are positive experiences.
2. Give some reasons why exam review sessions can become stressful; describe what you can do to relieve the stress.

The Most Effective Reviewing Methods

Adapt any of the following methods of active reviewing to help yourself study for exams. The point is to use your time wisely.

Some students waste time on passive busywork that does not produce the desired results. For example, mechanically recopying your lecture notes word for word takes too long and helps you too little. Instead, use your notes to make concise review sheets, using your own words to summarize the concepts. You are thereby actively rethinking and internalizing the material.

The review techniques we describe next reinforce your learning by visual (seeing), aural (hearing), and tactile (writing, diagraming) means. By involving several senses at once, you give yourself backup reserves when it comes to remembering.

Make Review or Study Sheets

Making *review* or *study sheets* is a highly effective technique for reviewing. It produces brief, condensed notes of essentials that you can review at various intervals—and one final time just before the exam.

First, reread a manageable section of your lecture notes or reading notes. Read quickly if you are familiar with the material and more deliberately if you are not. Then make a *condensed version* of your notes on lined $8\frac{1}{2}'' \times 11''$ loose sheets or in a large spiral-bound notebook. If you use separate sheets, you can reshuffle your notes more easily, putting the topics you have mastered aside and concentrating on the more difficult ones.

On these sheets, condense your notes on one lecture to about half a page. Reduce reading notes on one text chapter to a page or two.

As you work, rethink each concept until it is totally clear to you, and rephrase it briefly in your own words. Figure 11–1 shows reading notes from a text; Figure 11–2 shows a review sheet based on these reading notes.

The point is (1) to identify what is most important, and then (2) to create the most concise version of it for later review. In addition, you may want to put a star next to whatever needs more study.

Add Recall Clues to Your Notes

The technique of adding *recall clues* to the left margins of your notes will help you review both reading and lecture notes. Also add recall clues when making your condensed review sheets.

As you are reviewing your lecture or reading notes, periodically add a recall clue—a word or phrase that will jog your memory about a whole cluster of related information. In Figure 11–2, a student uses "4 floral parts" to recall a key page of her reading notes.

One way to use these recall clues is to cover the right-hand side of your notes, and, using the cue word to trigger your memory, recite or write down what you recall from your notes.

Use Index or Flash Cards to Memorize Essential Information

For information that you need to memorize, such as formulas or definitions, prepare index cards (or small slips of paper) with recall clues on one side and the answer on the other. Then shuffle the cards and review. (Carry these cards with you to study in your spare moments.) Once you know a card well, put it into a second pile, and concentrate on the cards you do not know. See Figure 11–3.

Create Study Questions Based on Key Topics or Themes

Many students find it helpful to create study questions. They compile and write down a series of questions based on the major topics or themes they identify in their lecture notes or reading notes. (Often they use the chapter headings to suggest additional study questions.) Later in their review, they answer their own questions, aloud or in writing, and then check to see how well they did. See Figure 11–4.

Think of Questions You Would Ask If You Were Making Up the Test

Some students find that they often can think of questions that the teacher in fact does ask. Others say they *rarely* think of the questions that actually appear on the test.

In any case, write down—and answer—questions that you would put on the test if you were the instructor. It is another way of approaching your review, and gets you out of simply rereading your notes mechanically.

Figure 11–1: Reading Notes—Informal Outline

Plant Reproduction

A. 4 sets of floral parts—each grows in ring or whorl

　　1. Sepals – outermost ring (all sepals together
　　　　　called calyx)
　　　　– usually green, are most like leaves
　　　　– protect unopened flower bud

　　2. Petals – next inner ring (all petals together
　　　　　called corolla)
　　　　– bright colors to set off from green leaves
　　　　– function is to attract pollinators to
　　　　　nectar (sweet liquid)
　　　　– provide pollinators a landing platform
　　　　– protect vital inner floral parts
　　　　– as pollinator (insect) drinks nectar, dusted
　　　　　with pollen and carries it to other flowers

　　3. Stamens – male flower part
　　　　– each stamen consists of long stalk (filament)
　　　　　topped by anther
　　　　– anther releases pollen grains containing male cells
　　　　– pollen released in large amounts through slits

　　4. Carpels – female flower part (also called simple
　　　　　pistil)
　　　　– stigma: sticky surface to capture pollen
　　　　– style: a thin stalk that supports stigma
　　　　– ovary: within are ovules or eggs; when
　　　　　fertilized develop into seed

B. In some species, male and female flowers grow
　　on different plants, called dioecious (holly)
C. In other species, male and female grow on same
　　plant, called monoecious (beech tree)

Figure 11–2: Review Sheet (Condensed Version of Reading Notes in Figure 11–1) with Recall Clues in Left Margin

Plant Repro

4 sets of floral parts

4 floral parts

1. sepals
   —outermost ring, green (like leaf), protects bud
2. petals
   —next ring, bright color, attracts and dusts pollinators, protects
3. stamens—male
   —filaments topped by anther; anther releases pollen
4. carpels—female
   —stigma (sticky), style, ovary (develops into seed)

monoecious
dioecious

monoecious: male and female on same plant
dioecious: male and female on separate plants
seed develops from fertilized ovule

Make Synthesis Sheets to Integrate Lecture and Reading Notes

If it applies to your course, try the technique of making *synthesis sheets.* When both lectures and readings cover the same topics or themes but each adds new material, integrate ideas from both sources on the same sheet. (Depending on how useful it is, add relevant material from handouts, additional readings, and so forth.)

This method encourages you to examine how the same topic is treated by your professor and by the textbook authors. You can see who gives a topic more emphasis, how it is connected to other topics, and how it applies in other contexts. Any study method that makes you actively work with the concepts in new ways will help you.

Make Yourself Visual Aids

On blank sheets of paper, experiment with making diagrams, drawings, or maps to help you visualize relationships. Then show connections by lines, boxes, arrows, stars, or circles. With this method, you picture key information to help you recall it.

Figure 11–3: Reviewing with Index Cards. The recall clue is on the right; the answer is on the left.

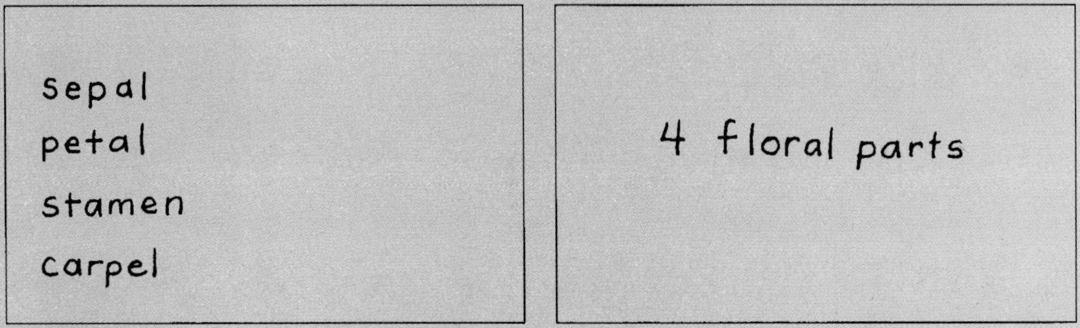

sepal
petal
stamen
carpel

4 floral parts

Figure 11–4: Questions Developed from Recall Clues in Figure 11–2

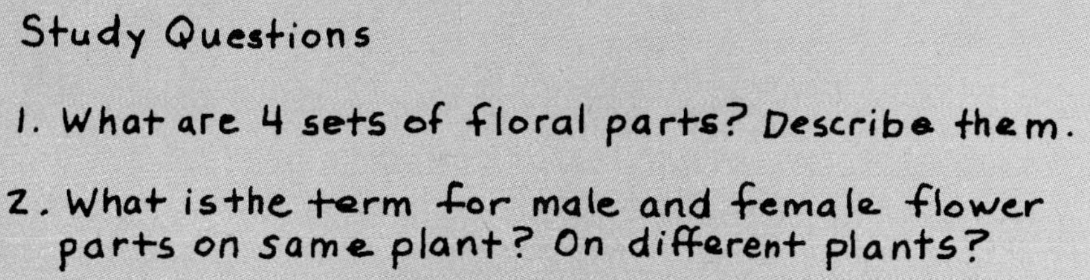

Study Questions

1. What are 4 sets of floral parts? Describe them.

2. What is the term for male and female flower parts on same plant? On different plants?

The student trying to remember the four rings of floral parts drew a rough diagram of the rings and labeled them (Figure 11–5).

Test Yourself

Self-testing can take many forms. If you have made up flash cards or written cue words in your notes, cover the answers and self-test by reciting or writing. Or use the study questions you have compiled earlier to test yourself.

Whatever form you use, self-testing is an active and effective study method. To use time efficiently, continue to review only those questions that you could not answer correctly.

Figure 11–5: Student's Diagram of Floral Parts

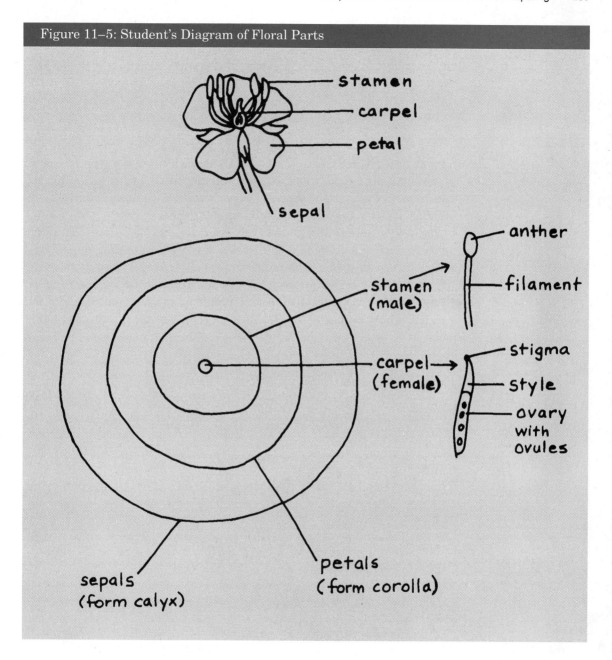

Ask Your Instructor If Computerized Review Material Is Available

In some courses, your teacher will steer you to computer-assisted reviews and study guides. If available, these are worth investigating.

Use a Tape Recorder

If appropriate, make a tape of selected items you want to remember and play it back to yourself.

Rework Problem Sets

In math and science courses, completely rework homework problems in old assignments without looking at what you did before to refamiliarize yourself with the thought process. Rework some of your old quizzes since a similar problem may appear on the upcoming exam.

Check your new work against your old answers. Make sure you thoroughly understand every step and how it derives from earlier steps. Look for and work additional problems in your text if you need more experience.

Go to every review session where the instructor works new or old problems. Pay extra attention to problems you have missed, and try to clarify what confused you. Speak to your instructor if you need additional help.

Using Computers for Review?

If you are a good typist and comfortable with your word processor, consider doing some of your review sheets or synthesis sheets on the computer. But if your keyboarding is too slow and eats into your study time, go back to handwritten notes.

For those students who have physical difficulties with handwriting, the computer may be an excellent solution for producing readable and well-organized study notes.

A Method for Memorizing

Say you have a list of essential formulas you must memorize for a test. Try learning the equations this way:

Write the first equation

$$PV = nRT$$

twice, while looking at it.

Then turn over your sheet or index card, and again write it out twice. Go on to the next equation; look at it and write it out twice. Then shut your notes and write it out twice again.

After five equations, practice all of them again. Meanwhile, make up mnemonic sentences to help you.

$$PV = nRT \text{ or } \text{"\underline{P}et \underline{v}ipers \underline{n}eed \underline{r}eal \underline{t}reats."}$$

The funnier the better. Review these equations daily.

PRACTICE 3

1. In a course you are now taking, take the lecture notes from one lecture and make a useful review sheet; add recall clues. How much were you able to condense the notes? Did you have difficulty deciding what was important?
2. Make some flash cards to help you review a course you are now taking. What are some advantages of flash cards as a method of learning?
3. Make a diagram or chart to visualize all the effective review methods described in this chapter.

Planning Your Essay Answers

If there is any chance that your exam will include essay questions, anticipate those questions before the exam day arrives.

Outline or diagram your answers on a series of large note cards that you can carry with you and flip through in spare moments.

To anticipate essay questions and plan your answers successfully, you need to know about the types of questions instructors frequently ask. Here are five common kinds of questions.

Comparing and Contrasting

Many instructors include exam questions that ask you to compare (cite similarities) or to contrast (cite differences between) two people, events, or objects:

Although Malcolm X and Martin Luther King had different approaches to improving the position of African-Americans, there were some similarities. Compare and contrast their positions.

In anticipation of a question like this one, make a note card that itemizes specific similarities or differences as we have done:

Malcolm X	**Martin Luther King**
took militant approach	took peaceful approach
advocated separation of races	advocated civil disobedience
converted to a Muslim	remained lifelong Christian
went to study in Mecca	remained in America
fought racism	fought racism
at end, began to emphasize new world with integration of races	permanently changed attitudes on civil rights in America
assassinated in prime	assassinated in prime

Tracing a Sequence or Process

Be prepared for questions that ask you to trace or outline the steps, stages, or events making up some larger sequence or process.

> According to Piaget, human intelligence develops through a series of distinct stages. Write an essay that traces those steps.

There is no need to prepare for questions like this in paragraph form. Instead, make a rough diagram to help you visualize (1) the individual steps or events, (2) the order and time frame in which they occur, and (3) any key terms used to characterize the individual steps or events (see Figure 11–6).

Analyzing Cause and Effect

Instructors often will include questions that ask you to explain how one or more events (the cause) led to or produced another event or events (the effect):

> Write a brief essay in which you explain how fear affects the human body.

If you anticipate this type of question, prepare yourself by drawing a diagram that illustrates the cause-and-effect relationship, as shown in Figure 11–7.

Figure 11–6: Diagram to Prepare for Essay Question on Piaget

Piaget's Stages of Cognitive Development from Infancy to Early Adolescence

Stage 1 Sensorimotor
(birth to age 2)

Child learns by touching and manipulating objects. By age 2, begins to use symbols

Stage 2 Preoperational
(age 2 to 7)

Language is major learning tool. Can remember past and anticipate future; categorizes on basis of single thing; more symbolic

Stage 3 Concrete Operations
(age 7 to 11)

Uses logical approach to solving concrete problems; organizes objects and events into classes

Stage 4 Formal Operations
(age 11 to 15)

Thinks abstractly; uses deductive thought and scientific problem solving

---

Figure 11–7: Diagram in Preparation for Cause-and-Effect Essay

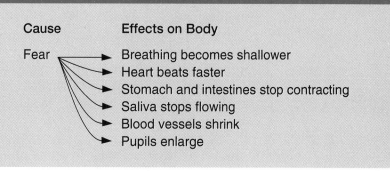

Cause	Effects on Body
Fear	Breathing becomes shallower
	Heart beats faster
	Stomach and intestines stop contracting
	Saliva stops flowing
	Blood vessels shrink
	Pupils enlarge

Characterizing or Describing

Some essay questions will ask you to characterize or describe events, people, or social change. The following is an example:

> How would you characterize the mood of America immediately following our failure to win the Vietnam War?

If you think you might be asked such a question, make a note card that lists key characteristics.

> **America After Vietnam**
> 1. Initial rejection of returning veterans
> 2. Sense of profound shock and disbelief
> 3. Needed more than a decade to come to grips with Vietnam
> 4. Americans polarized about how to view the war
> 5. Veterans angry and resentful

Giving Opinions Backed by Reasons

Many essay questions ask for your opinion. But the last thing the instructor wants in response is an *unsupported* opinion. Questions like the following ask you not only to take a stand but also to supply specific reasons for your position:

> During the last semester, we have discussed the controversy surrounding intelligence testing. What is your position on this issue? Do you believe that these tests accurately measure intelligence?

If you think you might face this type of question, formulate in advance a clear statement of your opinion. Then cite several strong reasons to support that opinion. Again, there is no need to write out the entire answer. A rough outline will do:

Opinion: Existing tests do not accurately measure human intelligence.

Reasons: 1. Questions rely on middle-class language and experience.
2. Tests predict success in school but do not predict success in later life.
3. Current research supports idea of many different kinds of intelligence that have to be measured in different ways.

Customize Your Review to Your Courses and Learning Style

No single reviewing technique works for every student or for every course. Customize your learning to suit each course and your personal learning style.

Develop an Overview of Each Course

As you study for your exams, take time to look for the overall framework of the course: Where did it start? Where is it now? What does it lead to? To see this framework, look only at the large topics or themes, and don't worry about the smaller issues and details. How do the large pieces fit together?

Make a visual illustration of the framework as you go. Use words and graphic devices—lines, circles, and arrows—to relate the key topics and show how they fit together. Refer to this diagram throughout your review.

Use the Study Aids in Your Textbook

Use your whole textbook—both what was assigned and any other useful sections—to guide your review. Use the opening pages of both the units and the chapters to help you grasp the *objectives* of the text. Check the *glossary* for definitions. Use the *index* to find where a topic is discussed in other places; use the *table of contents* and *preface* to identify the structure of the book, its major topics and subtopics. Make use of the *headings* in each chapter to aid your review and to help you formulate review questions.

If your text has them, use time lines, chapter objectives, summaries, and study questions. Many texts have built-in aids to assist your review—boldface type for terms; boxes; appendixes; and maps.

The Effectiveness of Group Study

Group study has some advantages. It will help you find out what others taking the course identify as important topics. And it may help you solidify your own learning if, for example, you can explain to others how to work problems. If it remains a serious study session, group study also can help you learn how to solve problems you could not figure out when working alone. Group study, however, is an inefficient method of studying if time is short. Usually not enough time will be spent on what *you* don't know.

Review in High Alert

It is almost useless to read your text or notes while in a tired or passive state. **Take over. Question and direct yourself.** The secret of good test preparation is to **be in the moment,** participating fully. To keep alert, give yourself directions like these:

1. **Is what I am reading right now important?** If yes, why? Should I make a review sheet now, or wait until I finish this section to decide how important it is?
2. **If this is a major principle, what can I associate it with** so that I can remember it? What are some examples of it?
3. If this is a minor point, should I spend time on it? Should I use it to remind me of how the major principle works? Or study it later if I have time?
4. *If this is an example,* is it the best one to explain the principle or point? How many examples do I need to write a good essay answer?
5. Since this is an anecdote in the text, I can skim it. But this instructor uses anecdotes in lectures to highlight his key theories. I'll learn those key theories.
6. If I can make associations, I can remember A leads to B leads to C; and A has four rings and B has seven parts. I will try to discover *patterns, repetitions,* and *similarities;* I can remember connected items more easily than isolated facts.
7. Since this section seems easy and self-evident, I'll move through it quickly—to save time for harder concepts.

Three Aids for Test Anxiety

Research shows that test anxiety can hamper the performance of good students as well as weak ones. Researchers recommend that greater self-awareness can help students manage and reduce test anxiety. As a first step, determine how you usually react to an exam.

Do you become distracted by worries about how you are performing during the test? ("I've only done three problems and I'm running out of time.") Do you feel the onset of physical symptoms, such as muscle tension or stomach cramps? Or do you suffer from an inability to concentrate on the test questions?

To combat these problems, learn in advance to direct your attention back to concentrating on the test questions rather than on distracting and self-defeating thoughts. The following three techniques are the ones most often recommended by researchers.

Reframing or Restructuring

With the technique of reframing (also called *cognitive restructuring*), you become aware of the worries that usually hamper you during the test. You face these worries head-on by verbalizing them or writing them down. Say you write down your typical test-anxious notion: "I'm not going to do well on this test." Then you quickly contradict and challenge your statement: "I have passed tests before, and I have made it all the way to college. Clearly I am capable of passing tests. I will even get a good grade if I keep to my study schedule." The reframing provides reassurance.

Muscle Relaxation

To induce muscle relaxation, first tighten and then release muscle groups in order to produce a relaxation response at the first sign of anxiety. With this technique, you tense each muscle group, hold it for a few counts, and then release the tension. Repeat this sequence for every major muscle group in your body.

Finally all the muscles are tensed together, held, and then relaxed. With repetitions of this technique, you will be able to induce relaxation when you need it. The idea is to become more attuned to tension and enable yourself to interrupt it at an early stage. For each muscle, tense and inhale; then relax and exhale. Prior to exams, do these exercises *slowly* for a total of fifteen to twenty minutes.

After several weeks, you should be able to stop tensing your muscles and promote relaxation simply by telling yourself to relax from head to toe:

Fists:	Clench your right fist. Hold. Feel the tension. Relax. Notice the difference. Again clench your right fist. Repeat with your left and with both fists.
Biceps:	Bend first your right, then your left elbow, tensing biceps.
Triceps:	Straighten arms; feel tension along the back of your arms.
Forehead:	Frown; wrinkle your forehead.
Eyes:	Shut your eyes tightly.
Jaw:	Clench your jaw moderately.
Lips:	Press together.
Neck:	Bend your head forward and backward, then roll it right and left.

Continue for the remaining muscle groups in your chest, stomach, lower back, thighs, calves, and ankles.

Imaginary Rehearsal

With this strategy, you rehearse a *desired behavior* in your mind, vividly imagining the scene. You might imagine yourself in the process of taking an exam, feeling strong and in control, and doing well. Then imagine yourself at the exam but the feared anxiety is setting in; immediately visualize yourself taking deep breaths and giving yourself positive instructions: "Focus on the exam, nothing else." Or repeat a short word cue such as "relax" or "be calm."

After several imaginary rehearsals, you should be able to use the cue words during the exam—and feel relaxation instead of anxiety.

Reduce Test Anxiety by Knowing More About the Test

Ask your instructor what kinds of questions to prepare for. Will the test be largely multiple choice, or should you prepare for essay questions as well? Once you know the types of questions, you can gear your reviews to the kinds of questions you'll be asked. You'll feel more in charge and better able to control any anxiety. For more on the various types of test questions, see Chapter 12.

Cramming as an Emergency Measure

Although, in an emergency, cramming *may* help you pass an exam, it is *not* an effective method of learning the material of a course. When you cram, you shortchange yourself. You master neither the subject matter nor the skills associated with preparing for exams (organizing material, selecting the essentials, and so forth). As a result, you might not be fully prepared to take more advanced courses.

Furthermore, cramming definitely increases anxiety levels because you know you are taking shortcuts in your studying.

Our advice—to study and review systematically throughout the semester—still holds true. But if you do get far behind in one course (or in one semester), here is some advice. If you must cram, make sure you have a method.

> * Cramming is *not* an effective method of mastering the material of a course.

A Six-Step Method for Cramming

1. Be highly selective about what you study.

Look over and list the most important topics that were covered in both your lectures and readings. Check the topics that received the most attention during lectures. Concentrate on these; they have the greatest chance of being covered in the exam. Yes, you do run the risk that the topics you ignore will appear on the exam, but you run an even greater risk if you try to study everything at once. Your mind will not absorb all that material in a brief amount of time.

2. Assess your strengths and weaknesses.

Now look at the topics you have checked. Are there any that you feel fairly confident about discussing (perhaps because you knew something about the topic before you took the class or because your personal interest in it made you pay special attention during the lectures)? Spend only one study session working your way through this material. Use most of your time to concentrate on the remaining topics, the ones you feel less sure of.

3. Determine your priorities.

If you have made the mistake of failing to prepare for *all* of your exams, don't, at the last minute, consider trying to cram for all of them. Decide which of your exams are most important in terms of your long-term goals and study for them the most. And by all means, speak to your counselor about strategies to tide you over.

4. Study in two-hour shifts, taking an hour break between them.

Marathon cramming without adequate breaks will confuse and exhaust you. Try instead to **schedule two-hour sessions throughout the day.** Every two hours, make sure you take an hour-long break to let yourself completely unwind; take a walk, play music, or jog around the campus. When you return to study, you will feel fresh and able to concentrate.

5. Use all of the review techniques described earlier in this chapter.

In the previous pages, we introduced particular strategies for making the most of your review sessions. Don't ignore them when you cram. On the contrary, they are even more essential when you have to make the most of every minute. Don't forget to make review sheets, develop recall clues, and anticipate test questions.

6. Know when to stop.

When you cram, **monitor the quality of your concentration.** If you take a break for an hour and return still feeling exhausted, it's time to quit and go to sleep. Don't assume that every hour spent studying will have an equal return in information learned. When you are overtired, the quality of your concentration decreases; in this way, you can spend time studying without really learning.

If, after cramming, you make it through your exams successfully, make a vow that in the future you will begin exam reviews much earlier.

Working Space

READING ASSIGNMENT

Read the following selection, "College Material" by student Alice Ellis. Then answer the questions that follow.

With the one exception of not having had much sleep the night before, I felt just about ready for my very first test at college.

I had in fact spent the last two weeks doing nothing other than studying chemistry reactions. As a newcomer to chemistry, I had done most of what my instructor had suggested to prepare for the hour-long test. I reworked problems, attended review sessions, and made dozens of review sheets on what to review. And I worried about the test now and then. I needed to pass my first college exam to prove to myself I was college material. And chemistry was, no question, my hardest class, serious stuff.

Although everyone—counselors, parents, my old high school teachers—suggested you get a good night's sleep before any tests, I hadn't done it. Not out at a party or out at a movie, but in my pajamas at about eleven, I pulled up the covers to my eyes and waited for the usual falling asleep, but I noticed I was awake whenever I checked. At midnight, I was still awake when I heard my roommate turn out her light. I hoped I wasn't going to have a problem with sleeplessness; I had had a sleepless night before my college entrance tests—not one minute of sleep the entire night.

My dorm room was located right next to the steeple of the chapel and I could hear the bells ring out in the pitch dark on the hour, the half hour, the quarter hour. It was a muted booming sound, usually very enjoyable. I thought of everyone else on the campus in bed asleep.

I thought of my dog who jumped all over you until you told her she was a good dog and you loved her. Then she calmed down. I thought how my parents were coming for parents' weekend and I would meet them right after my chemistry test, and I thought I would wear a new wool sweater my mother had bought me so that I'd look in style in college. I thought a little of my chemistry review sheets and started thinking of reactions. I thought of every thought in my head, to keep me from thinking that I hadn't yet fallen asleep. I thought the night away.

When my alarm clock was about to go off at seven, I decided to stop trying to fall asleep and to stand up and turn it off. I felt shaky as I stood up, as if I hadn't had enough sleep to function or think my best, but I would have to use whatever mind I had. I took a warm shower hoping to revive my thick head. I felt as if I could fall asleep very quickly if I lay down now. I put on the new wool sweater with the diamond patterns to look in good shape for my parents—to look as if I were college material.

As I took the exam in a big friendless hall, I noticed it was freezing cold for early fall, and no one had turned on the heat. As an added irritation, every time I went to write on my exam booklet, my new sweater kept getting caught on a little sharp nail that stuck out of the old desk. No matter where I put my writing right arm, the nail pulled out another thread of my wool sweater. After a bit, I thought I would have to sacrifice my new sweater. Later, Bob Pear, one of my friends from chemistry, asked, "Why didn't you ask the monitor to change your desk? The monitor would have let you; it was an honest problem."

I was new to taking exams in big halls; at my old high school, we took them in the classroom with the teacher, not some unknown monitor who was there to prevent anyone from cheating. "It never crossed my mind to ask," I told Bob Pear. "I was too busy thinking about how to do the chemistry reactions." I had scanned the test and I saw that a few of the problems at the end seemed doable, so I did those. Then I started doing a few at the beginning that seemed slightly familiar. But halfway through, I knew I would never finish—just too many problems that were too hard. If they had given me five hours, I might have finished all those problems. I began to feel as if I might not be college material after all. Maybe I could learn to drive a taxi or become a dog catcher.

And my sweater kept getting shredded as I would go to put down an answer. I began to feel worried about not even passing the test and thought how disappointed I'd would be, after putting in all those hours studying. If I hadn't studied at all, I could have failed just as easily.

Toward the very end, feeling that my mind was just not up to the challenge, I wrote in whatever little I could remember to show what I knew about various problems, but not enough to solve them. At my high school I used to solve the problems on my tests and finish in time. College was in some other league, filled with the brighter people from all over the state.

Right to the minute, the monitor announced, "Shut your exam books; the exam is over." I was writing down a final guess when the monitor stopped me with his command to quit, and I quit.

I then had to meet my parents, explain the threads hanging off my arm, and pretend I was not in academic trouble in my very first semester.

I went through the motions of enjoying the activities with my parents, but I kept thinking of the chemistry problems I had missed and seeing as I hadn't come close to finishing the test, I knew I couldn't have passed it.

I didn't have the heart to look when the grades were posted. Bob Pear said the average was low, that lots of people did a bad job. The grades were up for three days, but I felt too miserable to look.

At the next class, I was not surprised to get my exam book with a 59 in a circle, but I was surprised to see "Good job" written at the top. What was the instructor thinking of?

I had never heard of a curve—the professor putting all the grades on a curve so that my 59 was one of the less miserable marks. That totally amazed me. I had never heard of partial credit; all my little pathetic efforts to get going gave me partial credit that added up. And I had never heard of an exam too long for anyone in the class to finish it.

Despite all the misery of the last week, it looked as if I was, somehow or other, college material.

1. What are some of the things the student telling the story did not know about college exams?

2. What do you think the student means by "college material"?

3. What was one thing the student did before an exam that all advisers advise against?

4. What were some of the helpful things the student did in studying for her first exam?

WRITING ASSIGNMENT

Write a short personal essay about past experiences you have had with tests—both good and bad. Did you ever get a much better grade than you thought you deserved? When you did poorly, did you understand why?

JOURNAL ASSIGNMENTS

1. Describe the problems you have had with reviewing for tests in the past. Which of the techniques described in this chapter are you willing to try during your next exam period?
2. Discuss the following quote: "The time spent reviewing for exams allows the student to pull together and learn the material of the course and is therefore more valuable than the exam itself."

✔ Checking Out: Review Questions for Chapter 11

1. Describe three techniques you can use to reduce test anxiety.

2. What are recall clues and where do you use them?

3. What are some ways to self-test? Why is this a good way to review?

4. How do you prepare review sheets and what is their purpose?

5. Why is it important to revise your exam review schedule regularly?

6. What are synthesis sheets and what are they used for?

7. During exam reviews, how should you handle sleep and exercise? Should you study nonstop or take breaks?

8.   Name two advantages of overlearning.

9.   What are the advantages and disadvantages of a study group?

10.   What materials should you survey before setting up your review schedule?

▶ In Summary

The true secret of college success is to begin to study and review early in the term. Then begin your actual exam review early so that you can cover all the material you need to cover. Make up a review schedule by estimating the time it will take you to review lecture notes and text notes, to rework problem sets, and so forth. Your lecture notes are an important clue to what your instructor finds most significant.

Keep adjusting your schedule to reflect the actual pace of your reviewing. Select methods of active reviewing that will help you cover the material in your specific courses. Among the most useful study methods are creating review sheets, writing out study questions, using index cards, self-questioning, adding recall clues to notes, making your own visual aids, making synthesis sheets, and involving several senses in remembering.

Most important, always study in high alert, making ongoing decisions about how to review the topic at hand, how important the topic is in the course, and what study method you can use to learn it best.

Among the methods most useful for relieving test anxiety are the reframing of negative thoughts into a more positive mode, systematic muscle relaxation, and imaginary rehearsals.

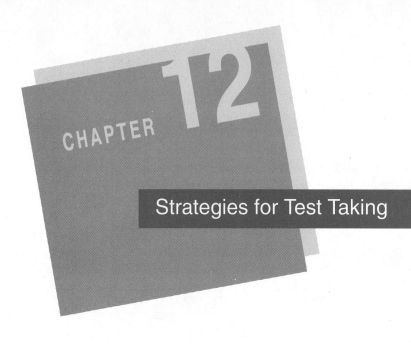

CHAPTER 12

Strategies for Test Taking

"Tests go on for as long as we live."
—Virginia Voeks, author

To do your best on a test or exam, learn test-taking strategies to maximize your performance. At the same time, learn how to avoid common mistakes that lower your grade—especially painful if you knew the answer. This chapter covers:

- Being ready on the day of the exam
- Learning strategies for passing objective tests
- Understanding the format of multiple-choice questions
- How to answer multiple-choice, true-or-false, fill-in-the-blank, short-answer, identification, and matching questions
- Solving numerical problems by equations
- Understanding essay questions

Being Ready on the Day of the Exam: The Right Mind-Set

You want to be at your best for the day of your test or your final exam. So consider the factors that will help you perform at your best.

Be Early Rather Than Late

Find out in advance where and when the exam is being held, and make sure you are there on time. It is better to be ten or fifteen minutes early rather than one minute late.

It's a good idea to sit quietly by yourself looking at your review notes or cards, ready for the concentrated work ahead. Keep yourself in a positive, confident state of mind, giving yourself encouraging messages.

Bring the Equipment You Need

Find out what equipment you'll need, assemble it the night before, and bring it to the exam. Do you need a calculator, sharpened pencil and erasers, a list of equations allowed for the exam, a handbook, cough drops? Be sure to think through what you need and bring it all. For example, make sure your contact lenses or glasses are clean and ready.

Bring Your Watch

Check your watch periodically to learn if you are running behind and need to change your strategy. When half the exam is over, you want to know if you have answered over half the questions.

If you are behind, shift gears and answer each question more quickly—and in less detail—in order to finish all the questions.

Wear Comfortable Clothes

Plan to wear loose, comfortable clothes. Bring along a sweater in case you feel cold, or be ready to take off a layer if you become too warm. Don't be caught in an itchy sweater or a tight pair of pants.

Be Wholly in the Moment of the Test

Sit at the front of the room. You will be able to hear what is going on, see what is on the board, and ignore what other students are doing.

Once the exams are handed out, your job is to give your full self and your undivided concentration to doing your best on the test. This is your time to prove what you know: to explain principles, to use good examples, to work problems efficiently, to **let the teacher know everything you have learned.** Do not be cautious about answering. Give full and complete answers. If you are unsure of how much to write, err on the side of providing too much.

Follow the Directions for Taking the Exam

If the directions ask you to answer only *three* of the five essay questions, and you forget and answer all five, you are putting yourself in avoidable trouble. You will be pressed for time to answer the remaining questions that count.

Instead of answering too much, some students neglect to turn the page to the last questions, and hurt their final grade by answering too little. Our very important point here is to **read the directions intensively several times,** underline key points, and refer back to them during the test.

If you are unsure of something, raise your hand for the monitor and ask for clarification.

Look Over the Entire Test Immediately

Preview the kinds of questions asked and the number of points allotted for each question. See if the exam is divided into sections and establish how much time and credit are given for each individual part. With this preview, you can begin to budget your time, allowing a few minutes at the end for proofreading your test.

Allot the Appropriate Amount of Time for Each Question

At the start of the exam, calculate the appropriate amount of time for each portion of the exam, giving the most time to those sections offering the most points. If the essay section of the test is worth 80 points out of 100, do not spend more than a few minutes on a multiple-choice section worth 20 points. Even if you get all the multiple-choice questions right, you still have only 20 points.

As you work, check your watch and notice when your time limit for each section is up. Too often, students get involved in completing one section of the exam and run out of time to complete the rest, a miscalculation that harms their final score.

Answer Every Question

Except in standarized tests where you may be penalized for guessing, it is a good strategy to answer every question. In multiple-choice questions, you can improve your chances of being right if you can eliminate a few wrong options. In short-answer questions, essay questions, or numerical problems, try to get as much **partial credit** as possible.

Don't Leave Early: Proofread and Check

Some students may leave the exam early, but you want to stay in your seat and (1) review what you have written, (2) **reread the directions one final time,** and (3) check to see that you have done each section and have answered every question. These final checks can keep you from making a foolish blunder.

PRACTICE 1   In a two-hour exam, how much time should you spend on two long essays worth 50 points, two short essays worth 30 points, and a true-false and a multiple-choice section each worth ten points (allowing time for previewing and proofing)?

Strategies for Passing Objective Tests

Good test-taking strategies will help you get the grade you deserve and often gain you some additional points. Even more important, these skills will prevent you from losing points that you should earn.

Most of the material on the exam you will probably recall from studying; some of it may cover material that you deliberately decided not to study and are therefore shaky about; and some may cover material that appears totally unfamiliar to you.

Obviously, you want to get credit for all that you know, so by all means first complete the questions you know and can answer well. For the remaining questions, you will have to answer by relying on common sense and your general knowledge of the subject; and you may have to do some intelligent guesswork.

Always Read Exam Questions with Care

Students make a common mistake when taking tests; they misread the question, give the wrong answer, and lose points on a question they knew how to answer—a sad but too familiar story. Don't let this happen to you.

Just before you take any exam for any course, remind yourself to **read each question with care;** do an attentive and analytical reading, mentally paraphrasing the question. Each additional reading will make clearer just what the question is asking.

Are You Asked to Recall or to Recognize?

Some test questions ask you to *recall* information that you have stored in your memory. When you are asked to fill in a blank or write a short essay, you have to access the information in your memory by some association or connection that you made as you studied.

With other types of questions, you are asked to *recognize* and select the correct answer from those given. In multiple-choice questions you must *recognize* the answer rather than *recall* it.

Since exams often combine different types of questions, it is probably safer to count on recalling information from your memory rather than to depend on recognizing the answer when you see it. In the former case, you have achieved a more intensive level of learning.

Understanding the Format of Multiple-Choice Questions

Multiple-choice questions are currently the most popular type of question on objective tests.

In multiple-choice questions, the student chooses the correct answer from among four or five options. In each case, only one of the options is correct. The others are incorrect choices known as *distractors,* plausible answers but not the right or the best answer. Distractors are intended to throw the less-attentive student off the track.

In one common type of multiple-choice question, an incomplete statement (the *stem*) leads to four or five possible endings, but only one ending completes it correctly or best. Usually all the endings have the same grammatical construction (they are either all nouns, phrases, or clauses).

stem
    The organization that preceded the United Nations in working for world peace was called

optional
answers
    a. the League for World Peace
    b. the League of Nations
    c. the Society of World Nations
    d. the Society for the Promotion of One World
    e. the United Nations of the World

(The answer here is the League of Nations.)

In the second common format for multiple choice, a complete question is followed by the optional answers.

What organization followed the unsuccessful League of Nations in attempting to achieve world peace?

a. the World Peace League
b. the United Nations
c. the League of World States
d. Nations for Peace
e. United Countries of the World

(The answer here is the United Nations.)

At times, you may be asked to mark not one but *all* the correct answers in a multiple-choice question, so, again, read the directions with care.

Tips for Answering Multiple-Choice Questions

1. For each multiple-choice question, **read the stem with every option** to determine which answer works best. Read with maximum attention; there may be only small differences among options.

    Some counselors suggest that you read the stem and then think of the answer *before* you read the options—to set you on the right track.

2. **Don't mark the answer until you have read all the options.**
   In some cases, you will be looking for the *best* answer, and you have
   to read all the options to find it.

3. **Cross out any options that you believe are incorrect.** For
   each option you can eliminate, you increase your chances of finding
   the right answer from those that remain.

4. **Even if the stem of the question sounds unfamiliar, read
   through all the options;** one of them might jog your memory.
   Some successful test takers say they (1) read the question to get
   the gist of it; (2) *read, analyze, and compare the optional answers
   very carefully;* and (3) finally go back to the question before making
   their choice.

5. **Pace yourself. Move on. Don't get bogged down** on one confusing question. Stay on each question only as long as the time allowed
   for each. Especially if most of a question is unfamiliar and you are
   stuck on it, force yourself to move on. You are hurting yourself by
   not turning to other questions that you know.

6. **Answer every question** (unless you know there is a penalty for
   guessing). A blank gets you no credit; a guess might get some. If
   you don't know the answer, make a quick guess based on common
   sense, picking an answer that sounds possible. See page 263 on how
   test-wise students make shrewd guesses.
   Since you have already spent time reading each question, *answer
   the questions in order, but put a check next to those you have doubts
   about*—in case you have more time at the end.

7. **Missing a few multiple-choice questions isn't serious**. Don't
   begin to feel anxious if you come across some unfamiliar questions.
   Usually enough questions are asked so that each one only counts a
   few points. You can miss some and still do well.
   Keep all your thinking concentrated on the questions, not on how
   you are doing on the test.

8. **Underline key words in the question,** those words on which the
   meaning hinges. Pay attention to verbs, to prepositions such as *except,* to qualifiers that limit the statement (such as *usually, sometimes, frequently, generally*), and to negatives that reverse the
   meaning of the statement, such as *not, never,* and prefixes that
   stand for *not* (*un*exceptional, *il*logical, *ir*replaceable).

9. Many students are confused when the answers have options such
   as *none of the above; all of the above; A, B, and D;* or *A, C, and D.*

As you read down the options, **mark next to each option *T* for true or *F* for false.** Then you can more easily see that *A, B, and D* are all true and thus the right combination.

10. If you eliminate options one by one but find that the last one is clearly not the right answer, start again.

What Test-Wise Students Know About Multiple Choice

Always try to answer the questions based on your knowledge of the course. If, however, you cannot answer the question without guessing, here are some tips from test-savvy students on how to guess.

We caution that these tips do not *always* apply, especially when the test constructors are alert to them.

1. The correct answer sometimes is longer and more detailed than the wrong answers.
2. The distractors are sometimes alike, and the answer is the one option that is different.
3. Grammatical awkwardness between the stem and the options may give away some of the distractors that are wrong.
4. Watch for all-inclusive terms like *all, never,* and *always;* they are more likely to be incorrect. On the other hand, the right answer is often signaled by qualifying words such as *sometimes, maybe, usually, generally,* and so forth.

For Those Who Have Trouble with Multiple Choice

For those who consistently do poorly on multiple-choice questions, we have a few suggestions.

1. **Do not overinterpret the questions** looking for subtle distinctions among the options. The answer is meant to be straightforward and not deliberately obscure. Look for the most obvious, direct answer.
2. **Reading and answering multiple-choice questions takes a great deal of mental effort.** It is not uncommon to feel mounting pressure. Just be aware that reading and thinking under pressure can be stressful and that some students feel more stress than

others. Most of all, assure yourself that, **under stress, you can still do well.**

3. A multiple-choice test *does not allow you to demonstrate all that you do know,* which can be frustrating if you have studied the material. You will have other opportunities to prove yourself.

4. *Practice taking all kinds of multiple-choice tests* to get used to deciding among four or more options; if possible, get earlier exams and try to answer the questions within the time limit.

☐ PRACTICE 2   Answer these multiple-choice questions.

1. A multiple-choice test is
   a.   a subjective test
   b.   an objective test
   c.   both subjective and objective
   d.   a test that requires little thinking
   e.   a test that requires recalling information

2. In the multiple-choice format, the stem
   a.   is misleading information planted in the question
   b.   is misleading information planted in the options
   c.   is a complete statement leading to the options
   d.   is an incomplete statement leading to the options
   e.   is intended to confuse unprepared students

3. In a multiple-choice test, read all the optional answers because
   a.   each gives information about the others
   b.   the right answer is usually near the end
   c.   it helps to write *true* or *false* beside each option
   d.   you want to cross out all the wrong options
   e.   you want to choose the most correct answer

4. If you don't know anything about the question,
   a.   don't bother reading the options
   b.   pick any option and mark it as correct
   c.   come back to the question if you have time
   d.   read all the options to jog your memory
   e.   mark as correct the shortest answer

5. If you see as an option "all of the above,"
   a.   mark it as correct
   b.   mark each option *true* or *false*
   c.   pick any option except this one
   d.   cross out all the distractors
   e.   look for the most plausible answer among the other options

6. A distractor is
   a.   an answer in disguised form
   b.   a plausible answer but not the correct one
   c.   one of the answers if the option says "a, c, and e"
   d.   the answer when "all of the above" is an option
   e.   usually a misleading fact in the question
7. Multiple-choice questions require
   a.   recall of the right answer
   b.   recognition of the right answer
   c.   a basic knowledge of test construction
   d.   that you rank options in order of correctness
   e.   that you pick the answer before reading the options

Tips for Answering True-or-False Questions

In true-or-false questions, your instructor asks you to decide if a statement is correct or incorrect. As in multiple choice, you need to recognize the right or *true* answer, not recall it from memory. But your odds of answering correctly on this type of question are higher than in multiple choice (two choices versus four or more).

1. Read every word carefully in true-or-false questions; you have less to read than in multiple-choice questions so think through the meaning of each statement.
2. Underline any phrase that you think might make the statement questionable or untrue. **If any part of the statement is untrue, it makes the whole statement false.**

   Leonardo da Vinci painted three of the most widely recognized paintings of the Renaissance: the mural *The Last Supper;* the fresco ceiling of the Sistine Chapel; and the oil painting *Mona Lisa.* T or F

   (Since one part is false—Michelangelo, not Leonardo da Vinci, painted the Sistine Chapel—this statement is false.)
3. Answer every question; when you guess, **you have a 50 percent chance of being correct** on each question; in multiple choice, you have only a 20–25 percent chance of guessing correctly.
4. Often the true-or-false section counts for only a small part of the overall score. Don't waste time to collect a few points when you can help yourself far more on other sections of the test.
5. Assume each question requires a direct, straightforward response.

Charles Darwin, in his highly influential book *Species Plantarum,* first gave accurate botanical names to plants and is considered the father of modern botany. T or F

To answer this question, you must recognize that Darwin's best-known book is not *Species Plantarum* but *On the Origin of the Species.* It is the Swedish scientist Linnaeus who is credited with giving accurate botanical names to plants. The statement is therefore false.

6. Students often are advised to mark true-or-false questions using all-inclusive words as false. These words (*all, always, every,* and *none*) often make a statement false because very few things are *always* true. But beware of the exceptions:

   All Chief Justices of the United States Supreme Court have been men. T or F

   (Even with the "all," this statement is true.)

7. If you are uncertain and have to guess, try guessing *true* because teachers often include more true than false questions.

8. **Remember to convert two negatives into a positive,** for example:

   "*not un*trustworthy" means trustworthy
   "*not un*clear" means clear

Tips for Answering Fill-in-the-Blank Questions

A fill-in-the-blank question requires that you *recall* or pull the answer out of your memory rather than recognize it from choices given to you. Students who are well prepared welcome fill-in-the-blank questions because they lack the possible confusion of multiple-choice distractors. If you know the material, you can pick up some relatively easy points.

1. Use as clues *all* the words given in the statement to be completed. Thinking about them together may jog your memory.
2. Use the length of the blank to guide you on roughly how much to write. But if you have more to say, fit it in the margin. It's better to say too much than not enough.

   Also check to see whether the blank requires a single word, a short phrase, or a longer clause to fill in the missing information.
3. If you have doubts, plan how to word your answer in the margin.

4. Be as specific as possible, using the dates, facts, concepts, definitions, and terms that you know.
5. If you know some of the answer but not all, by all means put down everything you know for partial credit.

   If you don't know a specific fact or date, try not to leave a blank; add some information that shows approximately when the event happened—or whatever else you know about it.
6. After you have filled in the blank, reread the entire statement to make sure your addition is consistent with what was given.

Tips for Answering Identification Questions

These questions usually ask you to identify a list of items—names, places, events, terms, dates, or numbers. You also want to add why the item is significant. Provide as much specific information as you can in the time allowed. If you have only a vague idea, put in as much as you know. Partial credit is always better than no credit.

Tips for Answering Short-Answer Questions

1. Just as in identification questions, you have to recall the answers to short-answer questions from memory. If you have studied your notes well, you probably can call to mind most of the answers fairly quickly.
2. Usually you will be asked to explain some event or concept discussed in the lectures or in the text. To develop your best answer (providing you have time), **plan what you want to say** in the margin, jotting down a quick list of points.
3. Here is your chance to **let the teacher know what you know;** you have more freedom than in true-or-false or multiple choice, so take advantage of it. Provide good examples to support your point, or back up your generalization with particular instances.

   If you see an unfamiliar question or one for which you neglected to study, don't waste time worrying about it. Your time and energy are better spent on the questions that you *do* know the answers to.
4. Check the directions to see if your instructor wants your answer in complete sentences or in phrases. If in doubt, use complete sentences; they are clearer for a reader to understand. If you are running out of time, however, a list with all the information is your best alternative.

Tips for Answering Matching Questions

In this type of question, you are given two columns of answers that you must match. Follow the directions on how to answer—whether with letters or numbers. Usually you are not allowed to draw lines to make the matches.

At times, the columns will have uneven numbers of items so that some items will go unmatched.

1. First, **read down both sides of the columns but do not mark any answers.**
2. Tentatively mark those answers you are most certain of first. If you make a mistake early in your matching, you create trouble for yourself later. **Cross out the options you have matched as you choose them.** Though the pool of choices will get smaller, the remaining choices will be less familiar to you.
3. Continue to make tentative matches until you think you have a good match for all the required items. Then write your final answers.

PRACTICE 3   Match the following items, using any reference works you wish.

_____ 1. Georgia O'Keeffe

_____ 2. Frank Lloyd Wright

_____ 3. Ralph Ellison

_____ 4. Henry David Thoreau

_____ 5. Martin Luther King

_____ 6. N. Scott Momaday

_____ 7. Mark Twain

_____ 8. Walt Whitman

_____ 9. Paul Revere

_____ 10. Ralph Waldo Emerson

a. designed silverware; hero of the American Revolution

b. painted flowers, skulls, the American Southwest

c. in his essays, urged Americans to write about American culture

d. wrote autobiography of a self-made man; studied electricity

e. wrote a long poem on the death of Lincoln

f. wrote *The Way to Rainy Mountain;* Kiowa Indian

g. designed "Falling Water"

h. wrote *The Invisible Man*

i. led civil rights demonstrations

j. wrote *The Adventures of Huckleberry Finn* and other comic works

k. wrote *Walden*

_____ 11. Benjamin Franklin

_____ 12. Langston Hughes

_____ 13. Harriet Beecher Stowe

l. wrote "A Dream Deferred" and other poetry

m. designed arch over the Mississippi River

n. wrote *Uncle Tom's Cabin*

o. was a well-known American composer

Solving Numerical Problems by Setting Up Equations

In scientific and engineering courses, chemical reactions, the flight of projectiles, the flow of electrical current, and the reaction of gases are a few of the physical phenomena expressed in equations.

As a simple example, you know that if you drive your car at a constant speed of 50 miles per hour for two hours, you will travel 100 miles. We can write an equation to express this result:

$$s = vt \qquad \text{[Equation 1]}$$

where s = distance traveled

v = the constant speed or velocity

t = time of travel

In Equation 1, s is called a *dependent variable* because it depends on the values of v and t: v and t are called *independent variables*.

Using Equation 1, you can find out the distance that your car travels by setting v = 50 miles per hour and t = 2 hours.

$$s = vt$$

$$s = 50 \ (2) = 100 \text{ miles}$$

In a more complicated problem, where two cars traveling at different speeds are involved, we will have to use some thought and common sense to apply Equation 1 to find a solution.

For example, let us assume that the distance between your school and your friend's school is 180 miles. If you and your friend leave your schools at the same time, how long will it take you to meet? How far will each car travel?

Assume your car goes at a constant speed of 30 miles per hour and your friend's car goes at a constant speed of 60 miles per hour.

To prepare to solve such a problem in a test-taking situation, first **read the problem carefully until you understand it.** Second, **draw a sketch** to show the physical situation.

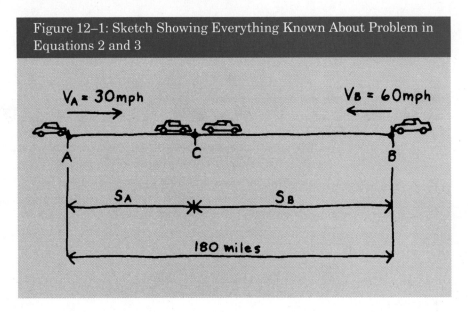

Figure 12–1: Sketch Showing Everything Known About Problem in Equations 2 and 3

Figure 12–1 shows your car, Car A, leaving your school and Car B, your friend's car, leaving hers, heading toward each other. We'll indicate the point at which they will meet by letter C.

Third, **write down everything you know about this situation.**

What do we know? Both cars will travel the same amount of time. Car B goes twice as fast as Car A and so will travel a larger distance.

In our sketch, we showed the distance (in miles) Car A travels to the meeting point, C, as S_A. We showed the distance Car B travels as S_B.

To solve for the unknown travel time and the unknown distances of this problem, we can use two equations. These can be supplied by using Equation 1 to express the distance each car travels.

For Car A,   [Equation 2]

$$S_A = 30t.$$

For Car B,

$$S_B = 60t.$$

We also know that the combined distance the two cars travel must equal 180 miles.

$$S_A + S_B = 180 \text{ miles} \qquad \text{[Equation 3]}$$

Substituting the values of S_A and S_B given by Equation 2 into Equation 3, results in

$$30t + 60t = 180 \text{ miles}$$

$$90t = 180 \text{ miles}$$

$$t = 2 \text{ hours}$$

To check the answer, we substitute $t = 2$ hours into Equation 2 and establish that $S_A = 60$ miles and $S_B = 120$ miles. So Car A travels 60 miles and Car B travels 120.

$$S_A = 30 \ (2) = 60$$

$$S_B = 60 \ (2) = \underline{120}$$
$$180 \text{ miles}$$

We now know that Car A travels 60 miles and Car B travels 120 miles, which equals 180 miles, the original distance between points A and B.

General Guidelines for Solving Numerical Problems

Here are some general guidelines for handling numerical problems in an exam.

1. **Read the problem several times** until you understand clearly what it is you are being asked to find.
2. **Identify the correct equation** that will solve the type of problem you are dealing with. Your instructor often will supply the equation if it is complex or will allow you to bring in a sheet with the equations related to the topics covered in the course.
3. To establish a clear understanding of the problem, **draw a sketch to clarify the known and unknown variables.** Indicate on the sketch every variable given in the problem.
4. Be sure to write down everything you know—all the variables given in the problem—and try to establish relationships between them.
5. **Solve the equation or equations** to establish the values of the unknown variables. **Do not skip steps** so that the instructor can follow your thinking more easily.

6. Whenever time permits, **check the solution** to verify its accuracy.
7. Your instructor usually will give you partial credit if your analysis of the problem is carried out in a logical manner. A neat, well-arranged series of steps or computations allows your instructor to evaluate the percentage of credit you have earned. (Deductions for math errors are usually small.)
8. If the solution to a problem is not apparent to you after you have made a sketch and indicated what variables you know, move to the next problem. After you have gone through the exam, return to those problems you did not complete.
9. Sometimes an exam is too long or too difficult for the time allowed, and you will not complete all the problems. In these cases, the instructor often grades on a curve. So if you earn 62 points on the exam, it might be worth a B.

Understanding Essay Questions

"I found that reading the essay questions more carefully pays off. I do much better on exams now than I used to."

—Leon Spearman, student

The first step in answering essay questions is to know precisely what you're being asked. Obvious as that sounds, many students do not spend enough time analyzing essay questions.

Faced with an essay exam, **give yourself time to do an analytical reading of the question.** While you read, ask yourself questions to help you understand what you are being asked.

1. What topic are you asked to discuss in your essay?
2. What kind of thinking are you asked to do? How should you develop your ideas? Are there any key words in the question that tell you how to proceed?
3. Are there any specific criteria you have to fulfill?
4. Does the question have multiple parts?

To show you how to apply these questions, we'll use this sample item from an essay exam:

Based on your reading, identify at least three methods television journalists use to make their news reports more exciting or interesting to the public. How would you evaluate the use of these techniques? In your opinion, do any or all of them lead to news distortion?

Managing Exam-Day Jitters

1. **Know that some anxiety is good for you.**
   A little anxiety before an exam is not a bad thing; it keeps you mentally active and alert. Don't panic at the first signs of nervousness. Instead, **manage your anxiety by telling yourself that you know the material and will do well.** There's no need to be unduly nervous.

2. **Get to the exam early and take a few minutes to compose yourself.**
   Rushing into class at the last minute, grabbing your exam, and hunting for your pen or pencil will produce stress. Instead, arrive early and get everything ready—before the exams are distributed.

3. **Use deep breathing to combat nervousness.**
   Breathing deeply can reduce anxiety. If at any time during the exam, you feel you can't concentrate, inhale deeply, counting to five while you hold your breath. Then exhale slowly, again counting to five. Do this three or four times, and you'll begin to feel calm.

4. **Don't look at your classmates while taking your exam.**
   Don't compare your progress with that of other students. Should the person next to you turn to page 2 while you are still on page 1, you'll assume that you are falling behind. In fact, your classmate may not have been able to answer the questions on page 1. **When you take an exam, work at your own speed.** Don't try to match anyone else's.

5. **Think positively.**
   Students who think they are going to do well on exams usually do. Obviously a positive attitude *without* thorough test preparation will not work. But if you combine solid preparation with a belief in your success, you'll increase your chances of doing well.

6. **Eat the right food before an exam.**
   Before an exam, don't fill up on soft drinks and potato chips thinking you'll get quick energy. Snack food has a negative effect on mental alertness. Instead, eat a meal low in fat and high in proteins—like yogurt, chicken, or eggs.

What is the topic you are asked to discuss? In this case, the precise topic is the news-gathering methods of television journalists.

Once you have established the topic, ask yourself "How should I develop my ideas about this topic?" **Look for key words** telling you what information to include in your essay and how to organize it. Often the verb tells you specifically what your essay should accomplish. The verb "identify," in our sample question, tells you to *name* and *describe* the methods television journalists use to make their reports entertaining or exciting. (For a list of other commonly used verbs, see pages 276–277.)

Next, determine whether or not the question establishes any specific criteria you must meet. Our essay question on television journalism states that a good answer must be "based on your reading." Therefore, avoid including information that might be accurate but is not drawn from the text you've been studying.

According to the sample question, a good essay answer must also identify "at least three" news-gathering methods. Although you can certainly include more than three, you will lose credit if you include fewer than three. After you read an essay question, **underline any words that identify the criteria your essay must meet.**

Note that our sample essay question, although not actually numbered, does have multiple parts. Part 1 asks you to identify three or more methods used to gather news. Part 2 then asks you to *evaluate* these methods; that is, *give your opinion* and *support it* by citing specific advantages or disadvantages.

After this kind of preparation, you are ready to write.

☐ PRACTICE 4   Read each essay question at least twice. When you are finished, answer the questions that follow.

1. Explain why we cannot tell merely by looking in the sky that stars in a given constellation are at different distances, while in a room we can easily tell that objects are at different distances from us. What is the difference between the two situations?

—Jay Pasachoff, *Contemporary Astronomy*

What topic are you being asked to discuss?

_____

What key words or phrases tell you how to proceed in your essay?

_____

_____

Does the question have multiple parts?

_____

_____

_____

2. Although the Portuguese made contact with China and Japan in the sixteenth century, both countries were still able to isolate themselves from foreign influence until the late nineteenth century. What happened in the nineteenth century to change this situation? In your essay be sure to compare and contrast each country's reaction to Western invasion.

What topic are you being asked to discuss?

_____

What key words or phrases tell you how to proceed in your essay?

_____

_____

Does the question have multiple parts?

_____

What specific criteria should you apply to your answer?

_____

_____

Verbs Commonly Used in Essay Questions

Analyze

Divide the whole into its individual parts and explain how these parts relate to one another.

"Analyze Alice Walker's story "Everyday Use" to show what each symbol—the churn and the quilt—contributes to the story's larger themes."

Argue for or against

Support a particular position or point of view, making it convincing through reasons, illustrations, statistics, or studies. Synonymous terms include *take a stand* and *prove.*

"Argue for or against President Truman's use of the atom bomb during World War II."

Compare and contrast

Compare means "point out similarities," while contrast means "show differences." If you are asked to compare and contrast two people, events, or objects, you should describe precisely how they are similar and different.

"Compare and contrast the approach to civil rights taken by Martin Luther King, Jr., and that of Malcolm X."

Demonstrate how

Give specific examples of how some generalization applies or functions.

"Demonstrate how Einstein's theory of relativity affected the world of philosophy."

Describe the effects

Concentrate *not* on the causes of some event but on the results or after effects. Synonymous terms are *explain the consequences; describe the aftermath;* and *how did . . . affect . . . ?*

"Describe the effects of long-term sleep deprivation."

Describe the sequence or process

List in chronological order the individual steps, stages, or events that led to some event, process, or happening. Synonymous terms are *outline* and *trace.*

"Describe the sequence of events that led to America's entry into World War I."

Discuss

Explain a point or concept, providing definitions, examples, and key points.

"Discuss the ways in which parents can detect signs of child abuse."

Evaluate

To evaluate some theory or contribution, list its pros and cons, explaining positive and negative points. A synonymous term is *judge the effectiveness of.*

"According to Daniel Goleman, self-deception plays a crucial role in both remembering and forgetting. How would you evaluate his claim?"

Explain why, how

Describe the causes of some event or happening. Analyze what factors contributed or produced the end result. Synonymous terms are *show how* and *trace the origins.*

"Explain why Harriet Beecher Stowe's *Uncle Tom's Cabin* profoundly affected the status of women writers."

Illustrate

Provide some specific examples of a broad generalization.

"Illustrate the way in which chemical pollutants have affected the environment."

Interpret

When you are asked to interpret a statement, you can respond in several ways. Although you can begin by paraphrasing the statement, you should also explain what it means to you and why, and what it means to other experts in the field.

"How would you interpret Freud's claim that dreams are the *royal road* to the unconscious?"

Justify

Give reasons that support an action or policy.

"Justify the presence of special-interest groups in government."

Summarize

Give only the gist of a longer work.

"Briefly summarize Carl Jung's theory of archetypes."

3. In the case of *Escobedo* v. *Illinois,* how did the Supreme Court's decision affect criminal procedure? What was the public's reaction to the court's decision?

What topic are you being asked to discuss?

_____

What key words or phrases tell you how to proceed in your essay?

_____

Does the question have multiple parts?

_____

What specific criteria should you apply to your answer?

_____

_____

4. What is the electoral college and how does it affect the way we choose our presidents? Throughout the years the electoral college has been the subject of controversy. In your essay, explain the source of that controversy.

What topic are you being asked to discuss?

_____

What key words or phrases tell you how to proceed in your essay?

_____

_____

Does the question have multiple parts?

_____

What specific criteria should you apply to your answer?

_____

_____

Guidelines for Essay Exams

Many students don't know how to answer essay questions effectively. Some firmly believe that the only good answer is a long one, and they pad their responses with extraneous or irrelevant information. Unfortunately, these students don't realize that pointless padding detracts from a good answer.

To make sure that you *do* know how to answer essay questions, here are some essential guidelines. Apply them to write the kind of clear, detailed, and concise answers that instructors look for when they grade your exams.

1. Make a rough outline.

Unless you are pressed for time, begin by roughing out your answer on a separate sheet of paper, briefly jotting down the points you want to make. Figure 12–2 provides an illustration.

Sample Essay Question

What effect did the two Supreme Court cases, *Escobedo* v. *Illinois* and *Miranda* v. *Arizona,* have on criminal procedure? What was the public reaction to the court's decision? Did that reaction influence the ruling in any way?

Figure 12–2: Planning Your Essay Answer: Make a Rough Outline of Key Points

Two Supreme Court Cases

Escobedo, 1964

1. Escobedo not informed of right to lawyer (when police questioned him)
2. Supreme Court reversed his murder conviction (vote 5–4)
3. Effect: Confession can't be used if suspect not allowed lawyer

Miranda, 1966

1. Police didn't inform Miranda of his rights
2. His confession (to kidnapping, rape) not allowed as evidence
3. Supreme Court reversed his conviction
4. Effect: Suspect must be read rights *before* being questioned:
    a. right to remain silent
    b. right to see lawyer

Public reaction and the court's response

1. Criminal treated better than victim . . .
2. Court did not overrule

A rough outline will help you clarify your thoughts and organize your information in a clear, sequential order. Before you hand in your exam, check your outline to make sure you haven't forgotten anything.

2. **In the first sentence or paragraph, give a general answer to the question.**

In an essay written for an exam, the first sentence should always be a general answer to the question asked.

> Television uses three methods to make news coverage exciting: staging, tape doctoring, and ambush interviewing.

If you have thirty minutes to write your essay, use the first paragraph to introduce your answer in general terms. Then use the remaining paragraphs to provide more specific supporting details.

> In gathering news for television, journalists employ a variety of techniques designed primarily to make the news visually exciting and entertaining. Three of the most common are *staging, tape doctoring,* and *ambush interviewing.* Staging occurs when an event is not filmed live, but reenacted. Tape doctoring is the practice of editing an interview to make it more controversial or shocking. Ambush interviewing is what journalists do when they approach a subject by surprise and ask him or her to comment on some current event without advance preparation.

> In essay exams, instructors are reading with one key question in mind. Do you know the answer to the question they have asked? Your first sentence or paragraph should tell them that you do.

3. **Don't skimp on supporting details.**

Often students skimp on details because they don't understand the role instructors play when reading exams. They assume that instructors know the material; therefore why spell it out? Unfortunately, this line of reasoning completely misses the purpose of exams as well as the role instructors play when reading them.

Your instructors give exams to discover how well *you* have absorbed the information introduced throughout the term. If you have understood the course, you should be able to explain the material to them in detail almost as if you were the teacher and they were the students.

When you write your essays, don't expect your instructors to fill in the supporting details. That's your job, not theirs.

4. Use transitions to help your instructor follow your train of thought.

If you are citing three different examples of the way in which animals respond to territorial invasion, help your reader sort those examples by using transitions. These can be words like *first, second,* and *third.* Or they can take the form of sentences that explicitly link your thoughts.

> In addition to the visual warnings previously described, animals use a variety of gestures or cries; the following are some examples.

Transitional sentences are useful if your essay question has more than one part, telling your instructor that you have finished answering one portion of the original question and are moving on to another.

> Having described three methods that television journalists use to make the news more exciting, I will now illustrate how these methods can and do distort the actual events.

5. Use new paragraphs to highlight shifts in thought.

At all costs, avoid long answers that go on for pages without a single indentation. Indent every time you take up a main point in your outline. Indent, as well, each time you answer a different part of the same question. New paragraphs will make it easier for your instructor to follow the development of your ideas.

6. Whenever possible, put your strongest ideas, explanations, examples, or reasons first.

The way in which you order information may be prescribed by the question you're asked.

> Name and describe the specific steps in the scientific method.

In this case, the order in which you present information is not up to you. There is an established sequence you have to follow.

Many exam questions, however, do allow you to decide how to order information. If so, start instead with your most persuasive point and show your instructor the depth of your knowledge.

7. Check your essay answer with the original question.

Before you hand in your exam, read the essay question again to make sure you have responded to every part of the question. Check also that you have fulfilled all specific criteria specified in the question. If your instructor asked for three examples, make sure your essay contains at least three.

8. Proofread for illegible words and mechanical errors.

When writing under pressure, many students forget about legibility. Faced with many exams to correct, few instructors have the time to decipher illegible words or mangled word order. If the answer to the question is not legibly written, most instructors won't try to analyze your handwriting until they figure out your answer. Even if they wanted to, they just don't have the time.

Whenever you write an essay, make it easy for your instructor to read it. **Write on every other line of the test booklet,** a practice that makes even the most cramped handwriting more legible. In addition, **proofread your answers** before you hand in your exam (see Chapter 16 for more on proofreading).

> ✳ To test your knowledge, instructors read an exam as if they were relatively unfamiliar with their own subject matter. You should therefore explain the material to them almost as if you were the teacher and they were the students.

PRACTICE 5   Here is one essay question followed by two student answers. After you have read the question carefully, read each answer; then decide which is better. In the blanks that follow, explain why you chose one answer over the other.

Essay Question

What effect did the two Supreme Court cases, *Escobedo* v. *Illinois* and *Miranda* v. *Arizona,* have on criminal procedure? What was the public reaction to the court's decision? Did that reaction influence later Supreme Court rulings in any way?

Answer 1

The *Escobedo* and *Miranda* cases profoundly influenced criminal procedure by rigidly restricting and controlling police behavior with accused criminals. In 1964, Danny Escobedo was questioned in regard to the murder of his brother-in-law. During the questioning, police repeatedly disregarded his requests for a lawyer. Nor did they inform him of his right to remain silent, and he incriminated himself through a confession. When Escobedo's appeal came before the Supreme Court, his conviction was reversed by a five to four vote. As a result, police were forced to inform every suspect of his or her right to counsel before questioning can take place.

That right was further extended by the *Miranda* v. *Arizona* case of 1966. In this case, Ernesto Miranda had confessed to kidnapping and rape after a two-hour interrogation session in which he was not informed of his right to remain silent or to have counsel. Once again the Supreme Court reversed the conviction, claiming that the confession was inadmissible evidence. As a result of this case, police had to be sure that each and every suspect had been "Mirandized." The suspect had to be explicitly told *before* questioning that he or she had the following rights: (1) the right to remain silent in order to avoid making incriminating statements, and (2) the right to an attorney. Furthermore, any suspect who asked for an attorney could not be questioned until that attorney was present.

The public was angry at the *Escobedo* decision, but it was the *Miranda* decision that really drew public outrage. Many saw it as a legal loophole that would allow criminals to go free on a technicality. Several movies made in the early seventies, like Clint Eastwood's *Dirty Harry,* reflected the public's dislike of both the *Miranda* and *Escobedo* decisions, and audiences cheered when Eastwood flouted police procedure in pursuit of criminals.

Members of the legal community who were opposed to these decisions argued that only those confessions that had actually been coerced could be considered illegal. From this point of view, Miranda's and Escobedo's confessions could not be considered illegal; the two men had not been coerced. They simply had not been advised of their rights. To a large degree, legal objections to the court decisions centered more on the interpretation of the cases themselves than on the way they affected police procedure.

Richard Nixon, aware of public feeling, promised in his 1968 presidential campaign to appoint justices who would overrule these two unpopular decisions. But despite Nixon's election and the resulting four conservative appointments to the Supreme Court, the decisions were not overruled. In 1984, however, the Supreme Court did formulate an exception to the *Miranda* ruling, which says that if concern for public safety leaves no time to issue warnings, confessions can be used as evidence.

Answer 2

In old-time movies about the police, scenes concerning the third degree were very popular, and it was commonplace to see criminals being brutally beaten by police who wanted to extract a confession. Aware that criminal defendants could be subjected to abuse, the framers of the Bill of Rights formulated the Fifth Amendment, which says that no person "shall be compelled in any criminal case to be a witness against himself." Since that time, many people, both guilty and innocent, have "taken the Fifth" in response to questions.

Research shows that most people believe that suspects have to be protected against the possibility of police brutality. But when the *Escobedo* and *Miranda* decisions appeared to favor the rights of criminal defendants, people were outraged. Both men had confessed to their crimes but were allowed to go free. It seemed as if the rights of the victims were being ignored while the criminal defendants were being treated with kid gloves. This is probably one reason for the success of films like *Dirty Harry,* where the detective hero simply ignored the rights of the criminals he pursued and used any means possible to bring them to justice.

Despite the public outcry against the *Escobedo* and *Miranda* decisions, the Supreme Court did not reverse itself. Even the conservative Supreme Court justices appointed by Richard Nixon have not reversed these decisions, although recent decisions have given the police more latitude in combating crime. These decisions are probably a reflection of the Supreme Court's current composition as well as a response to public interest in victims' rather than criminals' rights.

Which answer do you think is better, and why?

_____

_____

_____

_____

_____

_____

Working Space

READING ASSIGNMENT

The following selection by Donna Britt offers some suggestions for surviving a difficult semester. As you read it, evaluate the suggestions, asking yourself which ones you think are of practical value. When you finish, check off the ones you think you might use or suggest to a friend who is in a panic at the thought of facing finals.

Salvaging a Bad Semester

During the second semester of her freshman year at Wayne State University in Detroit, Michigan, Jeanette Bryant, eighteen, fell in love and fell off her academic pedestal.

Bryant faced her moment of truth one night late in the semester, several weeks after she'd decided that partying with her boyfriend was more exciting than cracking the books.

While cramming for an exam, the former B-plus student realized that she'd spent more time listening for the phone to ring than reading the chapter. "For the first time, I looked at my test scores and realized that I was in trouble in several courses," Bryant remembers. "Then it hit me: I'd either have to quit school or quit him and study. It was an easy choice—I decided to study."

Almost every student experiences the panic-prompting realization of possible failure, but freshmen are more likely to find themselves in such a situation. Nearly 25 percent of all freshmen at four-year colleges drop out of school, according to the 1985–1986 College Board's *Annual Survey of Colleges.*

How can you tell whether you're on your way to becoming part of this statistic? "Too often, students do lousy on a couple of tests in a few classes and think they're failing," says Robert Kriegel, the author of *The C Zone: Peak Performance Under Pressure* (Ballantine, 1985). "Some even drop out of school." If you usually earn A's but are making C's, stop worrying. You're not failing; you're just underachieving.

But if you acknowledge during the last two or three weeks of a semester that you're going into a final examination after missing more than half the questions on the midterm, or that your semester attendance totals three weeks' worth of classes, or that you really did blow off the term project that's due next week, you *are* well on your way to flunking. If you're not careful, a couple of bad grades can lead to academic catastrophe.

"Most students who drop out of college do so because they get intimidated when they see failure on their record," says Bert Ockerman, the assistant executive director of the American Association of Collegiate Registrars and Admissions Officers. "Often, students on the brink of failure are sure that they'll never raise their GPA, so they give up."

A bad first-year experience doesn't always mean that you should quit school, however. "If students can just make it through their sophomore year, they have an excellent chance of graduating," says Ockerman.

As corny as it sounds, you should adopt the credo of successful athletes: never give up. "No matter what the score or how far behind athletes are in a race," says Kriegel, "they give everything they've got. Sometimes the extra effort pays off."

It's also important to pinpoint exactly what's preventing you from doing well. For Bryant that meant having a serious discussion with her boyfriend. Together they agreed to limit telephone conversations and to adopt a new rule. If either of them scored below a C on an examination, the two would separate until their grades improved.

The plan worked—almost. Though Bryant received B's in three of her classes, she failed geology. "I was devastated and disappointed for letting myself get off the track that way," she says.

For others, the source of a late-semester grade crisis is less controllable. New York University law student Tanya Heidelberg was a sophomore in telecommunications at Syracuse University in New York when her grandmother suffered a stroke. A few weeks later, her grandmother died. Despite her grief, Heidelberg returned to school as if nothing happened, then watched her semester GPA fall to 2.4. "It was painful to see someone so strong and feisty become helpless, and I didn't have a chance to grieve," she says now. "My grades really suffered."

Although many factors contribute to flunking out of school, including homesickness, lack of preparation, and enrolling in the wrong school, students most often blame their lack of funds. But Ockerman believes that's merely a cover-up. "Low grades are the real reason so many students don't make it back on campus," he says.

Counselor Peg Taylor, who is the assistant director of the University of Kentucky's counseling center, agrees. "In nearly 75 percent of the cases, students haven't allotted enough time for studying," she says. "They're too busy partying and working, or they procrastinate because they don't like a subject."

If you think nothing short of a miracle will see you through this semester with passing grades, don't panic. Try some of these last-ditch efforts to rescue yourself from a late-semester crisis.

- **Realize that you have a problem.** Accepting that something is amiss is the first step in solving any problem. "One day I figured out that I'd created a pattern," says University of Georgia senior Dalerick Cruver, who admits to having survived many bad semesters. "I wasn't putting forth the effort; therefore, I wasn't performing up to my abilities. Once I became dissatisfied with my lack of progress, I began to work my way out of the poor-performance pattern."
- **Determine which classes are worth rescuing.** If you can't remember the last time you attended mathematics or chemistry class—or any class in which the professor teaches information cumulatively—your chance of pulling a passing grade is slim, even with marathon cramming. However, you may be able to salvage courses that require reading and memorization, such as American history, child psychology, and English literature.

  For courses that demand lots of reading, Taylor suggests that you create an information map, a spiderweb-type graph in which lesser ideas encircle the major theme of each chapter.
- **Reduce your class load.** Dropping an elective course gives you extra study hours to focus on the required classes. But be forewarned: Unloading a class late in the semester often results in automatic failure. Some colleges allow students to take an Incomplete and then make up the course the following semester. Check with the admissions office to learn your school's policy.
- **Obtain a copy of last semester's exam.** Some professors will give you a copy of an old exam if you'll just ask. If a professor refuses, ask a student who's already taken the course for a copy, advises Taylor. Note how the questions are phrased. For tests that quiz you on memorized information, study flash cards complete with dates, names, and definitions. Concentrate on those concepts and terms highlighted in the exam. Chances are that similar ideas will appear on your examination.
- **Hire a tutor.** Seek help from a tutor if you've tried hard in a course but haven't grasped the fine points, advises Rebecca Jones, who tutors Spanish at Georgetown University in Washington, D.C.

"A lot of times, students don't ask questions in class because they're afraid that their questions are silly," she says. "They feel more comfortable asking tutors."

But remember, even a terrific tutor can't help certain students. "If you haven't gone to class all year and really have no idea what's going on, hiring a tutor won't help," Jones warns. "A few hours of intensive tutoring won't replace an entire course."

To find a tutor, check with your professor or an administrator in the department that offers the class.

- **Consult a counselor.** Academic counselors can identify trouble areas and teach such study techniques as cramming. "Students should ask for help if they think they need it," advises Taylor. "Many students who bother to see me really *are* failing something, and I can usually help."

- **Make a deal with your professor.** Confiding genuine problems to your instructor can't hurt, according to Heidelberg, especially if you've already displayed a sincere interest in your class. Ask if you can turn in an extra-credit paper to make up for that failed midterm, or strike a similar deal. "Talking to a professor shows that you're concerned, and a concerned professor is more likely to give you hints about what's on the exam," says student Cruver.

  When Jeff Rivers was flunking a required health-education class at Hampton University in Virginia, he dressed in a suit, visited the professor, and explained the trouble he'd had balancing college's social life with academics. After completing an extra-credit paper, Rivers passed the course. "The professor was probably astounded to see me in a tie and figured the class had to be worth something to me," he says.

- **If you survive this semester, don't wait until it's too late next term.** If you take stock of your grades two weeks before final exams, you're playing a dangerous game. Assess your progress at regular intervals, and don't leave your studies until the last minute.

- **Take a break.** If you're floundering in school because you're unmotivated or unsure whether you even want to attend college, consider leaving for a semester or two. "Dropping out can be positive if students use the time to get some good work experience or to think about what they really want to do." But don't blow off school forever, Taylor advises. "College is the best place to grow up."

If all last-ditch efforts fail to save your GPA, hang in there. Remember that *one* bad semester may tarnish your academic career, but it won't end it. "A few bad grades aren't the end of the world," says Heidelberg. "Chances are, if you learned where you went wrong, you won't make the same mistake next semester."

1. According to the article, what is the real reason students flunk?

2. According to the article, "College is the best place to grow up." Do you agree? Why or why not?

3. If you had to say which of the suggestions for salvaging a semester was most crucial, which one would you choose?

WRITING ASSIGNMENT

Write a 500-word personal essay on exams, discussing one or several of the following.
1. Discuss the type of exam questions you think are fairest and allow you to show what you know.
2. Discuss the type of exam questions you feel most uncomfortable answering.
3. Do you think the amount of time you spend preparing for exams is reflected in how you do on tests?
4. Does test anxiety affect your grades on tests?

JOURNAL ASSIGNMENTS

Write on one of the following.
1. Can you think of another way for instructors to test how much their students learn other than by giving exams?
2. If you were a teacher, would you give final exams to help your students consolidate the material, or would you use some other method to help your students master the material?

✔ Checking Out: Review Questions for Chapter 12

1. What is the difference between recalling information and recognizing it?

2. What kinds of test questions require recognition? What kinds require recalling information?

3. If you don't understand the stem in a multiple-choice question, should you read all the options? Why or why not?

4. In answering essay questions, what should you try to accomplish in your first sentence?

5. What is the first thing you should do after receiving an exam?

6. Name two ways to combat test-day jitters.

7. In numerical problems, why is it always important to show your steps and make a sketch?

8. In true-or-false questions, should you answer every question? Why or why not?

9. Why is reading the test questions carefully a critical step?

10. What are some of the things you should do before you hand in your exam?

▶ In Summary

Tactics for test-taking are no substitute for solid preparation. But they can help you avoid the kind of pointless mistakes that result in a low grade. Why lose five points because you forgot to look at page 5 and didn't answer the last question? Why agonize over how quickly another student is finishing when, in fact, that student may not be answering half the questions? Now that you have at your disposal a repertoire of test-taking strategies, make sure you use to get the high grades you deserve.

5

UNIT

Becoming a Critical Thinker and a
Thoughtful Writer

CHAPTER 13

The Strategies of a Critical Thinker

The having of wonderful ideas is the essence of intellectual development.

—Eleanor Duckworth,
Harvard School of Education

In this present chapter, we will examine how critical thinking is applicable, and at times crucial, to many aspects of our everyday lives. And the same basic critical-thinking process you learn to apply to your personal decisions carries over to your academic work. Most important, it applies to complicated moral choices that all of us face throughout our lives.

- Applying critical-thinking strategies to everyday decision making
- Learning the characteristics of a critical thinker
- Being aware of the kinds of thinking commonly used for gathering and analyzing information
- Being open to new ideas; and being willing to rethink or modify your opinions
- Making moral choices; examining the kind of person you want to be

Applying Critical Thinking to Your Own Life

What do you do when you have a hard choice to make? Should you go to College A or College B? Should you go to the library to catch up or go hear your best friend's new band? Should you clean up the mess after a party or hope that someone else will? Everyone faces choices—large and small.

The term *critical thinking* describes the deliberate thinking that helps you decide what to believe about an issue or how to act in a given situation. Critical thinking helps you examine a problem or issue from many angles and reach the best possible decision. It helps you learn to think creatively and to find pleasure in ideas.

Critical thinking is by no means restricted to academic matters or to study skills; it encourages us to examine responsibly all the important issues and choices that we face in our lives and to deal with them productively. It means we have thought through the reasons for our actions and judgments, and do not act impulsively or emotionally.

Critical Thinking in Practical Decisions

At certain points in our lives, each of us faces some serious decision in which it is not clear what we should do. Take senior Sarah Boone's case. She has to decide between Job A (as a word processor) and Job B (as an assistant reporter for a local paper).

Job A pays considerably better but sounds like more routine work with little future potential. Job B pays less well but offers more opportunities to learn about the newspaper business, and the work offers more challenges. This is Sarah's first full-time job after college; she remains undecided about her long-range goals but is leaning toward getting a master's degree in special education.

Faced with this kind of decision, Sarah should sit down in a comfortable spot and weigh all the choices *and* their possible consequences. One way to do this is to list in separate columns all the possible benefits or advantages and all the possible costs or disadvantages. In other words she should make a list of every pro and con she can think of (as in Figure 13–1 on page 296). Then she should rank them in order of importance to her.

In making a decision, she should consider what is the worst thing that can happen to her in either situation. The worst thing in this particular decision is not too serious: both jobs are temporary situations in which she is learning more about herself, her goals, and the work world. But in other situations, the worst outcome might be something she does not want to risk.

If people do not take the time to make carefully thought-out decisions, they may instead make a spur-of-the-moment or an emotional decision that is not in their best interest.

After jotting down all the benefits and costs (both financial and psychological) of each choice, Sarah saw that she was deciding between a job with a larger starting salary (enough to save for tuition) and one with more future opportunities (but a smaller salary now). Making this decision forced Sarah to focus on her long-range goals. She realized that, most of all, she wanted a master's degree in special education and that, in her case, journalism would be a detour. Therefore she accepted the job with the larger salary to save for tuition.

Figure 13–1: Weighing the Pros and Cons of a Decision

Decision Making: Two Job Offers

Job A (word processor)
advantages
- earn more money—almost twice as much
- can save for next year's tuition

disadvantages
- dull, mechanical work
- no future
- won't learn very much

Job B (assistant reporter)
advantages
- more responsible work
- can learn about newspaper business
- Dad says I should give it a try

disadvantages
- only barely enough money to live on
- detour from main goal of getting master's

The Decision-Making Process

To make difficult personal decisions, it helps to think through your options using a systematic critical-thinking process. Rather than having confusing, contradictory thoughts floating in your mind, write down your ideas and see them in front of you. Follow the steps listed in Figure 13–2 whenever you face a difficult decision.

In everyday life, we constantly face situations in which we have to make decisions—even decisions between two good things. Some are small—whether to go away for a weekend vacation or to earn overtime by working all weekend. And some are larger and more difficult—whether to

Figure 13–2: Decision-Making Checklist

Making a Careful Decision

If you are trying to make an intelligent decision on any important issue, it helps to go through these steps:

1. Gather all possible facts and information: Study, read about, or re-search the problem. Ask many questions of yourself and others.
2. Write out a tentative statement of the decision you have to make. What are your realistic choices?
3. List the advantages and the disadvantages of each choice and rank them in order of importance to you.
4. Think of the long-range consequences to yourself and to others. Are these future consequences or risks acceptable?
5. Ask yourself if your expectations are realistic or too high.
6. Think hard—think critically—about your choices, discarding any that have clear weaknesses. After weighing your choices, make plans to take action.

	Advantages	Disadvantages
Choice A	1. ———————	1. ———————
	2. ———————	2. ———————
	3. ———————	3. ———————
	4. ———————	4. ———————
Choice B	1. ———————	1. ———————
	2. ———————	2. ———————
	3. ———————	3. ———————
	4. ———————	4. ———————

Your Decision:

accept a scholarship to graduate school or to accept a very good job offer that might not come again. In each instance we have a choice to make, and these choices, day by day, determine whether we take control over our lives or not.

Many adults have some regrets that they did not take more advantage of their opportunities when they were younger and freer of responsibilities. Make sure to take advantage of any opportunities to achieve more of your potential. Don't sit back: make things happen for yourself. Do some critical thinking about your life.

PRACTICE 1   Make a list of the possible choices, with advantages and disadvantages, for one of the following decisions.

1. You have misjudged your time, and your paper is due. You simply did not allow yourself enough time to finish. Should you (a) hand in a hastily written paper and try to do better on other grades, (b) speak to your instructor and ask for more time, or (c) not speak to your instructor, improve your paper, hand it in late, and hope for the best? What are the advantages of each choice? What are the disadvantages? What would you do and why?

2. You are about to graduate and have to make an important decision: should you continue in school to get a graduate degree (and borrow money for tuition) or look for a job right after graduating (and save up money for tuition)? What are some of the considerations you should weigh?

3. At age thirty, Louise Nevelson left behind her nine-year-old son while she went to study art in Europe for an extended period. Although she had briefly attended art school in New York, she wanted to study with Hans Hoffmann, the leading teacher of the new abstract art, and she sailed for Germany in 1931. Her son Mike was sent to live with Louise's parents in Maine. He wrote letters to her asking when she was returning; while she was away, she had serious doubts about her decision.

Even after she returned, Mike's young life continued to be disrupted by his mother's desire to find her way as an artist. After twenty-five years of struggle—to get money to live on, to develop her own style as a sculptor, and to find recognition for her work—Louise Nevelson became recognized as a leading American sculptor; her large wood constructions, often painted all black or all white, can now be seen in leading museums.

(a) Did Louise Nevelson make the right choice in leaving her young son and studying art?

(b) Should a person take care of his or her own needs first or put his or her responsibilities to others first?

(c) Have you ever been in a situation like Louise Nevelson where you had to decide between your own wants and needs and those of someone else? What did you decide?

4. Imagine a difficult practical decision you have to make: A friend invites you and your group of friends to his summer camp on a lake for the weekend. Everyone else is finished with exams, but your last hard exam is coming up the day you get back. How would you come to a decision?

Problem-Solving Strategies

As we have seen, the focus of decision making is on making a choice and then taking action. The focus of *problem solving* is on exploring the possible answers to a problem and then on identifying the best solution. (The best solution may or may not result in taking action.) And in some complex cases, a good solution may not be found.

In college, you face both problems of daily living (you can't find your keys) and academic problems (you can't figure out a complex assignment for your computer course). During and after college, you will encounter many kinds of problems that you must deal with. Some will require mathematical solutions; most cannot be expressed in numbers and will need verbal negotiations. Some will need both numerical and verbal solutions.

You need to bring different tool kits to solve different kinds of problems. For example, to solve a business problem, you need a practical approach that brings direct results rather than a theoretical or academic approach.

The following problem-solving strategies will help you work out reasonable solutions to many different kinds of problems.

State the Exact Nature of the Problem

Write down the problem in several versions and select the one that frames the problem most accurately, rewording it until you are satisfied that you have pinpointed the problem.

At times, people solve the wrong problem. When medical syringes and human waste washed up on New Jersey beaches, officials agreed that offshore dumping of garbage should be stopped at once. But it turned out that ocean dumping had nothing to do with what had washed up on the sand; it was caused by a faulty sewer system. The solution agreed upon had nothing to do with the problem.

Analyze the Problem in Detail, Looking at All Its Components

Say you are in a computer course that is too advanced for you. The other students in the course have considerably more background in the subject, either from high school or from previous courses. This one course is taking up all your time, and your other courses are being affected. You would like to drop it. But before you do, you should consider all the factors involved. There is, for example, a financial component to be considered; you may not be able to get a refund on the tuition if you drop the course. There is also a psychological component; you will feel uncomfortable telling your friends you were not able to keep up. What should you do?

Jot Down and Explore All Possible Solutions to the Problem

What should you do about your too advanced computer course? Say you come up with these ideas quickly:

- spend more hours a week studying, both to keep up and especially to review
- get more information from your adviser about dropping and making up courses
- speak to your instructor about filling in some of the background you need and learning enough to get a passing grade
- drop the course and feel less stress; worry about the results later

You might stop searching for solutions at this point, but often if you press yourself, you can come up with additional ideas:

- go to the computer lab and inquire about being tutored; it will cost less than repeating a course
- ask a friend in the course to give you some help
- call someone you know who works in a software company and ask for advice

Then you come up with another good possibility:

- buy the text for and, if possible, sit in on the basic computer class that meets before yours and learn some basics that way

If Necessary, Do Some Research

To find out any missing information that you will need to solve the problem, use the library or speak to knowledgeable people.

Identify the Best Solution to Your Problem

What would solve this problem best—a major adjustment (such as dropping the course), a moderate change (such as trying to study more hours and asking your teacher for help), or a wait-and-see approach (reevaluating the problem again after the next assignment is graded)?

Problems need to be analyzed thoroughly, and analysis should be followed by a period of *incubation,* in which you let your unconscious mind work on the solutions so that you can see the problem in a fresh light.

PRACTICE 2

1. Describe a problem, personal or academic, that you are facing now. What are some of your options for solving it?
2. Have you ever taken a course that put you under a lot of stress? What did you do to solve the problem?
3. At your part-time job shelving library books, you have a fellow worker who lets you do all the work. You feel he is taking advantage of you. What can you do to solve the problem?

Characteristics of a Critical Thinker

To become a critical thinker, set a high priority on forming your own independent viewpoint—and not simply adopting secondhand your friend's, your group's, or anyone else's viewpoint. To learn to think independently, consider these guidelines.

Avoid Making Inaccurate Generalizations

We all find ourselves, on occasion, making vague or sweeping generalizations:

"Women are overemotional, and men have no emotions."

"People from California take life too easy."

"Everyone from New York City is rude and aggressive."

Whenever you make such sweeping statements, ask yourself to think again and be more precise. Do you really mean *everyone,* or only a few people you have come across? How accurate are your estimates? Have you any supporting research or statistics? Are you exaggerating for effect?

Be on the lookout for careless generalizations in your reading, and stop yourself from making this kind of questionable statement in conversation.

Avoid Oversimplifying Complex Problems

Some problems by their nature are complex, and there are no simple black-and-white or correct and incorrect answers. When there are no clear-cut answers, learn to live with some ambiguity or uncertainty.

The question of capital punishment is a problem that is not easily solved. Opponents argue that an innocent person might be put to death. Supporters feel that some crimes are so outrageous that the criminals deserve to be put to death.

Supporters argue that the threat of capital punishment might deter others from committing future crimes; opponents argue that the possibility of the death penalty has no effect on criminals. Such questions are not easily answered.

Accept That a Diversity of Opinions Exists

Even if you have strong views about abortion, the death penalty, or other complex issues that divide society, recognize that your opinion is not the only—or necessarily the best—solution. Other people feel equally convinced about the opposite viewpoint.

Make sure that you know all the arguments on both sides, and patiently **try to convince your opponents by your persuasive arguments.**

Work Hard to Understand Another Person's Viewpoint

Try to take into account the experiences that helped form another person's viewpoint. President Reagan's press secretary James Brady was shot in the head during an unsuccessful attempt on Reagan's life by an unstable gunman; as a result of his wounds, Brady is confined to a wheelchair and has permanent debilitating injuries. He and his wife actively promote gun control through federal legislation. Even if you don't share the Bradys' position about guns, you should understand how people like the Bradys, whose lives are permanently affected by a stray bullet, should take such a strong position.

Recognize the Influence of Ideology

Examine the *ideology*, or firm set of beliefs, of those with strong positions, such as *liberals*, who favor active social change, and *conservatives* who feel that change has unknown risks as well as benefits and therefore often support the status quo.

Carefully examine the statements of those firmly committed to a particular ideology, people who take strong stands on given issues—for example, feminists, abortion activists, fundamentalists, and environmentalists. Often their outlook on many other issues is influenced by their underlying ideology.

When Hillary Rodham Clinton became First Lady, feminists predictably wanted her to take bold steps to define women's roles; liberals wanted her to work for social change; and conservatives argued that since she was not the one who was elected, she should stay out of the political picture.

Remain Open to New Ideas

Be willing to rethink your opinion if an author (or someone you know personally) offers good reasons for modifying your belief.

One student believed that she was hemmed in by her children, her tedious job, and her many home responsibilities. She was convinced that she had no choice, that her circumstances determined her situation. When she read the novel *Waiting to Exhale* by Terry McMillan, she was struck by a character who said, "If I want something to happen, I know I have to make it happen."

Acting on this idea, she vowed to change from someone who passively accepts situations to someone who actively makes changes. She began to look for a more interesting job, to delegate some of her home responsibilities to other family members, and to arrange financing for her last two terms of college.

Withhold Judgment Until You Are Convinced

Gather as much evidence as you can on a complex issue, and wait to take a final position until the evidence persuades you.

Was Darwin right or wrong in his theories of evolution—the survival of the fittest and natural selection? Find out about the issue and decide for yourself. What are the arguments? What are the counterarguments?

Ask Questions for Clarification

When addressing someone who holds an opposing view, ask questions to clarify the differences between you:

Do you have a good example of the point you are making?
Explain what you mean by the words _____ .
How do you define the term _____?
Let me restate your position to see if I have it right.
What are the advantages of X as opposed to Y?
What is the source (book or article) of your information?
Where can I find out more about this topic?
Can we look at this in another way? Reframe it?
What is your objection to point X?
Can we both work to find some middle ground?

Avoid Conventional or Stereotypical Thinking

With limited knowledge, people often think in stereotypes about cultures other than their own. Can you imagine what it would be like to be a minority in another culture? Are there minorities, people from other cultures, or handicapped students in your school or neighborhood? Do you avoid them, or do you try to make them feel comfortable and welcome? Do you try to learn from them about a larger world beyond your own?

Know yourself. Be willing to side with an unpopular view if you believe in it. Resist peer pressure; do not just go along with the crowd.

PRACTICE 3

1. Of the characteristics of a critical thinker listed on pages 301–304 do you feel describe you now, and which do not?
2. People have very different viewpoints about gun control. Those who oppose it argue that they need guns to defend themselves. Those who favor it argue that the availability of guns increases the violence in soci-

ety. Whereas the Constitution allows citizens to bear arms, the document was written long before the existence of automatic weapons. Some argue that the countless number of guns in the United States today puts innocent people at risk. Since even the police have recently spoken up for more restrictions on guns, those who favor gun control are beginning to see more support for their opinion. Although many children are killed each year in gun accidents, the National Rifle Association has long been an active opponent of gun control arguing that citizens have the right to keep weapons at home. What is your stand on this issue? What are your reasons?

PRACTICE 4   Which of the following statements are inaccurate generalizations or oversimplifications? Give a reason to support each answer.

Example: American men spend Sundays watching football on TV.
Answer: Inaccurate generalization. Not *all* American men spend Sundays watching football on TV.

1. The days of great movies are over; there will never be another Alfred Hitchcock or Humphrey Bogart.

   _____

2. The report listed various countries around the world that did not have democratic forms of government.

   _____

3. Government officials use their political offices to increase their personal wealth.

   _____

4. Every signer of the Constitution was a white male.

   _____

5. Europeans believe that American educators should discipline their students more and not let them have so much freedom.

   _____

6. Everyone watches too much television.

_____

7. Although B. F. Skinner's ideas are considered manipulative by some, his theory of positive reinforcement—a reward for a good job—seems to work.

_____

8. No one understands what happened in the last election.

_____

9. Canadians think Americans want to run the world.

_____

10. Everything has gotten worse in the last ten years.

_____

Methods for Gathering and Analyzing Information

The thinking strategies we have introduced to describe personal decision making and problem solving carry over directly to academic and creative work. In Figure 13–3 on page 308, we provide a list of some of the mental operations that specialists have identified. The list is arranged by the thought processes used to (1) **collect information,** (2) **examine or analyze it,** and (3) **evaluate or act on it**—the three steps most useful in problem solving and decision making. Can you think of any additional thought processes that should be added to this list?

Making Observations

One of the first steps of critical thinking in or out of school is **learning from observation.** Say you have a tentative idea or a *hypothesis* (a possible explanation of some unknown) that you want to study. How can you gather data to prove or disprove your idea? One convenient way, particularly for students, is to make *direct* or *controlled observations* and to take detailed notes on those observations. To make controlled observations means to make sure the process of carrying out the experiment does not change the result.

One high school student, for example, observed that teachers treated her differently when she wore her hair in a radical cut than when she wore it in a more conservative style. She decided to make a study of teachers' perceptions of their students and to investigate whether they favored students who appeared less radical. She won a Westinghouse Science prize for this sharp observation—one that she followed up with a written research report.

Collecting Your Data

Some observations can be carried out close to home; they usually require little special equipment or money. They often require time and patience. You might conveniently observe insect or animal behavior, for example, by studying closely a spider, an anthill, or a bird's nest.

Or to study government regulations of the TV industry, you might observe how many commercials appear on TV in an hour and how much time is left for programming. Or you might use yourself as a subject, and observe yourself, studying, for example, your energy levels at various times of the day. To emphasize its importance, a text on psychology states: "observation is the source of all psychological knowledge."

Another convenient way that a student can collect data is to conduct *interviews* or *surveys*. To study student attitudes about school, you might ask fellow students what they like most about their school, what they like least, and what they'd like to see changed. Or to study the leisure habits of students at your school, you might distribute a *questionnaire* asking how many times in the past month the student went to a movie, a restaurant, a bar, a rock concert, or whatever.

Another means to gather information is to administer a *test;* you might ask a group of students to answer test questions on cultural topics to find out how many students have knowledge of major cultural figures such as Picasso or Bach.

Another way to gather information is to search for local *artifacts,* for example, to study tombstones of early settlers to find out the average life span of early Americans. Or you might go to nearby museums to study Native American arts or costumes or to historic houses to learn more about the earliest settlers in your area. Even such items as old high school or college yearbooks yield information on the social history of earlier generations.

Figure 13–3: Mental Operations—Various Ways of Thinking

Ways to Gather Information

　　Review what is written on the subject (see Chapter 15)

　　Design a project or plan a study

　　Make careful, direct observations

　　Collect data

　　Take measurements in experiments

　　Imagine or invent (for creative projects)

　　Other: _____

　　_____

Ways to Analyze Information or Data

Make order out of unorganized material by using any of the following methods:

　　Compare items (for what is like, unlike)

　　Summarize large quantities of detailed or raw material

　　Classify items into orderly units; divide a whole into many parts

　　Hypothesize, that is, form a tentative explanation of the unknown

　　Interpret data by explaining what it means

　　Analyze by looking for underlying assumptions

　　Synthesize by combining the information into a new whole

　　Make analogies or create metaphors to explain the data

　　Make a mathematical model

　　Other: _____

　　_____

Ways to Evaluate or to Take Action

　　Draw reasonable conclusions from an analysis

　　Make appropriate decisions

　　Plan to apply findings to new situations

　　Criticize constructively

　　Make thoughtful ethical or value judgments

　　Write a report or give a presentation

　　Other: _____

　　_____

Analyzing Data

After collecting raw data, students and researchers must choose a method of analyzing their information (see Figure 13–3). Basically they try to classify their raw information into manageable groups and to determine what the data means. Scientists Watson and Crick, after observing the X rays of DNA crystals and the research of other biochemists, were able to work out the spiral structure of DNA—and also to win a Nobel Prize for their insight.

From their observations of the natural world, scientists first develop hunches or guesses that might explain what they are seeing. Their increasing degree of certainty is usually expressed in these terms:

hypothesis	a guess made by a scientist stated in a way that can be tested by experiments or by mathematical models
theory	a hypothesis that has been tested repeatedly and explains phenomena, such as Darwin's theory of evolution
law or principle	theories that have been widely tested over time and have been accepted as laws, such as Newton's law of universal gravitation

Newton's laws enabled scientists to plot the course of the astronauts to the moon and back; American astronauts were the first to observe firsthand the surface of the moon.

Scientists strive for objectivity. In order **for an experiment to be accepted as an objective finding, it must be replicated**, or repeated, in other laboratories by other scientists to guard against flaws or subjective reactions on the part of researchers.

Beyond Observation

How can we learn about what cannot be observed? How can we know about such abstractions as truth and beauty, right and wrong, good and evil? Such questions cannot be answered satisfactorily by the scientific method used by scientists. In college, many of these open-ended questions are discussed systematically in courses on the humanities—philosophy, literature, religion, art, and so forth. Each generation of scholars studies what has already been written about these subjects and then interprets and evaluates earlier conclusions, searching for fuller and deeper under-standing.

☐ PRACTICE 5

1. Stand at a checkout counter and carefully *observe* what people buy in a food market. Take systematic notes about their food purchases. Are they buying junk food? Vegetables? Candy? Frozen foods? Diet foods? How many of the people in your study appeared to pay some attention to nutrition and health? How much can you tell about a shopper's diet from your observations?

2. Make some observations on the type of clothing worn in your school.
   a. Make a simple list of what each male who passes is wearing (blue jeans, sweater, T-shirt, tie and jacket, and so forth) and what each female is wearing (pants, skirt, sweater, dress, coat, and so forth).
   b. After you observe about thirty people, decide which styles are most common in your location and whether the people you've observed are conformists or individualists.

Taking Moral Positions

By carefully questioning the viewpoints of others (scholars, experts, teachers, and friends) and by forming your own independent opinions, you will become a self-reliant critical thinker. You will develop your own views on an issue by determining whether or not the thinking behind someone else's opinion is reasonable. You will not go along with the crowd if you believe something seriously wrong is being done.

The most vital form of critical thinking is to develop your own moral viewpoint. Do you believe it is your responsibility to help others, or do you believe you are only responsible for yourself? Say you were in a boat accident; your motor boat overturned, and you and your friend needed help. Would you want other people boating in the area to decide your problem was none of their business, or would you want them to drop their own business and come to your rescue?

If you examine your own position on moral issues, you will become more alert to the type of person you now are and the type of person you want to become. Would you help someone in a situation like the boat accident? Some people want to aid anyone in trouble, without question, because that is the kind of person they want to be—thoughtful of others and giving of themselves. Others, more motivated by practical common sense, would go to the aid of those in the water because they themselves, in similar circumstances, would want help. Other people, a minority, would ignore the people in trouble in the water, letting someone else go to their rescue. What type of person are you?

Living with Moral Choices

In examining your moral choices, you must determine if you can live with your own decisions. And you also should consider what the long-term consequences may be. When U.S. Senator Joseph Biden, as a law student, copied several paragraphs, word for word, from a published article into one of his own papers (without footnoting them as another writer's words), perhaps he did not realize how serious plagiarism is. Perhaps he thought he would not get caught. When he decided to *plagiarize,* to use someone else's words as his own, he made a moral decision that he was willing to live with. In his case, the bad decision was discovered immediately; as a penalty, he did not graduate with his class and had to repeat the course and all the assignments for it.

Biden probably thought he had put the incident behind him; but when he had an opportunity to run for president in 1987, reporters began to accuse him of using other politicians' phrases in his speeches, and then someone remembered his old problem of plagiarism in law school. Biden decided that his campaign could not survive these questions of his poor moral judgment, and he withdrew as a candidate.

Critical thinking applies to every kind of moral issue, from stealing a library book to stealing someone's ideas in that book. No one is free from making moral choices. The Greek thinker Socrates said the unexamined life is not worth living. Critical thinking provides the tool for determining our choices and examining our lives.

Working Space

READING ASSIGNMENT

The following selection is from the *New York Times,* July 25, 1993. Read the article. Then answer the questions that follow.

A Trip Down a Utah Canyon Becomes
a Survival Quest

After months of training and preparation, five teen-agers and three adults from a Mormon youth group set out on July 15 for a high-adventure expedition into Zion National Park that was supposed to be the highlight of their summer.

But within three hours of beginning their four-day trek into the Narrows of Zion, two adult leaders had been sucked into whirlpools and drowned. The swift waters had swept away all but one of the party's backpacks and rope. And the last leader and the five teen-agers were stranded at the bottom of a 700-foot-deep canyon fighting the cold, the hunger, the fright and the deafening roar of Kolob Creek.

After four harrowing days, rescuers hoisted the survivors from the canyon late Monday. On Friday, the funeral was held for Kim Ellis, 37, while recovery teams searched for the body of the other drowned leader, David Fleischer, 27.

"We are now beginning to cope with what happened," Mark Brewer, 35, the group's surviving leader, said Thursday in an interview. "With the funeral, the reality of the deaths will set in."

Hazardous Route

Mr. Ellis, Mr. Fleischer and Mr. Brewer, all of South Salt Lake, were youth leaders at the Riviera Ward, their local congregation. They and the boys, Chris Stevens, 15; Mike Perkins, 17; Josh Nay, 16; Rick Larson, 16, and Mr. Ellis's 14-year-old son, Shane, had planned a challenging trip down the Narrows, an area where hikers wade through water in deep canyons. At some spots the sandstone walls stand four feet apart and tower 2,400 feet.

After obtaining a back-country permit from park officials, the group took on the most hazardous route into the Narrows, rapelling down 1,500-foot cliffs on the northern end of the park.

After walking several yards downstream, they began to see problems ahead. As the canyon narrowed to about five feet across, the ankle-deep stream at the beginning of the trek had turned into a deep, powerful torrent blasting through an alley of sandstone.

Negotiating Waterfalls

But there was no turning back. The cliffs were too steep to scale. "Once you are in there, you are committed to go downstream," Mr. Brewer said.

Tragedy struck when the hikers tried to negotiate a series of waterfalls. Mr. Fleischer jumped into a pool below the first falls, and he became entangled in the ropes he was carrying as a whirlpool pulled him under. Mr. Ellis jumped into the pool to help and the impact of his plunge pushed Mr. Fleischer out of the current, which then sucked Mr. Ellis under. Then Mr. Brewer dived in to assist.

"When I was first pulled under, I thought that was it, but I touched bottom and pushed off and pulled Kim out of the whirlpool with me," he recalled.

For 30 minutes the two men administered CPR to Mr. Ellis while the five boys waited above the falls.

Mr. Ellis never regained consciousness, and the group propped his body on a ledge where it could later be retrieved. Shane spent a few moments alone with his father, before moving on with the group to look for safe ground.

Danger Downstream

The two leaders moved ahead, carefully wading down the creek. Just as Mr. Fleischer tried to negotiate another waterfall, he was again yanked under water by a whirlpool.

As he watched his friend disappear, Mr. Brewer's first impulse was to jump in and try another rescue. But the thought of the teen-agers waiting upstream stopped him.

"It was the most difficult decision of my life," he said, "but there were five boys who had to be taken care of."

He trudged upstream against the powerful currents. As he made his way back to the shivering teen-agers, he could tell they sensed his anguish.

"When I got to them, I told them, 'Dave has died and now it is our job to live and be rescued,'" Mr. Brewer recalled.

Night was approaching, so they gathered cobblestones from the creek to build a six-foot-long ledge against the canyon wall, where they huddled above the rushing waters with a sleeping bag draped over their heads.

"There was very little sleep," Mr. Brewer said. "About every hour we would have a roll-call to make sure everyone was still with us."

While waiting for rescuers, they rationed a small inventory of pudding, granola bars and other trail snacks, but grew weak from hunger as each day passed. The tight cuffs of their wet suits caused feet to swell painfully. To keep spirits up, they talked about cars, clothes and family, sang hymns and prayed.

About mid-day Monday, a sign of help appeared as the group saw a helicopter. Unaware that the helicopter crew had spotted Mr. Ellis's body, the group's spirits plummeted when the craft flew away. About four hours later, an orange rope seemingly dropped out of the sky and dangled in front of them.

"I can't describe the exuberance we felt at that point," Mr. Brewer said.

Climbers from National Park Service and county rescue units hoisted the survivors out of the canyon and, with nightfall near, the group spent the night atop a mesa. They were taken to park headquarters the next day.

"We all gained a great perspective of what's really important," Mr. Brewer said. "All that matters is family, friends and helping others."

1. Describe the two moral decisions that Mark Brewer faced.

2. How much time did he have to make his decisions?

3. In your opinion, did he make the right decisions?

4. Can you think of anything that might have been done differently to prevent the tragic outcome of this adventure?

WRITING ASSIGNMENT

Write a short essay answering the question given at the end of the following quotation.

Over the last half-century, Americans have come to understand that a civilized society does not mistreat people because of what they are. It is unacceptable to assault someone because he is a Jew or deny him a job because he is black.

The question now is whether we are ready to apply that civilized standard to homosexuals. Are they to be despised and rejected because of what they are—because of a status that nature gave them?

—Anthony Lewis, *New York Times,* 29 January 1993

JOURNAL ASSIGNMENTS

1. Evaluate your abilities as a critical thinker. What are your strengths? What are your weaknesses?

2. A Polish-Jewish doctor, Marek Edelman, who lived through the brutal Nazi period of World War II and the later Russian takeover of Poland, said recently that he didn't think it mattered what country you were from or what politics you believed in. His simple morality was to help the person who was at the bottom of the pile and who was being beaten up by bigger, tougher groups. "Never mind who is being beaten," he said. "I believe you have always to take his side." Do you agree or disagree with this moral principle? Do you have a moral principle of your own?

3. Discuss this question in your journal: Is it better to suffer an injustice than to inflict some injustice on another person?

✔ Checking Out: Review Questions for Chapter 13

1. When making a major decision, why is it important to use critical-thinking strategies?

2. Why should you evaluate the long-term benefits and the costs of each of your choices? Why is it useful to consider the worst possible outcome?

3. What are the basic steps to follow for making a reasonable decision?

4. What are three characteristics of a critical thinker?

5. In attempting to solve any problem, why is it essential to collect as much relevant information as possible? What are some ways to collect it?

6. What are the basic steps for solving a problem?

7. When making moral decisions, why is it important to think for yourself and not follow the crowd blindly?

8. What are some methods students can use to make controlled observations?

9. What is the difference between a *hypothesis* and a *theory*?

10. Define *ideology* and give some examples.

▶ In Summary

Students who think critically about the issues they are studying remember the ideas longer than students who simply memorize facts or who are satisfied with surface knowledge. You will make an issue more meaningful for yourself if you find out how the separate facts are related in a broader context and what you personally think about a given subject.

Critical thinking is helpful in making productive decisions about things that occur in your daily life. The critical-thinking process carries over to academic issues; it requires that you gather all relevant information and then analyze the information in a thorough and thoughtful manner. In essence, critical-thinking strategies help you avoid making hasty or oversimplified judgments about an issue. You should remain open-minded and be willing to rethink your opinion based on the information you uncover.

Students who think for themselves take nothing at face value and do not accept an opinion merely because some friend supports it. Critical thinking requires that you examine the strengths and weaknesses of any argument, that you stay flexible, and that you do not look for simplistic right-or-wrong answers. Critical thinking helps you understand that many issues have no single answer and that many thoughtful people disagree over complex issues.

As its most important goal, critical thinking requires that you think hard about moral issues. You must decide how you want to act in relation to others and whether you can live with your own moral decisions. Thinking through the long-range consequences of any action will help you make a more responsible choice.

Critical Reading: Evaluating an Author's Viewpoint

"What we have to do is to be forever curiously testing new opinions and courting new impressions."
—*Walter Pater*

In this chapter we discuss how a reader should examine and evaluate an author's opinions, neither accepting nor rejecting ideas quickly. Then we explain how to find legitimate grounds for agreeing or disagreeing with an author's views.

Your willingness to question an author's opinions lies at the heart of critical reading and distinguishes an active reader from a passive reader. In this chapter, learn the basic tools for critical reading and creative thinking by:

- Developing a questioning attitude
- Looking for other possible sides to an issue
- Distinguishing objective fact from subjective opinion
- Learning to evaluate an author's opinion or viewpoint
- Recognizing bias or a one-sided argument
- Learning to detect your own biases

Becoming a Thinking Reader

By the very process of trying to decide whether to accept or reject an author's opinions, you begin to develop your own viewpoint. You engage the author in a two-way communication in which you become an active participant. You become caught up in the ideas under discussion.

Passive students make the mistake of accepting everything on the printed page as written by an authority and therefore not open to question. But active students always probe the statements and opinions they read, asking themselves whether they agree or disagree with the writer's views—and for what reasons. If they own the book, they make notes in the margins—one place they can be more honest than polite.

Teachers look for students who do more than merely repeat the information in the text without thinking about it deeply. They want students who apply what they have learned to new contexts. What sets apart skillful students from average students is the ability to think critically—to think for themselves—when they are reading.

By challenging an author's viewpoint, you can help yourself in several ways. You can offer your own independent views in class discussions. Your disputes with an author's opinions will often provide you with excellent topics for writing assignments or essay exams. And by thinking critically, you are learning to **push yourself to new levels of awareness** that lead to creative work. You are not just repeating what scholars have told you; rather you are learning to question as scholars themselves must question in order to make new discoveries.

Developing a Questioning Attitude

Advertising has already taught most of us to adopt a questioning attitude about what we view on television commercials. We take it for granted that a product is probably not as good as the manufacturer claims, that the detergent does not take out every stain instantly without scrubbing—or at least not as quickly as the TV commercial indicates. And you know you will never become a star tennis player just by wearing a certain kind of sneaker. The sneaker may, however, turn out to be a well-made brand that will improve the comfort of your tennis game. In any case, sensible people question the information they receive from advertisers and do not simply assume it is accurate.

In a similar way, skillful students do not simply assume that everything they read is accurate or up-to-date—or even the complete picture.

Instead they challenge and probe what they read by asking themselves questions like these:

- Am I convinced by what the author is saying?
- Does this information sound reasonable to me?
- Based on my personal experience, does this make sense?
- Can I think of any other examples like it?
- Does this explanation apply in every case?
- How does the writer know this information?
- Does the writer give me any sources for checking this information?
- Are these studies or statistics recent or out-of-date?

You should always ask yourself these or similar questions as you read. And read with an openness to new ideas—almost as if you are on a search for good ideas to improve your life.

If you heartily agree with the author because the information makes sense to you and matches your own past experiences, jot it down in your journal as something worth remembering. For example, one student was attracted to this sentence in her reading:

> I, however, can help, provided that I think not of going out to make the world a better place, but only of going *in* to make the world a better place.
>
> —Richard Mitchell

Our student wrote in her journal: "This author means I can help make the world a better place by making myself a more thinking, more capable person. And there's something to it because I often get discouraged about how little difference anyone makes. But Mitchell shows me how to have a small effect."

If you heartily disagree with an author, bring the point up during a class discussion or probe it further as an essay topic. Be demanding of all writers; challenge any writer whose opinions you believe are questionable or wrong.

Asking questions as you read is not just an academic skill-building exercise. When you raise questions and answer them as well as you can, you make the ideas far more meaningful for yourself by evaluating them according to your own experiences. You begin to sort out your own values and to understand yourself better by pinning down what you think and why.

Say you come across this statement in your reading: "It has long been known that people periodically need new challenges at work if they are to remain highly motivated." You should routinely ask yourself a series of probing questions about such a statement.

- Do I think the statement is generally correct?
- Do I personally agree or disagree with the statement?
- Does my personal experience lead me to think it is a good explanation of human behavior?
- Where does the author claim this information comes from?

One student responded: "On the one hand, the idea of people at work needing new challenges rings true. People get jaded by routine tasks and repetition. On the other hand, 'it has long been known' is not very specific; have studies been done on what motivates people at work?"

By asking yourself such leading questions, you probe the author's view as well as your own view of the issue. One characteristic of creative people is that they tend to question from many angles what other people simply accept.

In many cases in the past, you may have depended on the guidance of others—teachers, authors, experts, friends—to form your opinions. But we urge you to become less accepting and more assertive as you read your assignments. Confront the writer with your questions and disagreements. Jot down notes in the margin on whatever seems questionable or debatable.

Develop a questioning attitude. Take on the writer of whatever you read in a lively, ongoing debate.

> **✳**   One characteristic of creative people is that they tend to question from many angles what other people simply accept.

PRACTICE 1   Read the following statements carefully. Develop some questions you should ask yourself to probe these statements—both about the author's statement and about your personal response to the statement.

Example: "A cathedral, a wave of a storm, a dancer's leap never turn out to be as high as we had hoped." (Marcel Proust)

Answer: "Is what the writer says true, and do I agree? Yes, our hopes are always much too high. We expect too much and then are disappointed."

1. "Parental loss of control is quite common. All eighty parents in an interview study of two-parent families reported hitting, and 90 percent reported yelling. Forty-three percent of the families reported loss of control, which was defined as treating the child with a greater degree of physical or verbal aggression than the parent found acceptable. However, no child is going to be damaged for life by an occasional parental temper tantrum, particularly if the parent briefly apologizes and offers to explain later."

   —Marilyn Heins, M.D., and Anne Seiden, M.D.

2. "American students increasingly are expected to compete in an international marketplace, dominated by high-tech, readily changing demands. Teachers who once were content to emphasize rote memorization and repetition of facts must now teach students how to think for a living and how to continue learning on the job."

   —Dr. John I. Goodlad

3. "When college becomes a search for Mr. Right, young women narrow rather than expand their professional and personal options."

   —Joan Jacobs Brumberg, *New York Times*

4. "There is the road of short-term pleasure and long-term pain. There is the road of short-term pain and long-term pleasure. . . . If you sniff cocaine, shoot heroin in your veins, put dope in your veins, rather than hope in your brain, you made a decision. It's short-term pleasure, but it's long-term pain."

   —Jesse Jackson

5. "College core curriculums, those courses that supposedly represent the core of learning that each institution wants to instill in its graduates, are undergoing a reformation. . . . The major battle in this revolution pits those who believe the core should be based on the Western canon [the traditional works of Western culture] against those who support a broader, multicultural base rich in the voices of women, minorities, and foreign cultures."

   —William Celis, III

6. "Ms. Falco's recommendations for freeing Americans from the drug scourge place greater emphasis on private and community efforts, especially through education. She holds that school prevention programs can reduce the likelihood of children's using drugs; that neighborhoods and local police officers, working together, can drive dealers off the streets; that businesses can create programs to reduce drug use among employees."

   —Herbert Mitgang, *New York Times*

7. "I think the free public education, and the push we make to educate *all* our children, at least through high school, is one of the reasons for our greatness as a nation."

—Joseph A. Fernandez, Chancellor of New York City Public Schools, *New York Times Book Review*

Identifying the Other Sides of an Issue

One way to think critically is to look for the other possible sides of an issue. Search for any opposing opinions that might be used to counter an author's statement. For example, some author might argue that the main purpose of a writing course is for students to learn to express their personal viewpoints and that correct grammar and the mechanics of spelling and punctuation are of secondary importance.

To argue against this statement, you might say that such students could be judged unfairly at some later point because of their weaknesses in spelling and punctuation. In fact, these obvious errors might prevent a future employer from even reading through a job applicant's letter to discover his or her personal qualifications. You might also argue that such weaknesses are not readily overlooked in the business world and that therefore grammar and spelling should be given some emphasis in a writing course.

Examining an Issue from Different Perspectives: Pesticides

Sometimes you will be able to identify more than two sides of an issue. Take the controversial issue of how much pesticide and fungicide farmers should apply to farm crops to control insect damage and prevent crop losses. In an article taking the farmers' perspective, you may read that farmers want to continue to use chemicals and sprays to ensure high-quality, profitable crops and to keep prices down for the consumer. Without such spraying, their crops—eaten away by all kinds of insects and pests—are smaller and less desirable to consumers.

But you may also read that environmentalists take the opposite position; they are concerned that chemicals applied year after year may be harmful, over time, to those who eventually consume these crops. They believe the fruits and vegetables may retain some of the pesticides, which may accumulate in vital organs, and eventually harm consumers. Moreover, they complain that wildlife is endangered by unrestricted use of synthetic chemicals that run off into lakes and streams.

Then you may read about the average consumer, who is aware of the overuse of pesticides but nevertheless wants to buy reasonably priced and attractive fruits and vegetables.

Examining the issue of pesticides, you can identify at least three different viewpoints—the farmer's, the environmentalist's, and the consumer's.

Then say you read a recent newspaper account about a chemical that once was credited with helping Florida farmers produce acres of prize cucumbers, peppers, and cabbages but that now has turned that same farmland into wasteland where not even weeds grow. Tons of plants treated with Benlate, a fungicide, have had to be buried, and the farms cannot be replanted until the soil and water is free of the substance. The episode has forced farmers to ask themselves hard questions about their reliance on a whole range of chemical sprays and pesticides.

Taking everyone's needs into account, what, in your opinion, is a reasonable position on the issue of pesticides?

You do not have to *resolve* similar complex questions as you read, but you should at least *raise* them. Remember that you want to avoid simplistic, black-and-white thinking; and **recognize that several viewpoints often coexist,** each view held by various experts and each view having some merit.

If you investigate all the sides of an issue, you will come to a deeper, more complete understanding of the problems involved. To identify the opposing views of an issue as you read, call on all your previous knowledge, reading, memories, and experiences about it. Use all these resources to help you find support for *your* own opinion. If you want to find out more information about a specific issue, investigate the subject in the library (see Chapter 15).

> ***** If you investigate all the sides of an issue, you will come to a deeper, more complete understanding of the problems involved.

PRACTICE 2   For the following statements, give the other side or sides of the issue.

1. Each nation of the world must take care of its own hungry people.
2. Abused children should be taken from their parents and brought up by others.

3. It's a waste of time trying to rehabilitate juvenile drug users.
4. Every child should go to a school of equal quality; therefore, parents should be able to choose which school they want their children to attend, no matter what neighborhood or town they live in.
5. It is easy to define *pornography.*
6. The Native American was well-off living safely apart on reservations and was always well treated and protected by the government in the past.
7. As the only nation with enough military power, the United States should actively keep peace throughout the world and not let a dictator who abuses human rights take over any country.
8. Instead of worrying about birth control and overpopulation, we should concentrate on raising more food to feed everyone.
9. Varsity college football players should be given special treatment and be allowed more time to pass their courses. After all, they have to spend a lot of time at football practice.
10. Student newspapers should be supervised by teachers who decide what material is appropriate and censor the paper accordingly. Students have only a limited right to free speech because they at times lack judgment.

Matters of Fact and Interpretation

To develop critical-thinking skills, a reader should distinguish between a writer's factual information and his or her interpretation of these facts.

A writer, for example, might list the legislation passed during Franklin D. Roosevelt's terms as president; these are matters of fact that most scholars would agree upon. However, if the writer goes on to say that these legislative bills indicate that Roosevelt did not accomplish as much as he should have, this interpretation of the facts would probably find other scholars disagreeing strongly.

As readers, we often come across passages that interweave factual information and interpretation, and we are called upon to sort out the facts from the writer's interpretation of these facts.

Facts Can Be Verified

What is factual information? For practical purposes, a fact is something that we can count on as being reliable and accurate. It is a piece of information that can be verified by research (by checking in an encyclopedia or other reference book), or by making repeated measurements, such as in a laboratory experiment.

Here we have a sentence that can be verified in the library:

> Abraham Lincoln was assassinated on April 14, 1865, by John Wilkes Booth—just five days after the Civil War ended at Appomattox on April 9.

Reasonable people will accept these pieces of information without question.

We can also verify the dates of medical breakthroughs (an artificial heart was first used in 1963), of inventions (the Xerox machine was invented in 1946), and of scientific achievements (the first humans walked on the moon in 1969) as bits of factual information.

Historians know more facts about recent events than they do about earlier historical periods from which surviving records are scarce. Scholars, for example, would like to know far more facts about the life of William Shakespeare, whose education and activities remain largely a mystery.

A fact usually is expressed in *concrete* language—that is, by words that refer to physical measurements, time, distance, or weight. Scientists speak of their bits of factual information as *data*.

To verify their findings, scientists repeat their observations and experiments many times, trying to obtain the same results in independent laboratory tests. Through these efforts, they attempt to remove subjective factors and obtain objective results. Only in the frontiers of science, where many unknown factors remain, such as what explains the pull of gravity or what triggers certain diseases, do scientists differ on their interpretations of the data.

Opinions Are Open to Debate

In contrast to factual information, a *subjective opinion* is a statement of personal judgment or evaluation. It is based on relative values and individual beliefs and as such is not the final word on a subject. However, writers should *support* their opinions by supplying the reasons, evidence, assumptions, and facts that explain their thinking.

What are the critic's reasons for recommending a movie or praising a short story? What are a writer's examples for blaming the increase of violence in American society on the influence of television? **Critical readers expect writers to provide careful support and evidence for**

their opinions. If writers don't justify their opinions, critical readers remain unconvinced.

Look for clues in the language to see whether a writer is presenting you with facts or opinions or, as is often the case, a mixture of the two. Opinions often can be detected by comparisons ("more efficient than," "as disciplined as"), by adjectives ("careless," "determined," "pretentious"), and by evaluations ("this questionable approach," "a basic misunderstanding of the situation").

Interpretation of the Facts

Two writers might look at these two facts and interpret them in different ways:

- Lincoln's words on slavery: "My paramount object in this struggle is to save the Union, and is not either to save or to destroy slavery."
- Lincoln's delaying until 1862 the freeing of the slaves in the South (when he issued the Emancipation Proclamation).

Reading these pieces of information, one writer might conclude:

Lincoln was a shrewd and practical leader who spoke out against slavery cautiously, trying to reach a compromise with the South to save the Union.

Another might conclude:

Despite the myth of Lincoln as the Great Emancipator, he was a hesitant and even a questionable moral leader, who was willing to drag his feet on the great issue of freeing the slaves far too long.

Even when such opinions are stated quite firmly, the reader has to realize that these are the writer's own *interpretations* or evaluations of the facts. It is up to the reader to distinguish between the factual information (yes, the Emancipation Proclamation was issued in Lincoln's second term) and the writer's personal evaluations (seen in the descriptive adjectives *shrewd, practical, questionable*).

Whereas facts are generally agreed upon by reasonable people, opinions and interpretations are often subject to heated debate. In many instances, issues are complex and cannot be solved by simple black-and-white thinking. Unknown or ambiguous gray areas remain for future thinkers to debate.

To analyze differences of opinion among scholars, you need to use critical-thinking skills. After you have studied the issue in depth, form your own opinion of Lincoln's position. Was he a shrewd and practical politician, waiting until the time was right to act, or was he a weak moral leader?

Expert Opinion

A scholar who has spent many years studying the life and times of Lincoln will have opinions on Lincoln's view of slavery that should be given serious consideration. In academic areas, professors are often the experts on specific subjects within their discipline. Readers should give more weight to the opinions and interpretations of specialists in a given field than to, say, a journalist who is writing on the subject but has only studied it briefly and is not considered an authority.

> **✳** Even when opinions are firmly stated, readers must realize that these are the writer's own interpretations of the existing facts.

PRACTICE 3   In the following sentences, decide which information is (1) probably factual information, (2) a personal opinion, or (3) a mixture of fact and opinion. Give reasons to support your answer.

Example: Robert Frost, who was asked to read a poem at President Kennedy's inauguration, is America's finest poet.

Answer: mixture of fact and opinion; the fact that Frost read at Kennedy's inauguration can be verified, but whether or not Frost is America's "finest poet" is a matter of opinion

1. Blood circulation in mammals is a closed system in which the heart pumps blood through the body to deliver oxygen to the tissues.

_____

_____

2. A person who weighs 160 pounds is supported by 206 bones that weight a total of about 29 pounds.

   _____

   _____

3. Although he was slow to speak as a child, in the world of science no one compares to Albert Einstein.

   _____

   _____

4. Joe DiMaggio still holds the record for getting a hit in the most consecutive games (56 straight games) of the regular baseball season (1941).

   _____

   _____

5. Self-centered and ambitious, Paul Gauguin was an amateur artist who left his family responsibilities in France in order to become a painter in Tahiti.

   _____

   _____

6. The mother of twelve, Anne Hutchinson was banished from Boston in 1637 for her outspoken and controversial religious beliefs, considered by her judges as inappropriate for a woman.

   _____

   _____

7. The most important factor in choosing a career is how much satisfaction the daily work brings you.

   _____

   _____

8. The best-trained athletes in the world are Americans, followed by the Russians, and then the Japanese.

_____

_____

9. In his personal manner, Ronald Reagan was an effective and well-spoken president, but as it turned out, his administration was plagued by many problems (including the savings and loan scandal and the soaring national debt) that suggest he was not paying attention to business.

_____

_____

10. Everyone agrees that Prince is the greatest entertainer of our day; no one is a better singer and he moves like the finest of dancers; his presence is electrical.

_____

_____

Evaluating an Author's Viewpoint

When analyzing any piece of writing, look into how well the author has interpreted the various facts and conflicting opinions surrounding an issue. In other words, examine and **evaluate an author's viewpoint or position on an issue.** How, for example, do we evaluate the viewpoint of a historian who thinks Lincoln dragged his feet and didn't make bold moves? Is this viewpoint right or wrong? To find out, ask yourself a series of questions.

Ask Questions About the Author's Sources

Ask yourself where the writer's facts came from and what sources (books, magazines, journals) the writer has quoted. Can you verify these sources through information given in footnotes or endnotes? If the author does not give you the sources of the information, consider why he or she does not.

Ask Questions About the Quality of Support

Does the writer back up his or her opinions with **support,** that is, with facts, reasons, evidence, or examples, which, taken together, lead you to understand the author's viewpoint? Does the author discuss the possible opposing views or assume there isn't any opposition? Are the facts, as given, consistent? Are the opinions reasonable?

Ask Questions About Documents

Does the writer refer to original or **primary sources,** that is, letters, writings of witnesses, or authentic papers, say, in Lincoln's handwriting? Or does the writer use **secondary sources,** that is, works of other writers commenting on the original documents?

Ask Questions About the Author's Credentials

What do you know about the author's background? Has he or she written anything else on the subject? Is the author considered an expert in the field? Is the writer on the faculty of a major university or in an important position in the government, such as the head of the Internal Revenue Service (IRS), that gives authority to his or her views on taxes?

Ask Questions About Language

Is the language neutral and reasonable ("he's undoubtedly made some regrettable errors")? Or is the language emotional and exaggerated ("philandering, pot-smoking draft dodger" were the words used by Mary Matalin to describe the then presidential candidate Bill Clinton)? Is the writer appealing to reason and fairness, using arguments based on legal principles or moral values, or is the writer appealing to prejudices and passions, using name calling ("that bozo"), using insults, using vague and imprecise language?

Ask Questions About Bias

Does the author attempt to be objective? Or does the author appear openly *biased* or one-sided in favor of a certain group or position? Does the author openly represent and defend a political cause—for or against gun control, for or against abortion? Or does the author try to disguise a bias? If the writer is employed by a company, be skeptical, or at least cautious, about anything he or she writes about the company's products or interests. For example, be cautious if someone employed by a chemical company writes about the pesticides the company produces. And be sure to look at what the opposing side has written about the issue.

If the writer is not openly employed by a political group or cause, you still should look closely to **see if the author consistently takes a one-sided position.** For example, when writing about the women's movement, Phyllis Schlafly, who is known to support traditional roles for women, will predictably oppose feminist positions. Gloria Steinem, who is known for her support of equal rights for women, will consistently support feminist positions. You as a reader have to be vigilant in detecting these biases—both those that are openly stated and those that you have to read between the lines.

Ask Questions About the Author's Purpose

Does the author want to *inform* you—that is, does he or she want to present evidence on the opposing sides of an issue and let you come to your own conclusions?

Or does the author try to *persuade* you? In other words, does he or she give you both sides but persuade you to favor one side? Or does the author only give you a one-sided view of the issue?

Ask Questions About Dates

Is the study up-to-date? Is it the most recent study available? What is its date of publication? When was the research carried out? Is the author aware of the most recent research?

Can you find a more up-to-date study? Since many fields are changing very rapidly, be sure you have the most recent publications whenever possible.

What Is Your Evaluation of the Author's Work?

After all your questioning, do you generally agree with the author's conclusions? Do you think the approach is objective—with the opposing viewpoints presented fairly? Is the author making valuable points?

◻ PRACTICE 4   If you come across the following information about an author, what would you think of his or her credentials? Put a check in the space that you think describes the author's qualifications.

1. Stephen Jay Gould teaches biology, geology, and the history of science at Harvard University. He frequently writes a column for *Natural History Magazine* and has written many collections of essays, including *Ever Since Darwin*.

   As a writer on Darwin's theories, the author is
   Very qualified _____ Qualified _____ Not well qualified _____
   Not enough information given to decide _____

2. Judy Syfers Brady is the author of a very popular essay titled "I Want a Wife," which originally appeared in *Ms.* magazine in 1971 and has been republished many times. Brady writes about herself: "I am not a 'writer' but really am a disenfranchised (and fired) housewife, now secretary. I have published other articles in various types of publications (one on abortion, one on union organizing, for instance) and have edited . . . a newsletter for school paraprofessionals in San Francisco."

   As a writer on American unions, the author is
   Very qualified _____ Qualified _____ Not well qualified _____
   Not enough information given to decide _____

3. On the cover of Hayden Herrera's 1983 biography of the Mexican artist Frida Kahlo, it reads: "Hayden Herrera is a New York critic specializing in twentieth-century American and Latin American art. She spent much of her childhood in Mexico. . . . She received her doctorate in art history from the City University of New York and has contributed numerous articles to scholarly and popular publications. This is her first book."

   For information on the paintings of Frida Kahlo, the author is
   Very qualified _____ Qualified _____ Not well qualified _____
   Not enough information given to decide _____

4. Iris Lee is a graduate student in anthropology at the University of Arizona. She is now writing a master's thesis on the Pima Indians of Arizona. The present article on the Pima culture is her first published work.

   As a source on the Indian cultures of the Southwest, the author is
   Very qualified _____ Qualified _____ Not well qualified _____
   Not enough information given to decide _____

5. Leon Edel is a biographer who has specialized in the life and works of the American novelist Henry James. Edel's five-volume definitive biography of James was completed in 1972.

    As a writer on the short stories of Henry James, he is
    Very qualified _____ Qualified _____ Not well qualified _____
    Not enough information given to decide _____

Examining Your Own Biases

In addition to noting the biases of other writers, you should check out your own possible biases. Sometimes we are unaware of our own prejudices, and adopt some of the negative attitudes within our culture without even examining them. Do you have any personal negative feelings toward any group, considering everyone in the group as just alike rather than as unique individuals? Make sure that you want to hold such opinions and that you are not just maintaining someone else's old prejudices.

Working Space

READING ASSIGNMENT

Should farmers use chemical pesticides to spray their crops? Read the following two recent articles on pesticides. Then answer the questions that follow.

Both articles discuss the present laws on the use of pesticides. The Delaney Clause now bans the use of certain pesticides in *processed* or packaged foods, such as juices, jellies, flour, and baked goods. However, the present laws do allow some of these pesticides on *fresh* foods. Farmers can protect their crops, but at some risk of having traces remain in the fresh fruits and vegetables we eat. Think about each author's viewpoint carefully.

Article 1

No More Pesticides for Dinner
AL MEYERHOFF

The debate over pesticides will provide an early test of the Clinton Administration's pledge to enhance environmental protection.

Of all interventions into the natural order, perhaps none has stirred so much debate as the creation and use of chemical pesticides in agriculture. Starting with the biochemical revolution after World War II, alchemists have brewed as many as 50,000 new concoctions in America alone. The use of pesticides has increased dramatically, now approaching three billion pounds a year.

No one can deny that the formulation of some 600 ingredients has been a boon to mankind. Still, a price is paid when society relies so heavily on toxic chemicals: 68 pesticide ingredients have been determined to cause cancer. One out of every 10 community drinking-water wells contains pesticides; agriculture is the largest source of surface-water pollution in America.

Farmers exposed to herbicides have a six times greater risk than others of contracting certain cancers. Children in homes using pesticides are seven times as likely to develop childhood leukemia.

And overall, the bugs are winning, with nearly 500 species resistant to pesticides. . . .

A consensus is emerging that our pesticide laws, with their contradictory standards, inadequate enforcement and encouragement of long delays in taking products off the market, need fundamental reform.

The laws regulating pesticides in food were enacted nearly 40 years ago. There are two fundamentally inconsistent approaches. Pesticides in raw commodities such as fresh fruits and vegetables are subject to a cost-benefit test, allowing dozens of carcinogens[1] in food, often at unacceptably high levels of cancer risk. Pesticides that concentrate in processed foods such as juices, oils and flour are governed by the Delaney Clause,[2] prohibiting any residue of carcinogens.

The central premise of the clause is simple and powerful: what we understand best about carcinogens is the limited extent of our knowledge. As a result, the clause is grounded in prevention: prohibiting carcinogens in processed food, since the nation would otherwise be routinely exposed to them in its daily diet.

Much has changed since the clause was enacted in 1958. The use of pesticides has increased at least tenfold. Because of improved detection methods, we now know we are being exposed daily to dozens of carcinogenic toxic agents in many different foods, with no attempt to calculate the aggregate risk to health. At the same time, the

---

[1]carcinogen: substance believed to cause cancer
[2]Delaney Clause: a current law prohibiting any trace of pesticide in processed food

incidence of many forms of cancer, including breast cancer and childhood cancer, is on the rise.

Congressional action on pesticide reform legislation appears likely. Some may argue that the Delaney Clause must remain inviolate, but of far greater importance is fulfilling the statute's underlying purpose by reducing exposure to toxic substances at the source.

New legislation should adopt strict standards for all residues of pesticides in food, raw and processed; phase out pesticides most likely to cause cancer, and reallocate research dollars to promote alternative technologies and substantially reduce pesticide use.

The philosophy behind the Delaney Clause—preventing unnecessary exposure to hazardous substances—should be preserved. We still do not know whether humans are more or less sensitive than laboratory animals to carcinogens and whether one carcinogen may increase the cancer-causing effects of another. We do not know the cumulative impact of dozens of carcinogens permitted in the food supply and environment.

Rachel Carson was right in her book *Silent Spring*: "The ultimate answer is to use less toxic chemicals so that the public hazard from their misuse is greatly reduced. This system, however—deliberately poisoning our food, then policing the result—is too reminiscent of Lewis Carroll's White Knight who thought of 'a plan to dye one's whiskers green, and always use so large a fan that they could not be seen.' "

Article 2

Mother Nature's Pesticide Factory
MICHAEL FUMENTO

In the environmentalists' war against technology, nowhere are the stakes higher than the assault on pesticides. The current battleground is the Delaney Clause of the Food Additives Amendment of 1958, which bans anything that causes cancer in humans or rodents from being added to processed food.

The new Administrator of the Environmental Protection Agency, Carol Browner, in February asked Congress to review the clause, calling it an anachronism that threatened the U.S. food supply. Environmentalists objected loudly, and the E.P.A. quickly retracted her remarks. But Ms. Browner was right: this outdated law should be changed.

One problem with the environmentalists' argument is their claim that the tiny amount of pesticide residue left on food puts us all at risk of cancer. (About 1 percent of fruits and vegetables have residues above the legal limit; most have none at all.)

This stems from assumptions that a human will react the same way to a chemical as a rodent in a laboratory will. But 30 percent of the chemicals that cause cancer in rats at high doses do not harm mice, and vice-versa. With such a discrepancy between closely related species, what does that say about extrapolating[1] from either of them to man?

Another questionable assumption is that chemicals that cause tumors in rodents when administered in huge doses will cause tumors in humans at a fraction of those doses. It ignores the scientific axiom "only the dose makes the poison." The iron in a tablet that many adults take regularly has killed babies. Eating a lot of salt-cured meat can increase the risk of stomach cancer, but people must have some salt to survive.

Half of all synthetic chemicals tested in animals have caused tumors. But only the most dogmatic chemophobe believes that half of all man-made chemicals are carcinogens at the levels to which humans are exposed. And those who believe it must accept the sobering fact that half of the chemicals that occur naturally in foods have also been found in tests to cause cancer.

Four years ago, a CBS "60 Minutes" report panicked the nation with the claim that a chemical used in apple-growing, Alar, was the "most potent cancer-causing agent in our food supply." The evidence against Alar was that a chemical into which it decays may have caused tumors when fed in huge doses to mice (rats suffered no ill effect).

But two cancer researchers at the University of California at Berkeley, Lois Gold and Bruce Ames, pointed out that organic apple juice often contains up to 137 naturally occurring volatile chemicals, of which five have been tested. Two of these five have been found to be carcinogenic in laboratory animals. Another, alcohol, is a human carcinogen. Yet the Delaney Clause has not been applied to organic juice.

The two scientists also observed that in a cup of coffee there are 17 carcinogens that can affect rodents. They wrote in *Science* in 1990: "One cup of coffee contains 10 milligrams of known (natural) rodent

---

[1]extrapolating: projecting into an unknown area

carcinogens, about equivalent in weight to the potentially carcinogenic synthetic pesticide residues one eats in a year." They estimate that 99.99 percent of all pesticides, by weight, are generated naturally. Monsanto, Dow and Uniroyal are amateurs compared to Mother Nature's pesticide factory.

There is no scientific rationale for banning synthetic pesticides while leaving the natural ones alone. Notwithstanding this, the National Resources Defense Council[2] last year won a Federal court decision upholding the strictest enforcement of the Delaney Clause. This decision will likely remove from the market 35 different chemicals that appear in more than 10 percent of the basic pesticides farmers use.

The clause needs to be updated. Just as the Founding Fathers put no provision in the Constitution allowing for an air force, it could not have occurred to Congress 35 years ago when it passed the Delaney Clause that in testing rodents with massive doses we would find that half of all chemicals cause cancer. Nor could anyone have known that the clause would be used to exclude the tiniest amounts of manmade carcinogens while allowing huge amounts of natural ones.

Nobody is stopping environmentalist extremists from shopping at organic-food stores where they can pay far more for food. But as the evidence continues to grow that eating fruits and vegetables helps prevent cancer, we cannot allow special-interest groups to declare their superstitions as science.

1. Describe the viewpoint of each author on the issue of pesticides. Which one is in favor of using them and why? Which is in favor of limiting them and why?

2. Do you think pesticides should be banned from the food supply or not? What evidence do you think is the strongest?

---

[2]National Resources Defense Council: an environmental group

3. Do you agree that natural chemicals found in food are the same as synthetic or man-made chemicals?

4. Do you agree that the huge dose of chemicals given rats in experiments differs from the dose people probably eat in food?

5. If the evidence is still unclear, what do you think is the safest course?

WRITING ASSIGNMENT

Men are programmed to provide for their families economically while women are programmed to take care of their families emotionally and physically. As a result men put more effort into their jobs than women. The net result is a difference in work intensity that leads to that 40 percent gap in earnings. But there is no discrimination against women—only the biological facts of life.

—Lester Thurow

In a one- or two-page paper, agree or disagree with Lester Thurow's viewpoint, raising any questions you think are appropriate and looking for other sides of the issue.

JOURNAL ASSIGNMENT

Do you think it is possible for anyone to be purely objective in his or her thinking, or do you think everyone has a subjective point of view depending on his or her individual background?

✔ Checking Out: Review Questions for Chapter 14

1. Why is it a good strategy for the reader to agree or disagree with a writer's opinions and to challenge any of the writer's statements that seem questionable? How does this help the reader?

2. After considering a writer's opinions, why should the reader play devil's advocate and search for opposing sides of the argument?

3. What are some ways in which you can distinguish between fact and opinion?

4. What are appropriate questions to ask about an author's credentials?

5. Why is an author who gives the sources of his or her material more useful to a reader?

6. What is a biased viewpoint and how can you detect it? Why is it important to know if a writer represents some special group or interest?

7. What are primary sources? How are they used by scholars? What are secondary sources?

8. What are some questions you can ask yourself in order to examine an author's statements?

9. Name some current controversial issues where equally valid opinions coexist.

10. What are some of the ways a reader can evaluate a writer's viewpoint?

▶ In Summary

To become a critical reader, raise questions as you read. Agree or disagree with the writer continually, and examine your own point of view by reflecting on the author's views. Use your own past experiences and knowledge of the world to help you evaluate an author's viewpoint. When reading, compare your own opinions and personal experiences to those of the author.

A skilled reader acts as devil's advocate and brings up all opposing views. By looking at all sides of an issue, the reader can get closer to the heart of the matter. We have given you a checklist of questions (pages 330–332) to raise when you want to evaluate an author's credentials. Examine in particular the sources of an author's information and decide whether or not the author presents a one-sided or biased viewpoint. And check the dates of the author's research; in general you want to be familiar with the most recent studies on an issue.

To analyze an author's viewpoint, distinguish between objective facts and subjective opinion. You can often determine by a writer's use of language whether or not he or she is attempting to be impartial and neutral, or subjective and opinionated.

In this chapter, we have discussed how to use critical-thinking skills when evaluating a single writer's viewpoint. In the next chapter, we will discuss how to use these same skills when evaluating the conflicting views of several authors as they discuss the same issue.

CHAPTER **15**

Using the Library for Research

"The library is a school and the librarian is in the highest sense a teacher. . . ."

—*Melvil Dewey, librarian*

If you are asked to write an informal or personal essay, you can make use of your own experiences, memories, and knowledge of the world. But if you are assigned a more formal research paper, you need to find additional sources of information written by specialists in the field.

To locate useful sources of information, become familiar with your college library and its collection of books, journals, newspapers, and microforms. To help you learn how to gather material for a research paper, read about:

- Finding out what resources are available in your library
- Planning a strategy for doing library research
- Carrying out research in card catalogs, by computer search, or with hardbound indexes
- Writing bibliography cards to keep track of sources
- Taking appropriate notes on note cards

For any subject that you want to delve into more deeply, the library is at your disposal.

Becoming Familiar with the Library

At the library, you can look up information on virtually any subject you want to learn more about. Do you need in-depth, detailed information or a general overview of a topic? To help you find what you need, the information is organized and classified by author, title, and subject. The material is there waiting for you; your job is to find it.

Learn What Is Available

Your college library houses traditional books, periodicals (magazines and journals), and newspapers—as well as computer and card catalogs to help you locate each item on the shelf. With the ongoing revolution in library services, your library probably contains audio and visual media, micro-forms (miniaturized print), and computer equipment of which you are not aware. Not all the material is in sight; less-used items are stored in stacks.

To do your research, feel at home in the library:

- **Master the computer catalog or card catalog.** Learn how to hunt for information by using these catalogs, which give the call number for each item in the library.
- **Consult the reference librarian** on how to search for information and how to use the catalogs and computer terminals. This person's job is to help you.
- **Learn how to use indexes to journals and magazines.** These will give you a list of the titles in back issues of journals and magazines. The indexes are available in hardcover volumes and often on computer terminals as well.
- **Learn the floor plan,** including where you can find books on reserve (reserved for you by your professor), where reference works and periodicals are shelved, where various media are stored, and so forth.
- If possible, **take a tour to introduce yourself to the library** and its resources.

✳   The primary job of reference librarians is to help readers find the information they are looking for.

Discovering a Topic for Your Research

When assigning research papers, instructors usually give their students a general list of research topics to choose from. Here, for example, is a list from a freshman composition course:

Eating disorders
Environmental hazards
Domestic violence
Medical mysteries
Alcoholism
Animal rights
Virtual reality
Sexual harassment
Victims' rights
Cults
Natural disasters
Organ transplants
Prison reform

In their present form, however, all of these topics are too broad and sweeping to be covered in a ten- to fifteen-page research paper. Just consider for a moment the many subtopics that fall under a large general heading like alcoholism—causes, symptoms, effects, cures, and so on.

To get started on your research, choose a topic and then find an aspect or area of that topic that you can focus on. Some students claim that this is the hardest part of writing a research paper. Selecting and narrowing your topic won't be a problem for you, however, if you follow just a few simple guidelines.

Start with a Subject That Interests You

If you are not remotely interested in eating disorders, don't make this subject the topic of your research. You will be working on your paper for a lengthy period of time. Excitement about and interest in the subject are essential to maintaining a high level of concentration and motivation while you are doing your research.

Choose a Subject You Know Something About

Unless you are prepared to spend a good deal of time learning about an unfamiliar topic, you would be wise to pick an area in which you have some knowledge. Say that you are interested in organ transplants and cults. If you have read a few articles about cults in America and know next to nothing about organ transplants, plan on making the former topic the subject of your research.

Narrow Your Topic

Once you have chosen your general topic, think of ways to focus or narrow it, given the length of your paper and the amount of time at your disposal. You cannot tackle the whole subject of adoption; instead you need to find one aspect of it that you can handle. To focus your topic, try one of the following:

Browse   Browse quickly through a book written for the general reader, one that covers your topic broadly, and then try to identify one specific area for your research. Or find and read a few articles on the general topic. **The more knowledgeable you become, the easier it will be to discover a manageable topic.**

Restrict Yourself to One Area   Jot down various aspects of the topic and then select the one that holds your interest. For the general topic of adoption, you might consider focusing on one of the following aspects:

- the rights of the adopting parents
- the laws on adoption
- the interests of the adopted child
- the rights of the birth mother and father

Then you should narrow one of these subtopics even further. You might research the adoption laws in your state and compare them to those of another state. Or you might write about the need for uniform adoption laws among the states.

Look for a fresh perspective   Think of a fresh way to approach the topic. You may want to focus on the well-being of adopted children and argue that their needs should come before the legal rights of either the birth or the adopting parents.

Rethink or change your topic   You can always rethink your topic as you learn more about it. If you find something more appealing to write about, by all means change your topic. If you cannot find enough information, or you are missing a key book from the library, do not feel locked in. The more you are convinced about the importance of your topic, the better your paper will be.

Gathering Your Sources of Information

Let's assume you have a tentative subject, a subject that you're interested in learning more about. It's time to develop your **working bibliography,** a list of sources you plan to explore. To begin to gather information on your subject, act like a detective and follow leads. Here are some ways to get started:

- Ask your instructor for a few key books or names of authors to start your research.
- Speak to a person knowledgeable on the subject and ask for some leads.
- Speak to a reference librarian, describe your subject, and ask for advice on a good search strategy. Particularly with the new computer technology, reference librarians can save you time by pointing out the right terminal and giving instructions for using it.
- Use the computer catalog, searching for your topic under *keyword* or *subject.* Say you wanted to learn about women's impact on art; you might type in *women and art* or *women artists* until you find the right combination. Once you find one or two titles, you can usually find additional clues on the screen.
- Look at the *Encyclopaedia Britannica* for an overview of your subject and a bibliography.
- Check the *Readers' Guide to Periodical Literature,* which indexes articles in about 250 well-known popular magazines. You can use it to search for subjects, such as adoption, listed alphabetically.
- For the titles of articles in scholarly journals, find out the name of the *index* that lists them. These indexes, such as the *Education Index* (often available in hardcover and on computer) give the titles from numerous journals on education. Some give brief abstracts or summaries of the articles.
- Use the footnotes or bibliography of the first books you find to help you search for additional titles.

You will probably need to search in stages. It is usually more efficient to do a thorough search after you have completed some preliminary reading. As you learn more about your topic, you will have a clearer understanding of which sources are worthwhile. Though this means several trips to the library, it saves time in the long run.

Preparing Your Bibliography Cards

To keep track of your sources, **write a bibliographic card for each source** that you plan to read.

- Use 3″ × 5″ index cards or slips of paper.
- Record only one source (book, journal, newspaper article) per card.
- Distinguish between books and articles and take down the correct information for each (usually found on the copyright or title page).
- Even if you photocopy an article, make a bibliography card because the interior pages of the article will not have the full information (such as the volume number) you need later for your bibliography list (the works used in your research).
- Always take cards to the library to help you keep track of your sources.
- Always jot down a call number in case you need the book again.

Record the following information for books:

1. author's *full* name (or authors if there are two or three; if four or more authors, list only the first author and add "and others" or "et al.")
2. complete title, *underlined*
3. city of publication (add the state if the city is not well known—such as "Englewood Cliffs, N.J.")
4. publisher (usually the short form of the name—Knopf rather than Alfred A. Knopf, or Princeton UP for Princeton University Press)
5. year published

Record the following information for popular magazines and scholarly journals:

1. author's full name (as for books)
2. full title of article, set in *quotation marks*
3. name of journal or magazine, *underlined*
4. volume number plus issue number (or month or season if no issue number)
5. year published
6. page or pages on which the article is found

Note: You do not need city or publisher for articles; you do need volume and issue numbers.

Record the following information for newspaper articles:

1. author's full name
2. full title of article, set in *quotation marks*
3. name of newspaper, *underlined*
4. full date (day, month, year)
5. page or pages on which the article is found

See Figure 15–1 on page 350 for some sample bibliographic cards showing how to record the correct bibliographical information on a book, a scholarly journal, a popular magazine, and a newspaper.

Finding a Book: The Computer Catalog

More and more libraries are closing their traditional card catalogs and moving to on-line computer catalogs. These terminals are convenient, fast, and usually easy to operate. They can tell you whether the book you're looking for is or is not checked out.

The computer can help you locate a book by author, title, subject, or key word. The most unrestricted way to search is to type in a **key word** (or key words) on your topic and then to use any clues on the screen to continue your search.

By using the computer catalog, student Margaret Murano hoped to find some useful books on *utopias,* communities that strive for a better way of life. She elected to search by a key word since she didn't know the names of any specific authors or titles. Margaret started by typing in *utopias* when the computer asked for a key word. The computer responded with 297 titles, describing utopias all over the world. Faced with too many choices, Margaret had to restrict her key word. Since she was interested in American communities such as the Shakers, she typed in *American utopias* and was pleased to see only three titles appear on the screen.

She chose one title, *Seven American Utopias,* as a promising starting point, a book that would give her information on seven utopian communities. The computer produced the screen shown at the top of page 349.

The computer also produced additional subject headings, including *millennialism,* another term for the movement describing such communities. So Margaret was in luck; she saw on the screen that her book was in the library and that it had a bibliography leading her to other books. Margaret copied all the information she needed from *Seven American Utopias* onto a small bibliography card, including the call number (see Figure 15–1, top).

```
Author     Hayden, Dolores   Keyword = American
                                              Utopias
Title      Seven American Utopias
Published  Cambridge, Mass.: MIT Press, 1976
Status     in library
Includes   index, bibliography
Call no.   HX653.H39
Subjects:  Utopias—United States
```

If Your Book Is Not on the Shelf

Research can be frustrating if you locate a promising book in the catalog only to find it checked out or not on the shelf where it belongs. However, the librarian can check the computer and give you information on the book's whereabouts—and when it is due back.

The computer can also tell the librarian what other libraries own the book and whether it is available for an *interlibrary loan.* Since books may not be immediately available, allow time in your schedule for delays.

If it turns out that the books you need are lost or otherwise unavailable, you might have to change or refocus your research topic.

The Card Catalog

Until very recently, every college library maintained a **card catalog** with every book in its collection listed several times on printed cards. Most libraries now have replaced their card catalogs entirely by computers; others still maintain their card catalogs. In the traditional catalogs, cards are kept in chests containing many small drawers, with alphabetized titles on the outside to identify the range of the cards within.

For its card catalog, the library usually makes from four to six (or more) cards for *each* book. One card is listed under the **author;** one is listed under the **title;** and the rest are listed under **subject headings** (that is, the three or four main subjects that the book discusses). The subject headings can help you search for additional or related sources; they are generally listed at the bottom of both author and title cards.

Figure 15–1: Bibliographic Cards to Track Sources

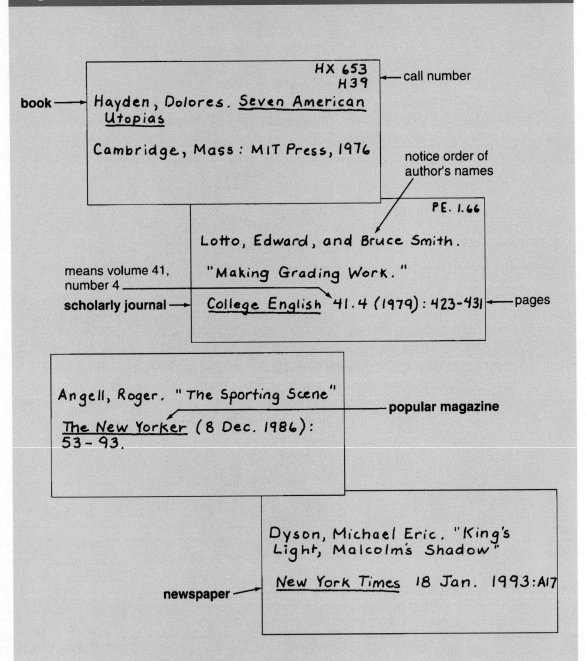

Useful Research Techniques

It is easy to spend too much time on unproductive research; use your time carefully to maximize results.

Be Alert for Leads to Additional Texts

Let one book help you find others; check its bibliography and footnotes for other related texts. If you locate one book on the shelf as you are researching, check the same area for other books that might be useful. Because libraries shelve related subjects together, you might stumble upon other good leads. Many researchers have found good books by happy accidents.

Read Selectively

Quickly check the index for the key concepts on your subject and for the pages where they appear. See if key words like *Shakers* or *utopia* are listed; go directly to those pages. Forget the old habit of reading from cover to cover; check the table of contents for chapters that cover what you want. Use exploratory reading techniques and skim until you come to material that will help you; then read more carefully. **Research requires selective reading;** you must **hone in on what is important to your topic**—at all times asking yourself, "How vital is this information to my paper?"

Review Frequently What You Have Already Discovered to Guide the Next Stage of Your Research

To get perspective on your research, read over the notes you have taken and see if you have found something unexpected, some point you want to study further, or some controversy you want to investigate. Do not continue to take notes aimlessly; stop to **check your progress**—to see what you have found and where you are headed.

Mull Over Your Research in Your Spare Moments

Mulling over your material in your journal or in your head is helpful as you begin to connect your ideas and put them into new relationships. Use spare moments to review what you have found out so far.

Reread Key Books Toward the End of Your Research

Sometimes it is helpful to return to a book or two toward the end of your research. When you have gained more insights on the topic, you may understand more clearly the author's perspective.

In doing research, learn enough about your topic so that you can write confidently about it and explain what you have discovered. You have to become fired up by it; you have to make it *your* own subject.

> ✱   Do not continue to take notes aimlessly; stop to check your progress—to see what you have found and where you are headed.

PRACTICE 1   Use the computer catalog or the card catalog to look up (1) two authors, (2) two titles, and (3) two subjects. Copy on note cards the information given to you by the computer screen or the printed card. If you cannot think of an author or a subject that interests you, look up sources on a well-known subject such as Martin Luther King, Jr., or the civil rights movement.

Searching for Articles in Magazines and Journals

Magazines and journals are rich sources of information for your research papers. Titles of articles, from both recent and past issues, can be found listed on computer catalogs or in hardcover volumes, called *indexes*.

These indexes cover virtually all the articles published in a large field, such as business or engineering. They are located in the reference section of the library. Some of these indexes are:

Readers' Guide to Periodical Literature	Lists titles of articles from 250 magazines (such as *Newsweek, Scientific American, Wilderness, The New Yorker*)
Humanities Index	Covers articles on the humanities (literature, fine arts, philosophy, etc.)
Education Index	Covers articles on education
General Science Index	Lists articles on science

It's not important to know the name of any particular index, but it is important to know that an index on every major field exists and to ask for the one you need.

Before computers, these indexes appeared as heavy hardcover volumes, listing by year all the articles published in a given field. Most of the indexes now also appear on computer data bases; find out which indexes your library has on line and what years they cover.

What kind of articles are you looking for—recent scholarly research or more general magazines like *Newsweek* or *The New Yorker?* Scholarly journals and popular magazines appear on different data bases. Try some of these tips for locating useful articles:

- Search for yourself. Look in the reference section to find out which index lists titles of articles on your subject. Learn whether your library has the index in hardcover volumes or on computer.
- Ask the reference librarian how to find articles on a subject such as adoption records. Should you, for example, look in journals in the field of social work or in sociology?
- **Use the computer terminal as a prompt;** many terminals have directions explaining what journals they cover and directions for how to use them.
- If you find literally hundreds of articles on the computer, type in a related key word or words to limit your search. Get help if you are not making progress.
- Use a hardcover index to browse for articles on your subject. For example, look in the *Readers' Guide to Periodical Literature* for articles on adoption. Such subjects are listed alphabetically. Each volume covers a single year, so to cover ten years, you will have to look in ten volumes.
- Decide whether you can find the information you want in popular magazines such as *Time* or in scholarly journals—or whether to use both.

One student called up *adoption* on the computer and was dismayed to find five thousand documents. This first try, however, produced a *see also* list of other subjects—such as *adoptees, biological parents, adoptive parents*—that helped her search further.

Next she tried the key words *"adoption—secrecy"* with no luck, but eventually she found the phrase *sealed adoption records,* giving her exactly what she wanted.

Use any clues on the screen, such as a list of related subjects, to help you hunt for additional titles. But if you are baffled and find yourself wasting too much time, ask for help.

Where to Start: Books, Articles, or Newspapers?

As a rule of thumb, start with books when researching historical events such as the nineteenth-century Shaker settlements, and with magazines when looking up more recent issues, like the ongoing discussions about AIDS.

In general, recent articles will give you the most up-to-date research on a given topic; but often the scope of an article is limited, and the reader does not get a full picture of the subject. A book, much wider in coverage, usually offers an overview of the entire subject. You may want to use a combination of both: books for the background information and the broad perspective; magazines for events that are relatively recent or fast-changing.

If some key event occurred on a specific date, consider starting with newspapers—for background on what else took place at the time. And by all means, read several papers for different interpretations. Check the *New York Times Index* as well as the indexes of other major papers, such as the *Chicago Tribune* and the *Washington Post.*

Whenever possible, try to locate several authors with opposing perspectives on your issue; such writers will give you a clash of views that you can attempt to resolve. Often authors mention other writers or scholars with whom they disagree.

For topics like the framing of the Constitution that have a complex past history and many sources covering them, find a few of what are considered the classic books on the subject. Then, if possible, look for recent authors who have questioned the thinking of earlier scholars.

Taking Notes on Note Cards

In addition to recording your sources on small index cards, use larger 4″ × 6″ index cards (or slips of paper) to take notes on your reading. Be sure to **label each card with the author's last name and the pages** on which you found the information. Also add a short title if you have two or more books by the same author.

The most difficult task, particularly at the start of research, is deciding what information to record on your note cards. Invariably you—like everyone else—will take notes on what you don't need, and you will not record what would have been a perfect quote. If you are determined, sometimes you can relocate the book with that quote.

Try to resist taking notes until you get a good grasp of your subject. Instead skim several sources to get an overview of your topic. As you grow more familiar with your material and develop a working thesis statement, you will be able to take notes more productively (see Chapter 16 for ways to develop a thesis statement). Record only one piece of information on each card. Give a short label or title to each card so you know what it contains, and review your note cards as you read and research so that you know what else you need to find.

What form should a note take? You have three options: direct quote, paraphrase, and summary.

Use Direct Quotations for Apt Remarks

Use a direct quote when the author's words are especially witty, controversial, to the point, or well phrased. For example, Oscar Wilde's words should be quoted exactly: "The only way to get rid of temptation is to yield to it." If you reworded it ("Oscar Wilde notes that if you give in to temptation, it usually goes away"), the sentence loses its bite.

Put quotation marks around the quote on your note card to remind yourself to transfer the quotation marks to your paper. When using a quotation in your paper, lead into it smoothly, so that it sounds natural in context.

Use Paraphrase to Restate the Author's Words

If, on the other hand, the author's language is ordinary or lifeless, factual or statistical, you may want to paraphrase it. In a paraphrase, you restate the author's meaning—but in your own words. (In a pinch, you may use no more than two of the author's exact words in a row.) Reproduce the author's exact sense but express it in your own words. Just as in the case of a direct quote, *you must cite the source of the idea* (see pages 382–383 on how to cite a direct quote and a paraphrase).

Use Summary to Condense Long Passages

Your third option is to summarize a long passage on a note card, boiling it down to essentials: "The author gives seven arguments for opposing the Equal Rights Amendment—none of them new: among them, whether women can be drafted into the army, whether we can manage single-sex bathrooms, and why we need the ERA if other laws cover it already."

You might also want to photocopy this author's long seven-point argument in case you need it later, and put your summary in your pile of note cards to have available when you are planning your paper.

To prevent later confusion, immediately label all photocopies with the author's name at the top. You might also want to use a highlighting pen on the photocopy to mark the key phrases that you have summarized. Figure 15–2 illustrates three types of notes: direct quotation, paraphrase, and summary.

Make Note Cards on Articles You Have Photocopied

Just as you take notes on your texts as a learning device, we think you should take notes on photocopies, even if you have them nearby. By making paraphrases and recording direct quotes, you engage with the material and evaluate its usefulness.

Make Note Cards on Your Own Ideas

As you read, you often will develop ideas and responses of your own that you want to remember. Put these ideas on note cards. Label them clearly so you know they are your own original ideas.

Switch Topics If You Cannot Find Sources

The key to searching for sources is to do it in a way that leads you to good results within a reasonable amount of time. If you have invested many hours and have come up with only a few sources, you may be researching a topic for which material is simply not readily available. In most cases, it is advisable to change your topic to one for which you can find more material.

Figure 15–2: Note Cards of a Direct Quotation, Paraphrase, and Summary

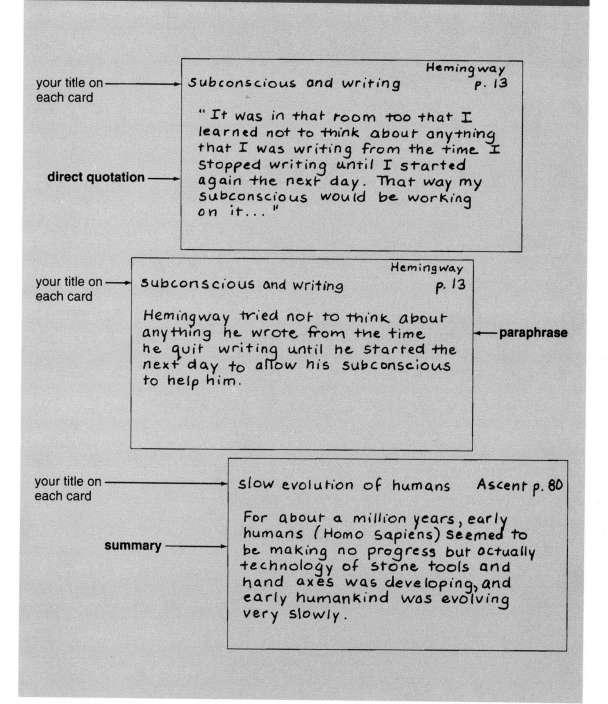

your title on
each card

direct quotation

Subconscious and writing   Hemingway
                                         p. 13

"It was in that room too that I
learned not to think about anything
that I was writing from the time I
stopped writing until I started
again the next day. That way my
subconscious would be working
on it..."

your title on
each card

paraphrase

Subconscious and writing   Hemingway
                                         p. 13

Hemingway tried not to think about
anything he wrote from the time
he quit writing until he started the
next day to allow his subconscious
to help him.

your title on
each card

summary

slow evolution of humans   Ascent p. 80

For about a million years, early
humans (Homo Sapiens) seemed to
be making no progress but actually
technology of stone tools and
hand axes was developing, and
early humankind was evolving
very slowly.

In this chapter, we have covered only the initial phase of doing research: locating library sources and taking notes. For more on developing the ideas that you have discovered into a research paper, see Chapter 16.

> * **The key to searching for sources is to do it in a way that leads to good results within a reasonable amount of time.**

PRACTICE 2

1. Find two passages that are suitable for quoting and make note cards.
2. Find two passages that are suitable for paraphrasing and make note cards.
3. Find two passages that are suitable for a summary and make note cards. Choose passages from a book or article that you have read with interest.

Working Space

READING ASSIGNMENT

Read the following essay by Russell Baker. How does he feel about the new technology? How do you feel about it? Would you prefer to study and do research at a computer in your room rather than go to a library? What would be gained and what would be lost? After you have finished the passage, answer the questions that follow.

Terminal Education

—Russell Baker

Ever since reading about Clarkson College's plan to replace its library with a computer, I have been worrying about what college students will do in the spring. I mean, you can't just haul a computer out on the campus and plunk it down under a budding elm and lie there with the thing on your chest while watching the birds at work, can you?

You can do that with a book, and it is one of the better things about going to college. With a computer, though, you've got to have a video terminal, which is basically a television set that rolls little, green, arthritic-looking letters and numbers across a dark screen.

It's not much fun reading a television screen, since, for one thing, the print has a terribly tortured look, as if it had spent four months in a Savak[1] cellar, and since, for another, you always expect it to be interrupted by a commercial. Which is neither here nor there, of course, since this kind of reading is not supposed to convey pleasure, but information.

The difficulty is that you can't take your television screen out under the elm tree and plug it into the computer—the information bank or the information center or the information conveyor, or whatever they choose to call it—since (1) television screens are expensive and fragile and no college president in his right mind is going to let students expose them to ants, dew and tree sap, and since (2) colleges aren't going to shortchange the football team to pay for installing electrical outlets in the tree trunks.

What this means for college students of the future—and Clarkson's electronic library is the library of the future, make no mistake—what it means is that students are going to be spending their springs sitting alone in stale air staring at television screens.

Give them a six-pack of beer or a glass of bourbon, you might say, and you have the ideal training program for American adult home life, which, one supposes, they will still be expected to undertake once they leave college stuffed with information. All I can say is: What does this have to do with education?

The answer comes from Dr. Walter Grattidge, director of Clarkson's new Educational Resources Center—Clarkson's term, not mine. "Education," he told a *New York Times* reporter, "is basically an information-transfer process." At the risk of sounding somewhat snappish, I say, "Fie, Dr. Grattidge! Fie!"

"Information-transfer process" indeed. Education is not like a decal, to be slipped off a piece of stiff paper and pasted on the back of the skull. The point of education is to waken innocent minds to a suspicion of information.

An educated person is one who has learned that information almost always turns out to be at best incomplete and very often false, misleading, fictitious, mendacious[2]—just dead wrong. Ask any seasoned cop or newspaper reporter. Ask anybody who has ever been the defendant in a misdemeanor trial or the subject of a story in a newspaper.

---

[1]Savak: Iranian secret police under the Shah
[2]mendacious: lying, untrue

Well, let's grant that Dr. Grattidge's opinion about being "basically an information-transfer process" is only 80 percent baloney. If you're going to learn the importance of mistrusting information, somebody first has to give you some information, and college is a place where people try to do this, if only so the professors can find out how gullible you are.

Knowing that, they can then begin to try to teach you to ask a few questions before buying the Brooklyn Bridge or the newest theory about the wherefore of the universe. I'm talking about the good professors now, not the ones who spend all their time compiling fresh information to be transferred to the book-buying public. Even the good professors, however, rarely have enough time to teach the whole student body the art of doubting, which leads to the astonishing act of thinking.

This is why so much of whatever educating happens at college happens in places like the grass under the elm where somebody has gone to read a book, just because it seems like a nicer place to read than the library, and has become distracted by the shape of the clouds, or an ant on the elbow, or an impulse to say to the guy or the girl crossing the quadrangle, "Let's chuck the books for a while and get a beer."

If the time is autumn, and the campus has an apple tree, who knows? Maybe somebody half asleep in an informational-transference volume will look up, see an apple fall and revolutionize science.[3] Not much chance of that happening if you're sitting in a room staring at a TV screen plugged into the Educational Resources Center, is there?

In there you are just terribly alone, blotting up information from a machine which, while very, very smart in some ways, has never had an original thought in its life. And no trees grow, and no apples fall.

1. According to Russell Baker, what is the real goal or purpose of education?

2. Why is he so opposed to Dr. Grattidge's claim that education is basically an information-transfer process?

---

[3]reference is to Sir Issac Newton and the theory of gravity

3. What is Baker's definition of an educated person? What is yours?

4. How does the art of doubting lead to the art of thinking?

WRITING ASSIGNMENT

Take your journal to the library and write several paragraphs describing one of the following.
1. Any activities that take place in front of you in your library reading room.
2. Some of the students and their various postures and expressions while studying.
3. The kinds of computer and microform equipment your library has (and any problems you had using it).
   In your description, try your hand at imitating Russell Baker's comic touch on pages 357–360.

JOURNAL ASSIGNMENTS

1. What do you think is the hardest part of writing a research paper? What makes the task difficult? What is the most rewarding part of writing a research paper? Why is it rewarding?
2. How do you feel about plagiarism? Do you think plagiarizing someone else's work should be severely punished with a failing grade or even suspension? Why or why not?

✔ Checking Out: Review Questions for Chapter 15

1. Explain the differences between bibliographical cards and note cards.

2. When making bibliographic cards, explain what information you need to cite about a book and what information you need to cite on a scholarly journal or a popular magazine. What are the major differences?

3. Describe how to search for sources using a computer catalog.

4. Name four ways to begin to find sources for your research paper.

5. What is a hardbound index to a discipline? Where are the volumes usually located?

6. What are key words and how do they help you locate an article?

7. Why is it important to keep reading, titling, and sorting your note cards as you continue to do research?

8. How do you decide whether to quote, paraphrase, or summarize when writing a note card?

9. If you find a book on your research topic, how should you use its index? How should you use its bibliography?

10. What is the *Readers' Guide to Periodical Literature?* How is it used in conducting research?

▶ In Summary

A library offers a wealth of resources that you can use to full advantage if you familiarize yourself with how your library organizes its collections. To search for sources, learn how to find books in a computer catalog, a card catalog, or both, and how to find articles in periodical indexes (bound by year, usually kept in the reference department) or by a computer search. To find and learn to use the various forms of miniaturized print or microforms, you must inform yourself about the various systems in your particular library.

Above all, ask the reference librarian for help. He or she can answer questions on the options for carrying out a search as well as on effective methods for searching by finding key words for the computer.

As a researcher, make bibliographic cards for all your sources (to incorporate later in your list of works used in your research), and make note cards on any information that contributes to your understanding of the subject. Take notes in the form of direct quotation, paraphrase, or summary; we recommend taking notes even on pages for which you have photocopies. And wherever you use information that you've learned from sources, you must cite the work. For more information on writing research papers, see Chapter 16.

CHAPTER 16

Writing as a Learning Tool: The Writing Process and the Research Paper

"You're finding out what to say as well as how to say it and that takes time."

—*Philip Larkin*

Learning to write well takes time and effort, but it will pay dividends long after college. You will be able to convey your ideas to others—to your employer, your newspaper, your representatives in government—and thereby make your voice heard.

Read this chapter to understand the writing process and for help with the research paper:

- Setting goals for improving your writing
- Discovering ideas you want to write about
- Learning techniques of brainstorming and freewriting
- Finding the best way to organize your ideas
- Writing a first complete draft
- Revising, editing, and proofing your draft
- Producing a research paper by following the writing process
- Citing your research; preparing a "Works Cited" page

Setting Goals for Improving Your Writing

Although teachers will give you helpful advice and comments on your writing, in the end you have much of the responsibility for teaching yourself how to improve your writing. The following five pointers encourage you to work on your writing in association with your other courses.

Find a Modelsur Writing

Look for a well-known writer whose work you find clear, direct, persuasive, or skillful. Many professional writers point to other writers whom they studied, and even imitated when they were first starting out. The English poet Philip Larkin mentions William Butler Yeats and Thomas Hardy as two writers he consciously studied as models.

First select a paragraph that you admire and study it for its content and ideas, the choice of vivid details and examples. Then analyze how the author constructs the sentences—the various ways the author combines phrases and clauses and uses fresh vocabulary. Look for strategies that you can adapt to your own writing.

Practice Your Writing

Try writing at least one paragraph every day, either as part of a course assignment or as a journal entry. You will gradually learn how to control words and sentences and make them mean what you want them to mean.

Learn How to Construct Paragraphs

The paragraph is the key building block of all forms of prose writing. In general, your paragraphs should begin with a sentence that introduces the main idea you want to discuss throughout the paragraph. This sentence, called the *topic sentence,* alerts the reader to the topic that you will take up in the rest of the paragraph.

When appropriate, use the opening sentence of a paragraph to make a transition between two paragraphs, explaining how your next paragraph is connected to the one just before it. Use a topic sentence to clarify immediately the point you will make in the paragraph and to avoid keeping your reader in suspense. As writer Annie Dillard says, "Suspense is for mystery writers."

Identify and Work on Your Own Weaknesses as a Writer

Identify the specific areas you need to work on in your writing. If you have trouble shaping your ideas into interesting and varied sentences, ask your teacher about sentence-combining techniques. If you are unsure of what is a complete sentence and what is a fragment, study English handbooks and workbooks that explain sentence structure; hone in on specific exercises to work out any problems you have with grammar or punctuation.

Read, Read, Read

Nothing will help you with your writing as much as reading widely. Any and all forms of written language can help you improve your writing—mysteries, sports columns, newspaper articles. Professional writers read other writers to discover ways to improve their craft. Writer William Trevor insists: "One can't write without having read widely."

In his memoirs, the critic Denis Donoghue describes reading with a purpose: "I always had a pen and a notebook at hand. If I found something interesting, I'd want to make note of it."

Discovering Ideas You Want to Write About

As a beginning writer, first look for ideas that interest you and that are important to you personally. Then think of how to interest your reader in these ideas.

Many beginning writers worry needlessly about having nothing to say; they assume incorrectly that they have no worthwhile ideas to write about. They have many more ideas than they are aware of, *if* they can learn to tap them.

Each one of us has observations about our families, about school, about what works and doesn't work in our community and country. You have much to say about how *you* view the world.

Learn to use all these resources—your own experiences, memories, conversations, your reading of newspapers and magazines, your reactions to events—as topics to write about. You have a lot to write about—all that you have learned about the world up to now.

Understanding the Writing Process

In general, it is useful to think of writing as a process in which you start with some uncertainty about what you want to write and gradually move toward a finished paper in which you have discovered what you wanted to write. It is this process of discovery that makes writing a satisfying experience. By the very act of searching hard for words to express exactly what you mean, you often discover ideas that you were not previously aware of.

Figure 16–1: The Writing Process

The writing process consists of roughly five phases (although you may want to repeat certain phases more than once):

1. In the **prewriting** phase,
   - use a discovery technique (such as brainstorming or freewriting; see page 368) to search for ideas
   - evaluate the resulting ideas and discard the weakest
   - from among your strongest ideas, select a tentative topic, the one that interests you most
   - draft a tentative main idea or **thesis statement** (what your overall paper will be about)
   - organize your best ideas in a rough outline
2. In the **drafting** stage,
   - write out a rough but complete first draft of the paper
   - rethink your thesis statement
   - do not worry about details of spelling or punctuation—just set down your overall ideas
3. In the **revising** stage, concentrate on the larger issues of improving and clarifying your overall ideas and organization
   - incorporate any new ideas you have
   - reoutline if necessary to improve organization
4. In the **editing** stage, correct problems in sentence structure, grammar, punctuation, and spelling
5. In the **proofreading** stage,
   - type (or neatly write) a final draft
   - proofread word for word to correct spelling, punctuation, typos

Narrow and Focus Your Topic

Because your paper has to be a specific length and must be finished by a certain date, don't try to tackle a topic that is too sweeping, such as "Drug Use in the United States." This topic covers so much ground that you'd never manage to cover all its aspects except very superficially. Instead choose one aspect of the whole issue that you can handle successfully. You may be able to identify your focused topic while doing library research, or you may have to wait until you have tried brainstorming (see below).

How can you narrow the topic? Instead of discussing the broad topic of drug use, limit the time period discussed (say to the last ten years) and limit the topic to one segment of the population (say to the effect of drugs on teenagers). The point is to select a topic that you can discuss knowledgeably and thoroughly within the designated length of your paper.

Brainstorm to Discover Ideas

Brainstorming is probably the fastest, most effective, and most direct method of searching for strong ideas. It helps you find your best ideas for writing any sort of paper. The following are basic tips for brainstorming.

- In the form of a list, jot down freely every possible idea about the topic you want to write about.
- Don't worry about the exact wording, just set down potentially useful ideas.
- Do not evaluate or organize your ideas at this stage.
- Explore; let one idea lead to another.
- Press yourself; ask "What else do I know about this?"
- Spend about ten or fifteen minutes; keep going until you are out of fresh new thoughts.
- Let the list grow messy as you connect related ideas with lines.

Cluster the Ideas from Your Brainstorming

Next, read through the ideas you have come up with while brainstorming and evaluate them, discarding the weakest ones. Now group the usable ones in *clusters*. For example, if you were brainstorming on the rights of adopted children, you might want to cluster your ideas under these simple headings:

- the perspective of the birth mother
- the needs of the adopted child
- the viewpoint of the adoptive parents

Once you have sorted your ideas into clusters (using arrows, circles, or stars to connect ideas), recopy your list so that it is more legible, and give each cluster of ideas a clear heading. From these clusters, you should be able to develop a brief rough outline to follow as you draft.

Try focused freewriting

Instead of brainstorming, some writers prefer to sit down and write out all their thoughts on a topic. They get down as many rough ideas as possible and pay no attention to matters of correct grammar or sentence structure. The idea is to **search for ideas on your topic by free association while continuing to write without pause.** Do not reread what you've written until you've finished. In freewriting, some rambling is expected.

Once the freewriting session is over, the writer must go back and remove the kernels of good ideas from all the material that is not useful. Some writers brainstorm after a freewriting session.

Shape and Sharpen Your Thesis Statement

At this stage of the writing process, **write out a thesis statement, a brief statement of the main idea you intend to discuss in your paper.** For short papers, you can usually draft this thesis statement in a single sentence; in a longer paper you may need several sentences or a paragraph.

But do not waste time perfecting your thesis statement until you have completed a rough draft. While in the process of writing your draft, you will find that you change some of your ideas, and you may want to change your thesis statement to reflect this new thinking.

At times, try writing a thesis statement that challenges conventional opinions. For example, instead of assuming that patients respect their doctors' skills, you might take the opposite view: "In recent years doctors have lost the faith of their patients." Then you would have to supply some support for your statement, such as: "Many doctors are perceived as not having time to know their patients as individuals."

Turn a Problem Statement into a Thesis Statement

If you are struggling to focus a thesis statement, sometimes it helps to write out a *problem statement* in which you set down some controversy or conflict. For example, you may set down this problem statement: "For many students, public schools are not doing a satisfactory job." Once you have described the problem, you can think about which of the following five perspectives you want to take.

1. **Identify the source of the problem:**
"Teachers are not paid adequately compared to what they can earn in business. Many fine teachers have left the profession, and the schools suffer."

2. **Identify a possible solution to the problem:**
"Private citizens must let local officials and school boards know that they support larger salaries for teachers."

3. **Prove that a problem exists:**
"Basic skills in reading and writing have dropped, and the schools have come under attack for producing students who lack these skills."

4. **Show that a misconception exists:**
"Many people think teachers will put up with low pay because they love to teach. The truth is many teachers feel exploited and no longer want to teach for too little money."

5. **Show a problem as well as a solution:**
"Loss of funds for sports and arts in public schools can be helped by organizing the community to pitch in and raise funds to help keep students off the streets."

☐ PRACTICE 1   Each of the following statements describes a controversy or problem. Turn the problem statements into working thesis statements, using one of the five perspectives we have just explained.

1. *Problem:* Some elderly people have no surviving friends or family nearby and suffer from acute loneliness.

Thesis statement: _____

_____

2. *Problem:* If abused as a child, a parent tends to treat his or her own children cruelly.

   Thesis statement: _____

   _____

3. *Problem:* Some people train for careers in fields that are suddenly glutted with qualified people.

   Thesis statement: _____

   _____

4. *Problem:* Many people who are very ill with diseases such as AIDS are eager to try experimental drugs; however, the Federal Drug Administration (FDA) needs time to test these drugs to make sure they are safe.

   Thesis statement: _____

   _____

5. *Problem:* Government and business computer files contain all sorts of private information about every citizen. It is impossible to know who has access to this information.

   Thesis statement: _____

   _____

Organize Your Ideas

Once you have brainstormed and have a tentative thesis statement, **make a rough outline** of the order in which you are going to take up your ideas. How can you find the best organization for your paper?

One possible way is to look at the clusters from your brainstorming list and consider several alternate organizations. Then **decide which is the best order for helping the reader grasp your points;** make your discussion easy to follow.

To take advantage of new insights that turn up as they draft, some writers prefer to draft and organize at the same time. On a separate sheet of paper, they jot down the actual outline that emerges as they draft. Especially if you have a computer or word processor, it is easy to draft and outline at the same time, moving whole paragraphs around if they work better in other places.

Write a Complete First Draft

Even experienced writers find drafting a challenge requiring their complete concentration. Remember not to try to polish anything; just get your overall ideas down simply and boldly. You can revise the rough spots and weaknesses later. Try not to slow yourself down by looking for a perfect word or checking a spelling.

Here are some general guidelines:

1. Be sure to *write out a complete first draft before doing any revision.* Push yourself to the end so that you can control the overall organization—shortening long sections and expanding sketchy ones. With a complete draft, you can see how long your paper will be (250 or 300 words per typed page).
2. As a first step, set down your tentative thesis statement (again, do not try to perfect it at this stage).
3. Whether you type or write by hand, *always double-space your first draft* to allow for changes.
4. Concentrate on getting your major ideas down forcefully. **Persuade the reader that your ideas are worth reading.**
5. Begin a new paragraph for each major idea you take up.
6. Connect your sentences by transitions (clauses, phrases, or words) that link your ideas.

   "As the Soviet economy worsened . . . (clause)

   "During those five years, ... (phrase)

   "Then, . . . (word)

7. Keep checking (or revising) your outline as you draft.
8. To improve your paper, **use the discoveries and ideas that come to you as you are drafting.**

Let Ideas Incubate

After you have finished a rough draft (especially for a major assignment), it is a good idea to put your paper aside and allow your ideas to incubate. When you return to your paper after a few hours, or even a few days, you are able to give it a fresh reading. Incubation is especially helpful in allowing you to switch roles from writer to *reader* of your paper. By reading your draft from a reader's perspective, you can see what might be confusing or unclear, and you can improve it.

Revise Vigorously

After you have put your draft aside to incubate, read it again with a fresh eye, pretending you know nothing about your topic except what is written on the page. Switch roles and become your reader. At this stage, you want to check that the major ideas are presented in the best order and as forcefully as possible. Here are some questions to guide your revision.

1. Has the reader been told enough to understand your main points? Should any basic information be added such as names, book titles, or dates? (If in doubt, it is best to provide the missing background information, even if your intended reader will know it.)
2. **What are the strongest ideas here?** Are they presented in the best order? Can you make them any more convincing by adding better examples or more detail? Can you restate a major idea to make it clearer or more persuasive? Are any ideas repeated needlessly? Does the paper ramble?
3. **What are the weakest sections?** (Mark or circle these for revision.) Don't be afraid to cut or totally rework passages.
4. Can you sharpen the thesis statement? Improve your introduction?
5. Are the connections between paragraphs clear?
6. What is your overall reaction—a good paper or one that needs more attention and thought?
7. Does your conclusion sum up the overall point of your paper?

Edit with Care

After you are satisfied with the ideas and the order of the ideas, it is time to check on smaller issues. Here is a basic checklist for editing papers. If you are in doubt about some of these issues, consult any one of the many handbooks for writers currently available.

1. Check for complete and correct sentences. Make sure that you have not included any unintentional fragments. Check that you have not run sentences together that need periods (called *run-on* sentences), and that you have not used commas instead of periods (called *comma splices*).

2. Make sure the main subject and the main verb of your sentences make sense together. (Drop out any words that come between them to check that they work together.) The subject and verb must also agree in number, that is, a singular subject requires a singular verb, and a plural subject requires a plural verb.

3. **Always check for apostrophes.** Any noun that shows possession needs an apostrophe:

   Clintons address (incorrect)

   Clinton's address (correct)

4. Check that contractions have apostrophes:

   Im (incorrect)

   I'm (meaning I am) (correct)

5. Watch for problems with *it's* and *its*. *It's* always means "it is." Unless you can substitute *it is* in your sentence, you need to use *its,* (which expresses ownership):

   The car isn't working any better since its battery was replaced. (correct; *it is* cannot be substituted for *its*)

   It's not a good car. (correct; *it is* can be substituted)

6. Check for introductory verb forms ending in *-ed* or *-ing;* they must refer to the subject of the sentence or to the noun just before them. These problems are called *misplaced modifiers*.

   Dangling from the drawer, I put on my sock. (incorrect)

   I put on the sock, dangling from my drawer. (correct)

7. Use parallel construction to help the reader. A series of three or more similar elements (whether nouns, verbs, or phrases) punctuated by commas can help the reader follow your discussion.

   She ran a mile, swam laps, and played tennis.

8. Make a list of words you find confusing and learn their correct usage. *Principle* and *principal* confuse many people as do *affect* (usually a verb) and *effect* (usually a noun).

The effect on this company was devastating. (noun)

Overeating affects his weight. (verb)

They're, their, and *there* are also easily confused. Learn how each is used.

9. When a paper is returned, jot down any mechanical difficulties you had with grammar and punctuation, and speak to your instructor to remedy the problems. Then be sure to look for and *correct* those mistakes when revising future papers.

Proofread

Even if you are tired from all your work, proofreading is essential. If you let sloppy errors slip by, your teacher will get the wrong impression. After you have prepared your final draft, read it once again for careless mistakes—missing periods, misspellings, words left out in recopying. A neat correction is far better than a mistake.

PRACTICE 2   Identify which of the following statements describe your problems as a writer and discuss what you can do about them.

1. My problem is with finding ideas; I can't think of anything I want to write about.

   _____

   _____

   _____

2. I have plenty of ideas. I am brimming with things I want to say. But when it comes to putting my ideas into words, sentences, or paragraphs, I can't do it. Many sentences don't quite say what I want to say and they don't satisfy me.

   _____

   _____

   _____

3. My biggest problem is with the basics of spelling and punctuation, and sometimes I don't know whether I've written a correct sentence or not. All the comments on my papers mention these basics. My ideas are lost in the shuffle.

_____

_____

_____

4. My problem is time. I never leave enough time to do the writing project. I can never get concerned until the pressure is on, and then I have no time to do it right.

_____

_____

_____

5. My problem is I feel very uncomfortable when I have to write. It isn't something I do very naturally. It's a strain.

_____

_____

_____

6. My sentences sound too simple, like a beginner; I hate to read my own papers.

_____

_____

_____

7. I think some people have more ability at writing than others. I have a friend who can dash off a decent essay quickly. To write even a bad essay takes me hours and hours.

_____

_____

_____

8. I'm a perfectionist. I write one sentence, erase it, rewrite it, and never get beyond the first paragraph.

_____

_____

_____

Writing a Research Paper

A research paper is usually a major assignment in a course, one that will count for a significant percentage of your grade. It requires that you combine many skills. You will need to prepare a schedule; hunt in the library for information; read and take notes on various published sources; synthesize your findings into a new whole; and write your paper, citing all your sources.

All these tasks cannot be accomplished at the last minute. And even though you may want to postpone starting your paper, begin early and use our step-by-step method to make steady progress by facing one specific task at a time.

The purpose of the research paper is to encourage you to learn independently. You are asked to investigate a topic or an issue by looking up information from various sources (books, journals, magazines, newspapers) and to come to your own conclusion based on both what you have found in your research and your own thinking on the topic.

In most cases, your teacher wants you to do much more than mechanically string together bits of information from various published sources. You are expected to think critically about what you have read, to explain and evaluate different viewpoints on the issue, and finally to present your own synthesis of the material. A **synthesis** is a new combining of ideas, based on what is already known about an issue, to form a fresh coherent whole.

Figure 16–2: Scheduling the Research Paper

Planning the Tasks of a Research Paper: Sample Schedule

Researching: allow 4 or 5 weeks in all

1. Identify tentative topic or topics	Allow 1 week or less
2. Do preliminary library research to investigate topic and see if enough material is available	Allow 1 week
3. Narrow topic (find a focused topic your paper will cover) and look for a tentative thesis	Allow 1 week
4. Read sources and take notes	Allow 3 weeks
5. Reread note cards; label and sort them	Allow 1 week
6. Think about and create a new synthesis from the material of your sources	Ongoing

Writing: allow 2 weeks in all

1. Brainstorm, outline, refine thesis statement	Allow 1 day
2. Write a complete rough draft	Allow several days
3. Incubate	Allow several days
4. Revise, cite sources	Allow several days
5. Recopy, proofread	Allow 1 day

General Guidelines for Writing Research Papers

Step 1: Identify Your Tentative Topic

In spare moments, think over a workable topic—one that genuinely interests you and that you can handle in the time you have. Do not think that you have to identify your precise topic immediately. You may have to wait until you have done a good deal of library research or even brainstormed to find a final focused topic to write about.

If you do pinpoint a topic that you truly want to explore, it will make your whole task far more meaningful to you. You will be more interested in explaining to your reader what you have discovered and what you have concluded about the issue.

Step 2: Do Preliminary Library Research

In the library, make a quick survey of the books and articles available on your topic. (Review Chapter 15 on library research techniques.) Determine whether you will find enough material from these published sources to write a good paper. If not, choose another topic and search once again for available sources.

Step 3: Narrow Your Topic and Rough Out a Thesis

Narrowing your topic means finding a focused topic that you can cover satisfactorily given your time and length considerations. Though the final polished statement of your thesis statement can wait until you have done more research, you should begin to draft it in rough form (see page 369).

Do not expect to settle on a firm thesis until you have done your research and have evaluated other writers' viewpoints on the topic; just state as clearly as you can something specific you want to research. As you read your books and articles, you often will learn something to make you rethink or radically change your ideas—and even your thesis.

Step 4: Read Your Sources and Decide What Notes to Take

Use efficient reading strategies to evaluate your sources. For books, check the index quickly for useful entries and skim the pages mentioned to find what covers your topic directly. Read key passages analytically, taking notes on what you might want to incorporate in your paper. For magazines, skim the headings to find what you need. Take down on note cards whatever strikes you as a potentially useful idea (as explained on pages 354–356).

Step 5: Review Your Note Cards, Give Them Titles, and Sort Them into Related Clusters

As you continue to do research, be sure to reread, title, and sort your note cards. Most of all, think about what conclusions your research is leading to and what you need to explore further. Do not let the note cards pile up without reviewing them; if you do, you will research aimlessly and without direction—and waste a lot of your time.

As you continue to review the cards and sort them into clusters, you will begin to shape your paper. Whenever you have ideas or responses of your own, make "reaction" note cards, in which you comment on what you have found in the sources, identifying which writers you agree and disagree with.

Step 6: Create Your Own Synthesis

Review and think over the meaning of your note cards. Which sources do you agree with and why? Which do you disagree with and why? If you read an author who says experimental social structures such as the Shaker colonies are not successful because they are short-lived, do you agree? If another author says the art and crafts of the Shakers reveal that the self-contained communities were successful on their own terms, do you agree?

In your synthesis, try to integrate several viewpoints that you agree with while discussing and ruling out those views that you believe are misleading. By developing your own viewpoint, you synthesize or combine ideas in a new way and reach a coherent conclusion.

Once you have determined your conclusion, you can restate your thesis statement to make sure it reflects what you will conclude in your paper.

Step 7: Writing a Rough Draft

Once you have formed a thorough understanding of your topic, have looked into all good sources, and have reached a satisfactory synthesis, review and organize your note cards one final time. Have the material fresh in your mind for a productive brainstorming session. If you are deeply immersed in your research, the brainstorming should go quickly, and you should be able to generate an outline easily.

Write the first draft from beginning to end. Don't polish or edit. Just get all your ideas down on paper. (See page 372 for more on drafting.)

Draft when you are feeling fresh and have several hours of free time to work. When drafting, you will have to pull all your ideas together and express them in sentences. Drafting will be the most challenging step of your paper, but if you have reviewed and organized your note cards, it will go much more smoothly.

Step 8: Revise Your Draft

Let your paper incubate for at least twenty-four hours. Then go back and revise using the guidelines on page 373. Don't be surprised if you have to repeat this step. Most good writers revise at least two or three times before they are satisfied with their work—adding more convincing examples, rewriting sentences to make them clearer, or inserting an apt quotation.

Step 9: Credit Your Sources

To avoid plagiarism, credit any sources you have quoted or paraphrased. Check with your instructor to see if you should use parenthetical references within the text or footnotes at the end of the paper. Consult a handbook to be sure that you use the correct format for in-text references or end-of-paper footnotes. The two most commonly used handbooks for research papers are *The MLA Manual of Style* and the *Publication Manual of the American Psychological Association* (see Figure 16–3 on page 382).

Step 10: Prepare the Bibliography

Preparing a bibliography or list of works cited is the final step in your paper. If you have good bibliography cards, this step should be fairly straightforward. Just make sure that your sources are listed in alphabetical order and that you use the correct format for bibliographical information. Here again, it's crucial to find out what format your teacher wants you to use and follow it precisely (see Figure 16–3).

Step 11: Proofread

Students new to college frequently neglect this essential step. They assume that the quality of their ideas is all that counts. Unfortunately this assumption couldn't be more wrong. Instructors often deduct points from a paper that contains spelling, punctuation, and grammar errors. So be sure to fine-tune your paper by eliminating any careless errors. Make your corrections neatly. Whiting out errors and writing in a letter or two here and there is fine. But if you have a lot of corrections and the paper starts to look messy, you would be better off retyping. In this case, neatness does count.

Figure 16–3: Crediting Sources and Preparing a Bibliography

Citing Your Sources

When you quote or paraphrase from material that is not your own, you must let the reader know your source. To document your sources, follow the style requested by your teacher. Here are two common formats—MLA (Modern Language Association) style and APA (American Psychological Association) style.

MLA Style

For the in-text reference (inserted directly into your paper):

- Put the author's last name and the page number in parentheses at the end of the sentence in which you use a source:

  Jefferson found leisure to write about human liberty by employing as many as two hundred slaves (Hofstadter 23).

- Or use the author's name directly in your own text and put only the page number in parentheses:

  Hofstadter notes ironically that Jefferson found the leisure to write about human liberty by using the labors of about two hundred slaves (23).

For the Works Cited page (at the end of your paper):

- Explain each source fully on a **Works Cited** page, an alphabetical list of all publications used in your research, as follows:

For books

> Hofstadter, Richard. The American Political Tradition. New York: Knopf, 1948.

For popular magazines and newspapers (add day to date for newspapers):

> Mead, Margaret. "In the Best Interests of the Child." Redbook Oct. 1978: 100–103.

For scholarly journals:

> Ohr, Alan. "Concrete Language." College English 31 (1980): 158–60.

> (Note: 31 refers to the volume number; 158–60 to the pages.)

APA Style

The APA style is similar to the MLA style with some exceptions.

- For the in-text reference, the APA includes the date and the abbreviation for pages (p. or pp.):

  Anxiety is the tension that results from real or imaginary threats to one's security (Hall, 1984, p. 145).

- The Works Cited page is called **References.** The date is placed in parentheses right after the author's name:

  Skinner, B. F. (1948). Walden two. New York, Macmillan.

  (Note: Use only authors' initials; capitalize only the first word of a book title, and underscore the title.)

- For magazine, journal, and newspaper articles, lowercase the name of the article (except the first word); capitalize and underscore the name of the publication:

  Voith, V. (1984). Procedures for introducing a baby to a dog. Modern Veterinary Medicine, 65 (7), 539–541.

  (Note: 65 refers to the volume number, 7 to the issue number, 539–541 to the pages.)

  Weinberg, S. (1983, March 8). The answer to (almost) everything. New York Times, pp. A17.

Working Space

READING ASSIGNMENT

Read the following research paper written by student Meenekshi Bose. What points do you agree with and why? What objections might you raise? With three viewpoints involved in questions of adoption, how do you think issues can be resolved for the benefit of all?

Meenekshi Bose
Professor Flemming
Study Skills 101
9 April 1988

Adoption Files and Privacy

In 1971, adoptee Florence Fisher finally completed a
twenty-year search for her natural parents. She then
set up an organization titled "Adoptees' Liberty Movement Association" to help others locate their natural
parents, and to persuade states to change their laws on
closed files (Kupersmith 27). Unfortunately, the major-
ity of the states still favor closed files (Hitchings
85), supposedly to prevent all parties from being hurt.
However, many people today argue that adoptees must see
the files to complete their identities, and that they
should be allowed to choose whether or not they want to
meet their natural parents.

In the past, adoptive parents kept the adoption a
private family secret, and often tried to ignore it altogether. Previously, an adopted child received a new
name and birth certificate, and was virtually considered "reborn" to her adoptive parents (Mead 100). Agencies advised parents not to tell the child she was
adopted, and often matched children to parents who re-
sembled them so that outsiders could not guess the
truth (Soria 24). Only adoption officials had access to
the files revealing the child's true name and informa-

tion on the birth parents, who lost all claim to the child (Soria 86). Fortunately, today people realize that keeping adoptions secret could emotionally harm the child if she finds out, because the secrecy implies that it is something bad (Soria 26). In addition, many adoptees argue that being considered a natural child of their adoptive parents is fantasy, not fact, and that they have a right to know their heritage (Budgen 42). Thus, today many people agree that adoptive parents can no longer pretend the adoption never occurred, but must face the reality that the child has natural parents.

Often adoptive parents do not face reality because they consider searching for her natural parents to be a breach of faith by the child. To many adoptive parents, questions about the circumstances of the child's birth imply either that they did not take adequate care of the child, or that the child no longer loves them (Soria 28). They consider themselves her true parents because they reared, fed, and cared for her, and resent the child for wanting more than they can give (Kuper-smith 3). However, many psychologists today argue that searching for one's natural parents doesn't mean that the adoptive parents have failed in their duty (Hitch-ings 85). Hitchings notes that adoptees search for their parents for emotional reasons or a "deep-felt need" (85). In fact, many adoptees wish to find their biological parents to achieve personal peace, and find

out what really happened, not to form relationships
with them at all (Kupersmith 30). Surprisingly, a recent study of over four hundred couples conducted by
Nassau Community College professors in New York showed
that two-thirds of the adoptive parents supported open
files (Soria 86). Perhaps they realize that curiosity
is natural, and that it will be healthier for the child
if they aid her in her search, instead of forcing her
to keep secrets from them (Soria 28). Most adoptees
looking for their biological parents do love their
adoptive parents, but simply need to know their past.

  Some people argue that closed files protect the child
from learning about an embarrassing past as well as
from meeting inadequate parents. They feel that adoption files should be closed to prevent the child from
embarrassment if she is illegitimate (Kupersmith 32).
Sandra Soria responds, though, by saying the adoptee
had no control over the circumstances of her birth, so
she should not feel guilty about being "born out of
wedlock" (28). Kupersmith further states that today illegitimate children are not as ostracized as before so
this is an invalid reason for keeping files closed (320).

  Other adoption officials, however, believe that
closed files protect the biological parents from memories of an unpleasant past and the child from emotional
pain if her natural parents refuse to see her (Soria
86). Margaret Mead remarks that often the natural

mother either gives up the child of her own free will, or loses the child because the state deems her an "unfit mother" for reasons including drug problems, mental illness, or simply that the mother is not taking proper care of the child (188). In contrast, Soria states that many parents give up the child for reasons which prove they "had the child's best interests at heart" (28), such as poor financial status or lack of education (28). She firmly believes that biological parents have a right to find out what happened to the child (86). Therefore, adoption officials can no longer use the outdated issue of illegitimacy or the unfair term "inadequate mother" as reasons for keeping closed files.

Adoption officials say that even closed files are accessible for "good cause," and Kupersmith believes that when "needs for medical or psychiatric histories" arise, either side will be granted permission to see the files (29). Nevertheless, in 1981, <u>Newsweek</u> magazine covered a story on James Grant George, an adoptee suffering from myelocytic leukemia, or cancer of the bone marrow. He required a bone marrow transplant from a blood relative for survival. Unfortunately, the courts did not feel the circumstances justified opening the files to reveal who his natural parents were (Williams and Foote 60). However, in this case the courts lack good reasons for why the files should remained closed. No physical contact need ever be made between the parent and child in giving the bone marrow, so the adoptive parents need not worry about the child's reaction to meeting his natural mother. Likewise, the transplant should not disrupt the biological mother's private life, because the hospital will not reveal her name or past to anyone. Thus, parents and courts who still favor closed files in pressing circumstances such as these are indirectly committing murder.

Although adoptees must sometimes open files for medical reasons, more commonly they do so to achieve personal peace and complete their identities. Soria says that some adoptees can never relax or be happy until primary sources answer their questions, which may range from medical histories to why the parent gave up the child (28). In addition, she believes that adoptees searching for their biological parents are also searching for roots and identities (26). Several factors constitute one's identity, including physical features from one's natural parents, the way one lives, whom one lives with, and one's role models (Soria 26). However, because adoptees do not know their past, many feel that they either lack or have incomplete identities (Soria 26). For example, Soria quotes one girl who states, "Sometimes I get the feeling that my identity was given to me by my adoptive parents, and that nothing was really mine in the first place" (26). For the adoptees' curiosity to be satisfied and for their identities to be complete, they must be able to see the files and find their real parents. As Mead says, a reunion between biological parents and their child not only answers the mother's questions about what actually happened to her child, but also reassures that child and gives her an identity. She becomes more secure about herself and her fears of the past cease (188).

Whether or not the adoptees have questions pertaining to their past, they should have the right to choose if they want to meet their biological parents. Most adoptees agree with Kupersmith that minors should not see adoption records because the emotional pressure and worry may be too much to handle (29). However, she also agrees with the Adoptees' Liberty Movement Association that "the truth of his origin is the birthright of every man" (27). Kupersmith also argues that it is an adoptee's constitutional right to see the files and learn her heritage, and not allowing her to do so deprives her of "human dignity" (32). Similarly, Budgen states that adoptees want to find their natural parents to "find out where (they) came from, and to have a past" (43). Not allowing them to do so forces adoptees to accept their adoptive parents when they never agreed to give up their real parents (42). Mead compares the adoptee liberation movement to immigrants who become American citizens; they know their past, but choose to be Americans with their American past instead. In both cases, the person should have the "freedom to choose" what she wants (100C).

Adoptees should have the right to choose whether or not they want to see their adoption records. Though some adoptees may not question the circumstances of their birth, those who do have a right to find out their past, roots, and medical heritage. Although very few states, including Alabama and Kansas, presently allow open files, other states should soon follow suit. Nobody should be forced to live feeling incomplete and insecure.

WORKS CITED

Budgen, M. "Right to Rediscover Roots." Maclean's 4 Aug. 1980: 42–43.

Hitchings, B. "Adopted Children and Their Search for Roots." Business Week 6 Feb. 1978: 85–86.

Kupersmith, N. "Fight to Open Up Adoption Records." Reader's Digest June 1978: 27–30+.

Mead, M. "In the Best Interests of the Child." Redbook 151 Oct. 1978: 100+.

Soria, S. "Adoption: Searching for Answers About the Past." Teen Mar. 1984: 24+.

Williams, D. A., and Donna Foote, "I Do Not Feel He Is My Son." Newsweek 10 Aug. 1981: 60.

WRITING ASSIGNMENT

Write a short research paper on (a) the rights of the adoptive parents, (b) the rights of the adopted child, or (c) the role of the biological mother—with your perspective clearly presented in the thesis statement.

JOURNAL ASSIGNMENTS

What do you think a research paper should accomplish? Use any of the following views to trigger your ideas.

1. The research paper should be a writer's interpretation of an issue and not merely an information-gathering exercise.
2. It should allow the student to develop a thesis, collect a bibliography, gather supporting evidence, compare and organize the evidence, and convince the reader.
3. It should help the student learn scholarly methods and good research practices.
4. It should encourage the student to think critically.
5. Obviously it is a trial run and is usually based on secondary research, that is, research based on the original research of others. Professional research requires much more digging, more expertise, and more original findings.
6. It is a good way of gaining in-depth knowledge about a particular topic.
7. It allows the student to work independently and to understand how professional researchers strive for accuracy and verify their information by citing sources.

✔ Checking Out: Review Questions for Chapter 16

1. What major issues should you concentrate on when producing a complete, if rough, first draft?

2. Why is it important to see the whole first draft before you begin revising?

3. Explain the difference between revising and editing.

4. What are the three key tasks of a good revision strategy?

5. How do you decide what information from your sources to cite?

6. What are some ways to discover ideas for papers?

7. Why should you edit sentence by sentence?

8. Explain how the writer works out a synthesis in the course of writing a research paper.

9. What is a Works Cited page?

10. What kinds of problems should you look for when you are proofreading?

▶ In Summary

If you improve your writing skills so that you can express your ideas convincingly, you will feel more confident about handling college writing assignments and answering essay-exam questions.

One way to improve your writing is to study other professional writers—both what they say and how they say it. Choose authors whose writing you admire and analyze in detail their sentences and paragraphs and the vocabulary they use. Adapt some of their techniques to your own writing. Reading every day—whether fiction, nonfiction, magazine or newspaper articles, detective stories, or whatever—is good practice.

Another way to improve your writing is to understand the basic writing process discussed in this chapter. The prewriting step is an efficient method for generating your best ideas, probing your experiences, memories, knowledge from previous classes, and so forth. When brainstorming or freewriting, draw on these inner resources and come up with ideas that you want to write about and interest your readers in. If you follow the steps of the writing process, you gradually will improve the clarity and style of your writing. Be sure to identify your own weaknesses as a writer—say you have trouble with sentence structure—and focus on improving them.

When you are assigned a research paper, follow the suggested steps for carrying out research until you have a good understanding of your focused topic. At that point, you will be able to create a synthesis based on the ideas you have read in your sources, your own reactions to these ideas, and your overall conclusions to the problem or issue you are writing about. In your thesis statement, you will state precisely what you have come to understand through your research, and in the rest of the paper you will support your thesis.

Suggestions for Reading Science Textbooks

Few students have the background knowledge that encourages under-standing of science textbooks, and so they find these texts difficult to read. To compensate for the density of unfamiliar information, skillful readers process the material very slowly, fitting it together piece by piece until the author's message makes sense.

It's also true that illustrations in science textbooks play a more promi-nent role than they do in social science or humanities texts. That means you have to study the accompanying illustrations as carefully as you do the textual explanation. This is something many students are not used to doing, but it's something they must learn if they want to understand sci-entific writing.

Just because science textbooks are difficult to read does not mean that you can't improve your ability to understand them. You most certainly can. You just have to supplement your usual strategies for reading text-books with a few that are specifically adapted to the study of science.

Understanding Theoretical Explanations

Because scientists develop theories that explain or describe natural phenomena or what happens in nature, you need to be alert for those places in your textbooks where authors offer theoretical explanations of existing phenomena. When you find such passages, read them analytically using questions like the following to guide and focus your thinking:

1. What object, event, or process is the author trying to explain or describe?
2. Does the theory or hypothesis (a) explain a cause-and-effect relationship; (b) describe the *physical composition* of some object, structure, or being; or (c) outline a process?
3. What kinds of proof or research have been offered in support of this theory? Did any particular conditions or instruments have to be produced or did any events have to take place before the theory could be universally accepted?
4. Is the theory associated with any particular person or group of people? What did each person or group contribute to the theory's development? How did the theory advance existing knowledge?
5. Does the theory have any known flaws or discrepancies?

Scientists spend their lives trying to explain the world's mysteries. In our time many questions have been solved, but many remain to be solved—perhaps by your generation. Your job as a reader of science is to analyze passages that describe both what scientists already know, what they are still puzzled by, and what they cannot explain.

Understanding Classification

When you read history or psychology textbooks, you'll occasionally encounter a paragraph explaining a system of classification. The author will describe how some large group can be broken down into smaller subgroups or categories.

However, even a brief prereading of your science textbooks should tell you that passages explaining systems of classification play a more significant role than they do in nonscientific texts. In science books, passages dealing with classification are not only more frequent, they are also much longer. They often extend far beyond a single paragraph to encompass several pages. When this is the case, the author usually will open with a general statement telling you what the larger group is and how many subgroups comprise it. Subsequent paragraphs describe each subgroup in greater detail.

This selection is a good example:

> Sea-floor sediments can be classified according to their origin into three broad categories: (1) lithogenous ("derived from rocks") sediment; (2) biogenous ("derived from organisms") sediment; and (3) hydrogenous ("derived from water") sediment. Although each category is discussed separately, it should be remembered that all sea-floor sediments are mixtures. No body of sediment comes from a single source.
>
> **Lithogenous sediment** consists primarily of mineral grains which were weathered from continental rocks and transported to the ocean. The sand-sized particles settle near shore. However, since the very smallest particles take years to settle to the ocean floor, they may be carried for thousands of kilometers by ocean currents. As a consequence, virtually every area of the ocean receives some lithogenous sediment. However, the rate at which this sediment accumulates on the deep-ocean floor is indeed very slow. From 5000 to 50,000 years are necessary for a 1-centimeter layer to form. Conversely, on the continental margins near the mouths of large rivers, lithogenous sediment accumulates rapidly. In the Gulf of Mexico, for example, the sediment has reached a depth of many kilometers.
>
> Since fine particles remain suspended in the water for a very long time, there is ample opportunity for chemical reactions to occur. Because of this, the colors of the deep-sea sediments are often red or brown. This results when iron on the particle or in the water reacts with dissolved oxygen in the water and produces a coating of iron oxide (rust).
>
> **Biogenous sediment** consists of shells and skeletons of marine animals and plants. This debris is produced mostly by microscopic organisms living in the sunlit waters near the ocean surface. The remains continually "rain" down upon the sea floor.
>
> The most common biogenous sediments are known as *calcareous* ($CaCO_3$) *oozes,* and as their name implies, they have the consistency of thick mud. These sediments are produced by organisms that inhabit warm surface waters. When calcareous hard parts slowly sink through a cool layer of water, they begin to dissolve. This results because cold seawater contains more carbon dioxide and is thus more acidic than warm water. In seawater deeper than about 4500 meters (15,000 feet), calcareous shells will completely

dissolve before they reach bottom. Consequently, calcareous ooze does not accumulate where depths are great.

Other examples of biogenous sediments are *siliceous* (SiO_2) *oozes* and phosphate-rich materials. The former are composed primarily of opaline skeletons of diatoms (single-celled algae) and radiolaria (single-celled animals), while the latter are derived from the bones, teeth, and scales of fish and other marine organisms.

Hydrogenous sediment consists of minerals that crystallize directly from seawater through various chemical reactions. For example, some limestones are formed when calcium carbonate precipitates directly from the water; however, most limestone is composed of biogenous sediment.

One of the principal examples of hydrogenous sediment, and one of the most important sediments on the ocean floor in terms of economic potential, is **manganese nodules.** These rounded blackish lumps are composed of a complex mixture of minerals that form very slowly on the floor of the ocean basins. In fact, their formation rate represents one of the slowest chemical reactions known.

To read such passages skillfully, keep in mind questions like the following:

1. What is the larger group that is being divided?
2. How many subgroups are formed through this division? What is the name of each group?
3. What are the characteristics of each one?
4. Does the author offer any representative examples of the subgroups?
5. What are the crucial differences cited? Do the subgroups share any important similarities?

When you can answer these questions, you understand the passage well and can begin taking notes. For your notes, consider making a chart to represent the system of classification described, similar to the chart in Figure A–1 on page 398.

If you are taking several science courses, consider including charts in your repertoire of note-taking strategies. Like maps, charts give visual form to the underlying structure of the passage, making them useful for taking notes on long passages that explain a complicated classification. Such passages have a clear-cut underlying structure carefully built in by

From Frederick K. Lutgens and Edward J. Tarbuck, *Essentials of Geology,* (Merrill, 1986). Reprinted by permission of the publisher.

Figure A-1: Chart to Represent a System of Classification		
Lithogenous	**Biogenous**	**Hydrogenous**
1. Consists of mineral grains weathered from continental rocks 2. found in every area of ocean 3. 5,000 to 50,000 years for 1-centimeter layer to form but on continental margins more rapid. Ex: Gulf of Mexico 4. red or brown color due to water reacting with dissolved oxygen and forming a coat of iron oxide	1. Consists of shells and skeletons of marine animals; most common are known as calcareous oozes ($CaCO_3$) 2. Does not accumulate when depths are great because shells completely dissolve before hitting bottom 3. Other examples are siliceous oozes (SiO_2)	1. Consists of minerals that crystalize directly from seawater 2. Principal example manganese nodules, blackish lumps that form very slowly on floor of ocean basins

the author. The more you can mimic that structure in your notes, the more readily you will remember what you have read.

Analyzing and Interpreting Illustrations

Illustrations in social science texts highlight and emphasize key points and can be a clue to what is important in an author's explanation.

Within scientific textbooks, however, illustrations play a more fundamental role: they are an essential part of the explanations science writers provide for their readers. As you will see in the following excerpt, the authors consistently refer the reader to the individual line drawings accompanying the text explanation. It is largely through the drawings that the authors hope to make specialized terms like *internal force, deformation,* and *vertical displacement* meaningful.

Internal Forces and Deformation

Anything that carries load develops *internal forces* that cause it to deform. When lifting barbells, weightlifters experience internal forces within their bodies: their muscles elongate and contract. When a heavy truck goes over a bridge, internal forces develop in the structure that cause the roadway to *deflect,* that is, to bend. Because bridges are constructed of stiff materials such as concrete and steel, these deformations are small, too small to see with the naked eye. When a boy, however, crosses a think plank, supported on two sides of a small river bank, you can easily see the thin board bend or deflect, as in Figure A–2a.

Figure A–2a

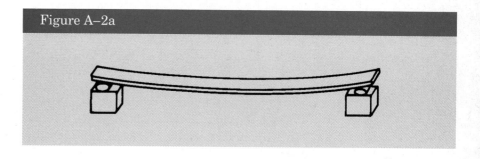

In the study of *statics,* which covers the behavior of loaded bodies at rest, computations are based on Newton's Second Law, which states that force equals mass times acceleration:

$$R = Ma \qquad \text{(Equation 1)}$$

where
R = resultant force acting on the body
M = mass [related to weight]
a = acceleration

In Figure A–2b, we see a workbench loaded by a piece of heavy equipment, a machine that weighs 400 pounds. The force exerted by the machine on the top of the table is represented by an arrow labeled *W.* The arrow indicates that the force of 400 pounds is pushing down on the workbench. Upward forces or reactions exerted by the floor on the table legs are represented by the letter *P.*

Figure A–2b

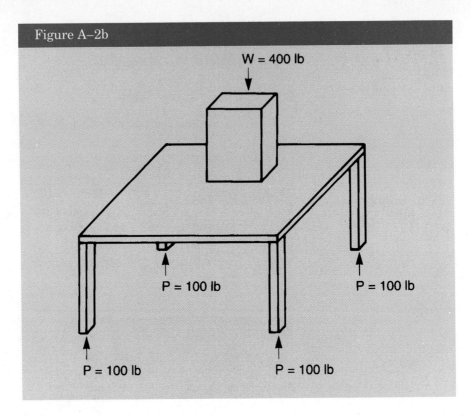

Since the table is obviously at rest, its acceleration equals zero: When a equals zero, the right side of Equation 1 equals zero, and we can write:

$$R = 0 \qquad \text{(Equation 2)}$$

Expressing R in terms of the forces acting on the table, we express Equation 2 as

$$4P - 400 = 0$$

and solving for P, we find

$$P = 100 \text{ lbs}$$

where a force acting up is considered positive and a force acting down is considered negative.

Physically, you can see there is as much force acting upward as acting downward. Equation 2 is called an equation of static equilibrium.

Vertical displacement or *deflection* occurs as the plank in Figure A–2a develops curvature when the boy stands in the center. Curvature is produced when the upper surface of the plank shortens and goes into a state of compression, and the lower surface of the plank is put into tension as the fibers of the wood at that location stretch. If the boy weighs 200 pounds, the reaction at each support is 100 pounds.

When the plank bends (see Figure A–2c), the distance from A to B shortens, and the upper surface is placed in *compression*. The distance from C to D elongates, and the lower surface is put into *tension*. The vertical displacement is labeled Δ (delta). This same kind of deformation and vertical displacement occurs in a bridge, but the small displacements produced by loads can only be measured by instruments—not perceived by eye.

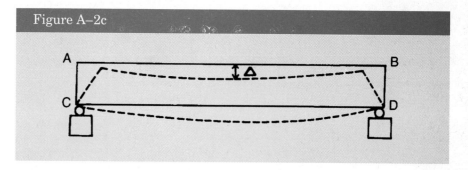

Figure A–2c

In responding to this passage, skillful readers automatically would **study the illustration each time the author refers to it.** They would mentally match up the labels and arrows in the drawings with the descriptions in the text in order to see, for example, how Figure A–2a represents the *deflection* or bending explained in the text. In this way, the reader could fully grasp the basic first steps of statics the author wants to explain.

In matching text and drawing, note that most authors try to place their figures *after* the first reference to it in the text. Also figures and tables are usually numbered by chapter number and then by sequence: Figure 9–3, for example, would be located in Chapter 9, after two earlier figures.

Process Diagrams

Process diagrams outlining the steps or stages in some event or happening are among the most common types of scientific illustrations and deserve particularly close scrutiny. Figure A–3 is a block diagram that outlines the process of "negative feedback."

Figure A–3: The Removal of Blood Glucose

The removal of blood glucose causes reduction of insulin secretion, causing more glucose to be retained in the blood, and an intermediate amount of insulin to be secreted. This results in a steady state of insulin and glucose concentration, and illustrates the way negative feedback can maintain homeostatic steady-state conditions.

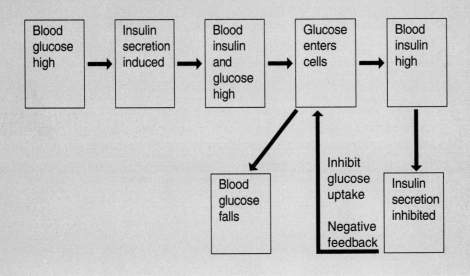

To understand this process diagram, **look carefully at the individual steps or stages represented by the blocks.** Study not just what happens in each one, but the order they follow as well. Remember, too, that diagrams of a process usually use arrows to indicate both the order of the steps and the relationship among them. If you want to understand the process described, you have to study the arrows, noting how one step stems from, leads to, or affects another step.

Tables

In scientific writing, authors frequently use tables to illustrate similarities and differences among members of the same class or group. In Table A–1, for example, the author uses a table to explain how chemotherapy—the treatment of disease with chemicals—actually works on the body. While the middle column identifies each chemotherapeutic agent, the "mode of action" column indicates *how* those agents work, and the "preferential use against" column indicates *what* bacteria they destroy most effectively.

Mode of Action	Chemotherapeutic Agent	Preferential Use Against
I. Antimetabolites	Para-amino salicylic acid	*Mycobacterium tuberculosis*
	Isonicontinic acid hydrazide (INH)	*Mycobacterium tuberculosis*
	Sulfonamides	*Escherichia coli* (urinary infection)
II. Cell wall inhibitors	Bacitracin	Gram-positive bacteria and *Neisseria*
	Cephalosporin	Gram-positive and gram-negative bacteria
	Cycloserine	*Mycobacterium tuberculosis*
	Penicillin	Gram-positive bacteria
	Vancomycin	Penicillin-resistant staphylococci
III. Plasma membrane inhibitors	Amphotericin B	Fungi
	Nystatin	Fungi
	Polymyxin B	*Pseudomonas*, fungi
	Chloramphenicol	*Salmonella*, rickettsias, chlamydias
IV. Inhibitors of protein synthesis	Erythromycin	Gram-positive bacteria and mycoplasmas
	Gentamicin	Gram-positive and gram-negative bacteria
	Kanamycin	*Escherichia coli, Proteus*
	Lincomycin	Gram-positive bacteria
	Neomycin	Gram-positive and gram-negative bacteria
	Streptomycin	Gram-positive and gram-negative bacteria
	Tetracyclines	Gram-positive and gram-negative bacteria, rickettsias, chlamydias
V. Inhibitors of nucleic acid synthesis of function	Cytarabine	Viruses
	Idoxuridine	Viruses
	Nalidixic acid	Gram-negative bacteria
	Rifamycin (used with INH)	*Mycobacterium tuberculosis*
	Vidarabine	Herpes simplex viruses

Table A-1: Mode of Action and Preferential Use of Some Important Chemotherapeutic Agents

When confronted with a table, study the left-hand column and the column headings to identify the kind of information listed in each column. Be prepared to compare and contrast the information provided in the individual columns, particularly if the author directs you to do so within the text. Follow the author's directions precisely and move your eyes from the author's words to the item cited on the table. This is the only way to fully understand the author's intended explanation.

Whatever type of scientific illustration you encounter in your reading—line drawing, process diagram, or table—study it carefully, keeping in mind these three pointers:

1. Each time an illustration is mentioned, look at it before you continue to read the text.
2. Read the captions. They explain the purpose or point of the illustration.
3. Note the direction of any arrows used. Study all labels that identify or separate parts of the illustration.

✳   Within scientific textbooks, illustrations play a fundamental role: they are an essential part of the explanations science writers provide for their readers.

Become Comfortable with Scientific Symbols in Text

When reading scientific writing, be prepared for passages in which authors move from words to mathematical and scientific symbols. Conventional language is often not precise enough to describe adequately a chemical process or physical phenomenon. At times more refined and precise symbols are necessary, particularly if an explanation in words would be too lengthy and time-consuming.

Compare, for example, these two versions of the same chemical reaction:

Zinc added to hydrochloric acid produces zinc chloride and hydrogen

or

$$Zn + 2HCl \rightarrow ZnCl_2 + H_2\uparrow$$

For precision, writers of scientific textbooks use scientific symbols. Familiarize yourself with the meanings of these symbols so that they do not intimidate you. In general, you should be ready to do the following.

> ✳ In reading scientific writing, be prepared for passages in which authors move from words to mathematical and scientific symbols.

Match Words with Symbols

In the sciences, textbook authors are aware that you are not generally familiar with many of the shorthand symbols they employ. They, therefore, make it a point to tell you initially what word each symbol represents. This is certainly true of the following example in which the author introduces Newton's law of universal gravitation first in words and then in mathematical symbols. Notice how each symbol is carefully defined:

> Every material particle in the universe attracts every other material particle with a force that is proportional to the product of the masses of the two particles, and inversely proportional to the square of the distance between their centers. The force is directed along a line joining their centers.
>
> In mathematical form, the magnitude of the force is represented by
>
> $$F_{gravity} = Gm_1m_2r^2$$
>
> where $F_{gravity}$ is the magnitude of the force, m_1 is the mass of one of the objects, m_2 is the mass of the other object, r is the distance between the centers of the two objects, and G is a proportionality constant (which is needed just to use units already defined for mass, distance, and force).
>
> —Nathan Spielberg and Byron P. Anderson,
> *Seven Ideas That Shook the World,* Wiley and Sons, 44

Your job as a reader is to read these passages analytically, carefully matching words with scientific symbols. You must understand the meaning of each symbol, word, and concept to grasp the meaning of this compressed passage.

Write Out All Scientific Formulas

As you write out formulas, make sure you understand each term of each equation and pay attention to every sign or symbol.

Learn the Standard Symbols That Represent Key Relationships or Operations

Some of the symbols commonly used to identify scientific operations or mathematical relationships are familiar to you. You will have little difficulty figuring out what + and − represent, but what about the arrows in this chemistry equation?

$$Zn + 2HCl \rightarrow ZnCl_2 + H_2\uparrow$$

To understand the process represented by this equation, you must know that the horizontal arrow pointing right indicates that the elements on the left-hand side, zinc and hydrochloric acid, react to form the combination on the right-hand side, zinc chloride and hydrogen, while the vertical arrow shows that the hydrogen formed was a gas and passed into the atmosphere. Authors usually explain the meaning of such symbols the first time they appear in the text, but from then on, it's up to you to remember their meaning.

Authors in the sciences often assume a certain level of mathematical competence and will sometimes use, without explanation, symbols they think you know. For example, when explaining Newton's law of universal gravitation, the author defined all the letters in the formula. But he assumed that the reader was familiar enough with algebra to know that the raised number 2 is an exponent indicating how many times a variable or number is to be multiplied by itself:

$$b^2 = b \times b$$
$$b^3 = b \times b \times b$$

When you find passages where mathematical symbols are used without explanation, learn what those symbols represent. You may have to review an introductory math (algebra or geometry) text where such terms are defined and explained, or you may have to refer to an introductory text in one of the basic sciences (chemistry, biology, physics).

Whenever Possible, Make Abstractions Concrete

Matching words with mathematical symbols is an important first step. Whenever possible, go a step further and try to relate those symbols to what you already know about the world, developing your own examples, analogies, images, or patterns. Let's say, for example, that you were studying the following formula:

$$Fe + CuSO_4 \rightarrow FeSO_4 + Cu$$

It represents the chemical reaction called *replacement,* which takes place when iron combines with copper sulfate. Yes, the first step is to recognize that Fe represents iron and $CuSO_4$ stands for copper sulfate. But to understand what that formula really means, you might also evoke the analogy of a dance between copper and sulfate where copper is left in the cold after iron cuts in. In this respect, reading scientific symbols is no different from reading words: much of your understanding depends on your willingness to interact with those symbols, looking for links between what you already know about the world and what you are learning.

When you encounter scientific or mathematical formulas in your texts, study them carefully. Do not skip any; decipher them one by one. If your own analytical reading doesn't do the trick, ask your instructor or a knowledgeable classmate for help. Chances are that these same formulas will reappear in later chapters, where you will be expected to know them. It's worthwhile to master scientific formulas when they are first introduced because at this point the author will provide the most detailed explanation of each symbol.